WORLD HUNGER

Since there are so many people in this world afflicted with hunger, this sacred Council urges all, both individuals and governments, to remember the saying of the Fathers: "Feed the man dying of hunger, because if you have not fed him you have killed him."

Gaudium et Spes 69

For Jerry

WORLD HUNGER

THE RESPONSIBILITY

OF CHRISTIAN EDUCATION

SUZANNE C. TOTON

ORBIS BOOKS
Maryknoll, New York 10545

The parable "My Son John" (pp. 166–67) is reprinted with permission of Macmillan Publishing Co., Inc. from *Love, Love at the End* by Daniel Berrigan, S.J. Copyright © 1968 by Daniel Berrigan.

Second Printing, August 1982

The Catholic Foreign Mission Society of America (Maryknoll) recruits and trains people for overseas missionary service. Through Orbis Books Maryknoll aims to foster the international dialogue that is essential to mission. The books published, however, reflect the opinions of their authors and are not meant to represent the official position of the society.

Manuscript editor: Robert J. Cunningham

Library of Congress Cataloging in Publication Data

Toton, Suzanne C.
  World hunger.

  Bibliography: p.
  Includes index.
  1. Food supply. 2. Food relief—International cooperation. 3. Agricultural assistance—International cooperation. 4. Church and underdeveloped areas. 5. Christian education. I. Title.
HD9000.5.T67   261.8'5   81-16906
ISBN 0-88344-716-9   AACR2

CONTENTS

Part III
EDUCATING FOR JUSTICE

Chapter 13
The Role of Religion in Maintaining the Status Quo

Chapter 14
The Role of Education in Maintaining the Status Quo

PREFACE

When the food crisis first came to the attention of the American public during the years 1972–75, its causes were attributed to shortages, bad weather, and overpopulation. Americans were advised to tighten their belts and eat less meat, while the poor in the Third World were admonished to limit their population growth. Both the identified causes of the crisis and the recommended "solutions" to it suggested a naive understanding of a problem of international importance. At about the time that hunger was becoming a widely recognized problem, I was working on the so-called development problem. I gradually became convinced that the Third World was not simply poor but was being made poor, and that the First World and the United States, in particular, played a significant role in keeping the Third World poor.

My research on the structural relationship between the Third World and the First World made me suspicious of the generally accepted analysis of hunger. I felt that there had to be some relationship between the structured dependence of the Third World and its hunger. I continued to research the trade, aid, and investment policies of the First World with the particular interest of determining whether those policies contributed to the hunger of the Third World. My findings were true to my original insight.

In recent years several books have been published on the problem of world hunger, including *Food First* by Frances Moore Lappé and Joseph Collins and *How the Other Half Dies* by Susan George. In terms of the analysis they present, both works are in basic agreement with my thesis. I believe that we have now reached the point in our society at which we must begin to respond to the problem.

For the last eight years I have taught social ethics and religious education in a Catholic college and university. During that time I have offered courses on development ethics and world hunger from a Christian perspective. In teaching these courses I have become increasingly convinced that Christian education has a responsibility for ending world poverty and hunger and can make a specific contribution to this effort. What that responsibility and contribution might be was the subject of my doctoral dissertation at Columbia University Teachers College.

My research revealed that critical material on the responsibility and role of education, in general, and of Christian education, in particular, to effect systemic or structural change were virtually nonexistent. To test this observation further, I wrote to several prominent educators in the United States and abroad who were active in the field of education and social change. In reply, all of them confirmed my observation, citing sources that I had already found.

It is apparent, therefore, that the relationship of education in general and of religious education in particular to systemic change is an area that needs to be explored in greater depth. This book is a step in that direction. It is an attempt to clarify what the responsibility and contribution of Christian education might be to change the systems and values that prevent the poor from feeding themselves. In short, this book is an attempt to work out the theory and practice of educating for justice with respect to the problem of world hunger.

This book, therefore, is addressed to Christian educators who teach in a variety of settings. It is written for Christian educators in Catholic or Protestant church schools and colleges as well as for teachers in Sunday schools, catechetical programs, and adult religious-education programs. Teachers of social ethics in seminaries, campus ministers, and educators who teach religion, values education, or social studies in public schools and colleges may also find it helpful. While the analysis and pedagogical practices presented are more appropriate for students in high schools, colleges, and adult programs, the book provides good background material for Christian educators involved with every age level.

In organizing this book I have tried to follow the methodology of the liberation theologians. We do not begin with the study of revelation and tradition but with the concrete problem of world hunger itself. Part I scrutinizes critically the theories of world hunger that have been advanced over the past two decades. We then examine world hunger from the "underside" of history, from the perspective of those who experience poverty and hunger most—the Third World. Because the underdevelopment of the Third World cannot be understood apart from the development of the First World, the contribution of the First World in general and of the United States in particular to the problem of poverty and hunger is examined in depth and placed within a theoretical framework. The conclusion drawn in Part I is that the problem of world poverty and hunger is fundamentally a moral problem. It is a by-product of an economic system and values that give precedence to the pursuit of goods over human well-being.

Liberation theologians argue that only after examining the economic, political, and social roots of the problem can we begin to examine it in the light of faith. Part II attempts to interpret the preceding analysis of world hunger and the responsibility of Christians in the First World from the perspective of the Hebraic-Christian tradition and the social teachings of the Roman Catholic and Protestant churches. It argues that the moral responsibility of Christians must extend beyond charity to working for systemic, structural, and value change. It shows how the struggle to bring about a more just social order is itself the struggle for the kingdom of God.

Since reflection, according to liberation theologians, becomes validated only in action, Part III focuses on the specific contribution that Christian educators might make to alleviating world poverty and hunger. It examines the obstacles to justice in religious and educational institutions in which Christian educators work. It provides a theoretical basis for educating for justice. And it suggests creative ways to teach about world hunger and to involve students, their families, and their community in this educational process.

The final section of the book contains an annotated list of books and organizations that can assist Christian educators to get started in educating for justice with respect to world hunger. The intention of this book, in short, is to provide a solid theoretical foundation and practical suggestions for educators interested in teaching about world hunger from a Christian perspective.

At the outset a few clarifications are needed. In analyzing the root causes of world hunger we concentrate primarily on the role of the First World in general and of the United States in particular. In doing so, I by no means wish to imply that the governments, the military, and the wealthy of the Third World have not contributed significantly to the poverty and suffering of the vast majority of their people. Revolutions in 1979 in Nicaragua and Iran have exposed some of the repressive measures that these groups employ to maintain the concentration of wealth and power in the Third World. They have also exposed the support that the United States lends to those who enforce repression. Most Americans are unaware of the fact that the military who maintain the internal "stability" of a number of Third World countries—frequently through measures that violate human rights—have received training either in the United States and other First World nations or from United States and other First World advisers. We assist not only in training members of the military but also by supplying them with the necessary military hardware. While that assistance may be awarded under the rubric of keeping the Third World free from communism, its use for domestic "security" purposes is no secret. Besides our military assistance, we help solidify the power of the wealthy in the Third World through technical and economic assistance. Many studies document the effect foreign aid has had in shoring up the wealth of the rich.

Besides the contribution of the Third World to its own poverty and hunger, we do not discuss either the contribution of countries with centrally planned economies, that is, the USSR, China, and other Communist nations, to the problem of poverty and hunger in the Third World. While their exploitation of the Third World cannot be denied, the fact of the matter is that their trade, aid, and investment in the Third World, while expanding, have up until the present been relatively small compared with those of the First World.

In the analysis of the problem of world hunger, we concentrate on the contribution of the First World in general and of the United States in particular for a number of reasons. Many of what we now call "nations" of the First World colonized the Third World beginning in the fifteenth century. After the colonies won independence, the First World continued its interests in the Third World by systematically integrating it into the world-market system. The contribution of the United States must be examined thoroughly because it is not just another First World nation but the very center of the world-market system. In the words of the American Socialist Michael Harrington: "America is at the center of a complex, structured and interdependent system, historically and presently suffused with capitalist values and priorities, which massively reproduces the injustices of a world partitioned among the fat and the starving" (*The Vast Majority,* p. 253).

Because our nation is at the center of the capitalist system, it has the power to significantly effect change on behalf of the poor and hungry of this world. Thus we who are citizens of the United States have an awesome responsibility and opportunity to make a difference in the suffering of the world's poor and hungry. Whether we work in education, religion, business, politics, or the arts, each of us must assume responsibility for the struggle for justice in our own field of expertise. This book aims to help Christian educators in the First World recognize and assume their responsibility to change the systems and values that keep the poor from feeding themselves.

Finally, this book would never have been possible without the help of others. I would like to take this opportunity, therefore, to formally thank them, my family, especially my parents, Helen and John Toton, who generously gave up the precious time that this work kept us from spending together. Rev. John McNamee introduced me to the struggle for justice many years ago. I am deeply indebted to Beverly Wildung Harrison of Union Theological Seminary for her encouragement and trust as well as countless hours spent in conferences with me throughout my doctoral studies at Columbia University Teachers College. Dwayne E. Huebner, Joan Dye Gussow, and Philip H. Phenix advised me and served on my doctoral committee.

I am also grateful to Margaret M. Reher, chairperson of the Religion Department, Cabrini College, for giving me support and freedom in developing new courses and trying new ideas early in my teaching career. John E. De-Turck of Cabrini College was the most delightful co-teacher anyone could ask for in the world-hunger course we taught together. A word of thanks also goes to Cabrini College's efficient and helpful librarians, especially Muriel Clouser, who tracked down and promptly ordered many obscure works for me. Silvio E. Fittipaldi and the administration of Villanova University granted me a reduction in teaching during one semester as I was working on this book. I give special thanks to my students for the challenges they posed, their responsiveness to issues and ideas, and their growth and development, which have always been my greatest joy. A sincere word of thanks is due to members of various organizations who generously received my army of students pursuing projects for my classes: Timothy H. Smith of the Interfaith Center on Corporate Responsibility; Janet Vandevender of the Interreligious Taskforce on U.S. Food Policy; Barbara Howell and Edward Brady, S.J., of Bread for the World; Jack Malinowski of the American Friends Service Committee; Sr. Carol Coston of Network; Dick Taylor of Jubilee Fellowship; Bob Smith of the Brandywine Peace Community; Eugenia Durland and William Durland, of the Center on Law and Pacifism; Bernard Evans of the Campaign for Human Development; William Callahan, S.J., of the Quixote Center; Joel Gajardo of Church World Service; and Armando Sonaggere of Catholic Relief.

Betty Reardon of the World Council for Curriculum and Instruction graciously gave of her time in conversations with me, lent me materials on education and structural change, and put me in touch with educators working in the area of education and change. The following people corresponded with me or furnished materials on education and social change: Christoph Wulf of the School of Education at the University of Siegen in the Federal Republic of Germany; Robin Richardson, Director of the World Studies Project in London; Garnet L. McDiarmind, Professor of Educational Theory at the Ontario Institute for Studies in Education; Cheryl Hollman Keen of the Harvard University Graduate School of Education; Magnus Haavelsrud, Executive Secretary of the Peace Education Commission of the International Peace Research Association and Assistant Professor at the Institute of Social Science, University of Tromso; Howard Rush of the University of Sussex, Science Policy Research Unit; and the World Hunger Education Service.

The following people helped with various parts of the book: Joseph Lombardi, S.J., of St. Joseph's University; Thomas Venables of the Graduate School of Education, Rutgers University; Nancy Bancroft; Denis Goulet of the Overseas Development Council; Richard Holm; Joseph Romano of Cabrini College; and James B. McGinnis of the Institute for Education in Peace and Justice. Brennon Jones carefully read Part I, and William and Barbara Miller scrutinized the entire manuscript and offered valuable suggestions.

Finally, how can I thank enough my husband, Jerome R. Zurek, Jr. He has helped me in countless ways, such as driving me at 5 a.m. to the Trailways Bus Terminal in a seedy section of town so that I could make a 9 a.m. class in New York, listening patiently to ideas that I needed to develop out loud, and even volunteering to type the first draft of the manuscript for the book on two fingers! So it is to Jerry for his incredible support, patience, and love that I dedicate this book.

PART I

THE PROBLEM OF
WORLD HUNGER

Chapter 1

CAUSES OF THE PROBLEM

More than half a billion people are undernourished or malnourished today. They lack the essential nutrients to live healthy active lives. Because of a poor diet, some become physically impaired. Glazed stares, swollen bellies, flaking skin, and general listlessness are the marks of undernutrition and malnutrition. Infants, young children, and pregnant or lactating women are hunger's prime victims. The hungry, for the most part, live in the Third World, although there are also a significant number of them in the affluent nations of the world. The largest concentration of hungry people are found in the following nations: Afghanistan, Bangladesh, Benin, Burma, Burundi, Cameroon, Cape Verde, Central African Empire, Chad, Egypt, El Salvador, Ethiopia, Gambia, Ghana, Guatemala, Guinea, Guinea-Bissau, Guyana, Haiti, Honduras, India, Ivory Coast, Kenya, Laos, Lesotho, Madagascar, Mali, Mauritania, Mozambique, Nepal, Niger, Pakistan, Rwanda, Senegal, Sierra Leone, Somalia, Sudan, Sri Lanka, Tanzania, Uganda, Upper Volta, Samoa, Yemen Arab Republic, and Democratic Yemen. All these nations have been classified by the United Nations as "most seriously affected" (MSA) countries.

The scope and magnitude of the problem of hunger gained worldwide attention during the food crisis of 1972–75, when a very great number of people in the Third World perished from lack of food. Numerous factors triggered that crisis, but were not its cause. Nor are they the cause of the chronic undernutrition and malnutrition that persists in the Third World today. To understand the nature of the problem we will be studying, therefore, we must begin by distinguishing the factors that triggered that particular food crisis from the more deep-rooted and enduring causes of hunger.

FACTORS IN THE FOOD CRISIS OF 1972–75

1. Cut-backs in production. In the decade preceding the food crisis, food, fertilizer, and fuel were abundant and cheap. The United States Department of Agriculture (USDA) in fact reported that at the beginning of the 1969–70 marketing year, the world's grain stocks reached a peak of 191 million tons.[1]

3

Surpluses are not a blessing, especially for producers in countries whose economies are based on a capitalist or free-market system. Such surpluses tend to drive prices down and reduce producers' margin of profit. In the fertilizer industry, for example, overproduction and overcapacity drove the price of fertilizer down from $90–$102 a ton for bagged urea for export in 1964 to $40–$45 a ton in late 1970.[2]

One way to reduce surpluses is to cut back production. This is exactly what the food and fertilizer industries did toward the end of the 1960s. The world's major grain-exporting countries cut back their grain production considerably, especially wheat production, between 1968 and 1970. The USDA estimates that the four major grain-exporting countries—the United States, Canada, Australia, and Argentina—reduced their wheat area from over 50 million to 33 million hectares between 1968 and 1970.[3] Their grain production fell by an estimated 20 million tons.[4] Also hurt by plumeting prices, the fertilizer industry began to close older, less efficient plants and to cut back investments in and construction of new plants in 1969–70. Thus when major crop failures occured in several parts of the world in the early 1970s, the world was already drawing on significantly reduced supplies of food and fertilizer.

2. Bad weather. Weather played a major role in triggering the food crisis. The Soviet Union's wheat crop, for example, was devastated by a winter kill followed by a dry summer. At about the same time, Argentina and Australia experienced a severe drought. Typhoons hit the Philippines, and India went through an inadequate monsoon.

3. Decline in world fish catch. While much of the world was experiencing poor harvests as a result of inclement weather, the world's supply of fish, another important source of food, began to decline. After World War II technological means were developed to exploit the world's oceans. Since then fish has become an important source of protein, particularly for the people of Japan and the Soviet Union. Fish is consumed directly or it can be fed to animals in the form of fish meal. Improved technology and the increasing appetite for fish eventually led to overfishing. In the Northwest Atlantic region alone, where 5 percent of the world's fish is caught, the fish catch rose from 1.8 million tons in 1954 to 3.9 million tons in 1968.[5] By 1970 it dropped 18 percent.[6] By 1972 the haddock catch amounted to only one seventh of its earlier level.[7] A similar drop occurred in the catches of cod, halibut, and herring.[8] Overfishing took its toll not only on the North Atlantic fisheries but also on the rich fisheries off the coast of Peru. Because of heavy annual catches in 1967, 1968, 1970, and 1971, the Peruvian anchovy fisheries virtually collapsed in 1972–73.[9]

After food supplies had been depleted by bad weather and the failure of many of the world's fisheries, some nations turned to imports to compensate for local food deficits. The increased demand for food placed an added burden on the world's grain supply, which had already been reduced by measures used to raise prices. The world's grain stocks suddenly dropped to a record low, while the price of grain rose to a record high. The price of wheat, for example, increased from $60 per ton in the second quarter of 1972 to $210 per ton in the first quarter of 1974.[10] Rice rose from $132 per ton to $570 per ton in the same period.[11]

As the result of an increased demand for food, more land was brought into production, and thus more fertilizer was needed. But fertilizer production had also been reduced in the late 1960s. The demand for fertilizer soon outran the supply. Like the price of grain, the price of fertilizer soared. Bagged urea, for example rose from $45 per ton in 1971 to $350 per ton in 1974.[12]

4. Rise in oil prices. To add fuel to the fire, the OPEC nations decided about the same time to raise the price of oil. The cost of a barrel of oil rose from approximately $2.00 in 1972 to $5.00 in late 1973 and to $8.00 in December 1973.[13] Escalating fuel prices affected both the grain and fertilizer industries, since without energy neither industry can function. As a result, the rising cost of fuel affected both the supply and the cost of food. The soaring costs of food, fertilizer, and fuel between 1972 and 1975 made it virtually impossible for poorer nations to compete on the world market with affluent nations for those commodities.

To summarize, production cutbacks in the food and fertilizer industries, inclement weather in several parts of the world, a decline in the world's fish catch, and a sharp rise in the price of fuel are the main factors that triggered the food crisis. The causes of hunger then and now, however, are much more deep-rooted and difficult to identify. We shall now try to understand these causes more clearly.

EXPLANATIONS FOR WORLD HUNGER

There is significant controversy about the specific causes of world hunger. Experts are divided as to whether it is a result of overpopulation or of political and economic systems. A prominent group of experts claims that the increasing population in the world's poor nations and the increasing consumption in the world's affluent nations are outstripping the capabilities of the major food-producing systems of the world. Another group argues that hunger is the result of political and economic systems that keep the poor from feeding themselves. Before offering my own analysis of the problem, let us review the arguments on both sides and point out some of their major weaknesses.

Views of Paddock and Paddock

William Paddock, a consultant in tropical agriculture, and Paul Paddock, a retired foreign service officer of the state department, were among the first to propose the theory that overpopulation is the source of the current problem of food scarcity and hunger. They argue in *Famine 1975!* (a book published in 1967) that the increasing population and static growth of agriculture in the poor nations makes famine inevitable. The population of the

Third World, Paddock and Paddock note, has been increasing more rapidly than its food supply. Although food aid from affluent nations has kept the Third World from experiencing prolonged and severe famine, famine cannot be headed off much longer, in view of the burgeoning population of the Third World. The introduction of modern medicine into the Third World accounted to a large extent for its accelerating population growth by reducing the death rate. Medical treatment enabled individuals to live longer and healthier lives. Since healthier individuals are more fertile they tend to reproduce more frequently. Paddock and Paddock maintain that nothing can prevent an impending catastrophe because more than half of the population of the Third World is of child-bearing age. The people who will cause the famines are already born and reproducing at an incredible rate. The agricultural system of the Third World, the authors maintained, further compounded its food problem. Most of the world's arable lands as well as its submarginal lands are already under cultivation. Moreover, its agricultural methods and technology are extremely primitive and incapable of producing higher yields. The authors' conclusion is dire:

> Thus, with no new technology and no new marginal land available the race between food production and mouths to be fed—the race which until then [1958] agriculture had at least been keeping up with—now began to be lost.[14]

When famine finally does strike and the world's grain reserves are exhausted, Paddock and Paddock argue that the major food-producing nations, particularly the United States, will have no alternative but to choose which nations among the needy will receive food aid. The war-time practice of triage, they maintain, should be applied to needy nations in times of food emergency. In their words triage is "the most clean-cut method of meeting the crisis."[15]

The Paddocks recommend that food aid should be allocated on the following basis:

1. Nations receiving aid must have a reasonably good chance of surviving if they are helped.

2. These nations must resolve to implement major population-control programs.

3. They must be of military, political, or economic importance to the donor nation.

As Paddock and Paddock succinctly state:

> . . . when such shortages and/or high prices do force the American public to change their diet, it is certain that our citizens will become dead serious about this food, food which they will forgo in order to feed distant foreigners. When this happens, I take for granted that American public opinion will demand that this food be distributed in a manner which will give them their "money's worth."[16]

Finally, the authors argue that famine will provide a rare opportunity for the United States to exert its influence in the world because of its strategic position in world food production. The United States can dominate in an era of famine if it uses its power wisely.

At the time of its publication in 1967, *Famine 1975!* was an important book because it predicted the famine that was to come in the early 1970s. Ironically, it also foretold the criteria that the affluent world would use to distribute food aid to hungry nations during the food crisis, although no nation would admit that it indeed practiced triage. Aside from its prophetic value, however, *Famine 1975!* does not present a thorough or critical examination of the factors contributing to hunger. For example, it does not examine why people in the Third World have so many offspring. Nor does it ask why the agricultural system of the Third World is so primitive—why does the Third World not have the agricultural imputs and technology it needs to feed its population? Moreover, the authors do not examine the Third World's relationship with the First World. They do not mention the colonial past or the Third World's economic and political ties to the First World today. No questions are raised about the types of agricultural commodities being produced in the Third World or about who controls that production and who consumes those commodities.

Finally, the Paddocks' recommendation that the United States should adopt a policy of triage toward the Third World raises serious ethical problems—problems about the authors' own system of values and about the level of morality of a society that would seriously consider such a solution.[17] In my judgment *Famine 1975!* is an ahistorical, apolitical, and amoral treatment of a historical, political, and moral problem.[18]

Views of Lester Brown

Lester Brown, one of the world's experts on world hunger, has attributed the problem of hunger to a scarcity of food brought on by an accelerated growth in the world demand for food since World War II. In the early part of this century, the global demand for cereals went up by about 4 million tons annually. But in 1950 the demand for cereal was increasing by 12 million tons annually, and in 1970 by 30 million tons annually.[19] This dramatic increase in consumption, according to Brown, is ecologically undermining the world's major food-producing systems of land, water, fuel, and fertilizer.

In Brown's view, the growth in population of the Third World exerts the greatest demand on the world's grain supply. He points out, however, that a rise in food consumption, particularly of beef in the affluent nations of the world, is exerting an increasing pressure on the world's food supply. He estimates that, of the average annual increase of 30 million tons in the world's grain supply, approximately 22 million tons are needed to meet demands brought on by population growth, while 8 million tons—or about one third of that required for increased population—are needed to meet the increasing consumption demands of the world's affluent nations.[20]

Thus the solution to the problem of world hunger, Brown argues, lies primarily in curbing population growth in the Third World and consumption patterns in the affluent world.

Brown stresses the need to initiate effective birth-control programs in the Third World. He points out, however, that family-planning programs alone will not bring down the birth rate in the Third World. In societies in which individuals have access to economic and social benefits such as health care, education, jobs, and credit, and in which income and social services are distributed equitably, birth rates drop significantly despite a low per-capita income and the newness or absence of birth-control programs:

> The relationship between socio-economic change and fertility is admittedly complex. In every country there are special cultural or religious factors that have implications for population growth, as do variations in the means available for reducing the birth rate. Yet there is increasing evidence that the very strategies that cause the greatest improvements in the welfare of the entire population also have the greatest effect on reducing population growth.[21]

Because people in affluent countries consume a greater amount of grain per capita in the form of meat and dairy products and because the food systems of affluent countries exert greater stress on the earth's ecosystems than does the Third World, Brown maintains that the affluent must curb their per-capita consumption of food and limit their intake of animal protein. There are economic, ecological, medical, and moral reasons for simplifying the diets of the rich. Cutting down on the consumption of animal protein, Brown maintains, not only reduces the individual consumer's food bill but also relieves some of the global inflationary pressure brought on by competition for scarce food supplies. Ecologically, simplifying the diets of people in the affluent world would cut down on the runoff of pesticides, fertilizer, and animal wastes into our fresh-water lakes and rivers. Medically, cutting back on the consumption of animal protein would reduce the incidence of heart disease. Finally, Brown argues that because rich and poor alike draw on common natural resources to meet their food needs at a time when these resources are becoming scarce, the rich who continue to consume a disproportionate amount of food deprive the poor of their share. Given the present situation of food scarcity and dwindling resources, therefore, Brown holds that it is unethical for the rich to consume an excessive amount of food when they are depriving the poor of their very survival.

In *By Bread Alone* Brown acknowledges the fact that a relationship exists between poverty and hunger:

> Historically, famine has been limited to relatively small geographic areas, as in Ireland in 1847 and in West Bengal in 1943. But advances in global and national food distribution and transportation systems now

ensure that food scarcity is allocated according to *income* levels, with scarcity concentrated among the world's poor, wherever they are.[22]

Unfortunately, Brown never really develops this insight much further. Yet this point is crucial for our gaining a perspective on the roots of the problem of world hunger. Brown never asks what prevents certain groups from acquiring enough capital to grow or purchase enough food. He never examines the global economic and political systems to determine their role in keeping the people of the Third World poor and hungry. Except for calling on people in the affluent world to simplify their diet, Brown does not correlate the appetite of the rich with the poverty and hunger of the poor. Even in his most recent work, *The Twenty Ninth Day*, where Brown shows more sophistication regarding the role that economic and political systems play in creating shortages, he still attributes the roots of hunger to overpopulation and overconsumption. In sum, Lester Brown's analysis of world hunger leaves out some of the most important parts of the picture.

Views of Georg Borgstrom

More than Brown or Paddock and Paddock, Georg Borgstrom, a professor of Food Science and Human Nutrition at Michigan State University, has involved the economic and political systems of the affluent world in the food and hunger crisis. For Borgstrom hunger is essentially an economic and ecological problem brought on by the pressures of overpopulation. The way Borgstrom defines "overpopulation," however, is the key to his analysis. A country is overpopulated, according to Borgstrom, when the basic resources within its territory are insufficient to feed its people. When a country is overpopulated, two things usually happen. A major portion of its population migrates to other countries. Or the country becomes dependent on land, pastures, or fishing grounds beyond its borders. Using this definition of overpopulation, Borgstrom claims that the affluent world is no less overpopulated than the poorer nations of the world. The major difference is that when the West was experiencing its population explosion between 1850 and 1950, its people were able to migrate to North America, Africa, Asia, and South America. There they extracted the labor and resources of those continents to ease their population problem:

> During the Golden Age (1850–1950), Europeans swarmed all over the globe. In the North American prairie they created a colony in tilled acreage, forest lands, and in mineral wealth far richer than the combined resources of all the European countries from which they came. In addition, the South American pampas were earmarked for their use. White man, in the guise of these European emigrants, also grabbed major choice pieces of the highland soils of Africa and took power positions of trade along the African coast. During this process India

became British; the East Indies became Dutch. Furthermore, the entire continent of Australia and its invaluable satellite of New Zealand had become part of the white man's booty. This world-wide grab induced the greatest migration in history. Nearly 100 million left the European continent, although about one-fourth eventually returned, for a net exodus of 75 million. These millions became the progenitors of hundreds of millions more of European descent around the globe, primarily in North America, Latin America, Oceania, and Siberia.[23]

The effects of the population explosion of the West on our ecosphere were devastating. We are currently experiencing them, Borgstrom writes, in our "depleted or eroded soils, irreversibly tapped groundwater resources, deforested lands, and in disturbed ecological relationships hitting back through the spread of diseases."[24]

Now that the population of the affluent West is stabilizing, the poorer nations are experiencing their own population explosion. Their population explosion has taken a further toll on our depleted resources. Unlike the people of the West, the people of the Third World have no new continent to which they can migrate. Moreover, their resources are still largely controlled by the affluent world to maintain the needs of its population. The affluent nations, Borgstrom points out, control not only the resources of the Third World but the terms of international trade as well. Because they dominate world trade, the affluent nations have been able to set to their own advantage the rate of exchange for products traded between themselves and the Third World. The net result is that the poor nations cannot generate enough capital from their exports to purchase more food or to invest in agricultural production so as to meet their domestic food needs. The ironic consequence is that the poor nations provide more protein (in the form of oilseeds, oilseed products, and fish meal) to the affluent world than they receive from the affluent world in the form of cereals:

> . . . the Western world is currently acquiring from the HW [Hungry World] one million metric tons more protein than is delivered to the HW through grains. In other words, the Western world is exchanging approximately 3 million metric tons of cereal protein for 4 million metric tons of other proteins which are all superior in a nutritive respect. This flow from the HW is depriving millions in tropical Africa, Latin America, and Asia of their major deficit commodity. The SW [Satisfied World] is thus taking no small amount of protein from the world's scarce supplies. In addition, close to half of the ocean catches are earmarked to provide feed protein and food fat to the SW—catches that largely originate in the waters of the two most protein-deficient continents of South America (Peru and Chile) and Africa (South and Southwest, and Angola). Europe alone is currently importing around 1.7 million tons of fish meal protein annually.[25]

Although Borgstrom condemns the "relentless greed" and "perverted goals" of the affluent world, he does not believe that fundamental economic or political reforms will solve the food needs of the hungry in the Third World. In his judgment, even if the economic disparities in the world were eliminated, it would be impossible to feed adequately all the earth's population because of the irreparable damage that overpopulation has caused to our ecosystem. Borgstrom comments:

> If all the food in the world were equally distributed and each human being received identical quantities, we would all be malnourished. If the entire world's food supply were parcelled out at the U.S. dietary level, it would feed only about one-third of the human race. The world as a global household knows of no surpluses, merely enormous deficits.[26]

In an effort to meet the insatiable needs of its population, Borgstrom maintains that the affluent world in particular has wrought such ecological devastation that it is virtually impossible to meet the basic food needs of the world's population. He argues, therefore, that while development programs, particularly agricultural development programs, must be stepped up in the Third World and while population must be controlled on a global scale, the food needs of all human beings will be met only when all nations, rich and poor alike:

> become truly economical in the use of such basic resources as soil, water, and minerals, and at the same time heed the fundamental laws of living nature and the obvious limitations of the globe.[27]

Although Borgstrom exposed the political and economic as well as the ecological dimensions of the problem of hunger, his response does not take the political and economic aspects of the problem seriously into consideration. The question that he should have faced is whether it is possible for nations to exercise restraint in the use of the earth's resources if their economic systems are founded on and foster unbridled consumption, greed, and waste. In order for there to be fundamental ecological change, that is, a change from the abuse and squandering of the earth's resources, is it not necessary to have systemic change—a change in the systems that generate and legitimate ecological devastation? In addition, Borgstrom does not deal with the following issue: Once the ecological balance has been restored—without a change in the global systems that govern the production and distribution of food—what is to prevent the affluent nations from hoarding or using the food produced for their own purposes? Certainly an increase in the volume of food produced does not ensure a just and even distribution of food. If there were enough food to feed the entire human race, is there any guarantee that the entire human race would indeed be fed without the political and economic mechanisms to ensure that they would be fed? In short, although Borgstrom's analysis of the roots of hunger is more critical and convincing than those of Brown and of the Paddocks, his response to the problem does not equal the economic and political insight that he brought to bear on the problem.

Views of Lappé, Collins, and George

The World Food Conference of 1974 offered a new perspective on the causes of world hunger. It acknowledged the fact that world hunger is not solely the result of overpopulation and natural causes but rather the result of political and economic systems that exploit the poor and keep them hungry. Two publications—*Food First* by Frances Moore Lappé and Joseph Collins and *How the Other Half Dies* by Susan George—examine the economic and political roots of hunger from this new viewpoint.

In *Food First* Lappé and Collins attempt to dispel some common myths and misconceptions about hunger by offering the following new analysis of the situation:

1. The control of food production exercised by the rich and by multinationals. Lappé and Collins hold that every nation has the capacity to feed itself, but is prevented from doing so by an economic elite in the poor and rich nations and by a few powerful multinational corporations that control agricultural production for the purpose of producing profit rather than for meeting the basic food needs of all people. Lappé and Collins argue that the elite and the multinational corporations monopolize land, capital, labor, credit, research, and technology in both the rich and poor nations of the world. Consequently, the poor majority are cut off from controlling their own food production which ultimately affects their food consumption. The authors cite countless examples of how land, labor, and capital, particularly in food-deficit countries, have been diverted from producing food for domestic consumption to producing luxury crops for the minority who can afford them in the Third World and for export to the First World. Here are a few of the examples they give:

—Africa is a net *exporter* of barley, beans, peanuts, fresh vegetables, and cattle (not to mention luxury crop exports such as coffee and cocoa), yet it has a higher incidence of protein-calorie malnutrition among young children than any other continent. . . .
—Mexico now supplies the United States with over one half of its supply of several winter and early spring vegetables while infant deaths associated with poor nutrition are common.
—Half of Central America's agricultural land produces food for export while in several of its countries the poorest 50 percent of the population eat only half the necessary protein. (The richest 5 percent, on the other hand, consume two to three times more than is needed.)[28]

Thus, Lappé and Collins hold that food and natural resources are not scarce in food-deficit countries. They are merely owned and controlled by the economic elite and multinational corporations that use them for their own commercial purposes.

2. The undermining of the poor's food security by governments, multinationals, and the rich. Lappé and Collins further argue that the governments in both the poor and rich nations work hand in hand with the landed and corporate elite to undermine the food security of the poor. The governments of many Third World countries encourage foreign control of their agricultural systems by providing credit and tax incentives for large landowners and foreign agricultural investors. The same is true of the governments of many First World countries. To encourage the development of new operations in the Third World, governments make available low-interest loans and grants to the agricultural firms of their own nationals. Thus small farmers in the Third World find themselves in the unenviable position of having to compete with large domestic and foreign firms for credit, agricultural inputs, and markets.

More than any of the authors thus far discussed, Lappé and Collins show how the affluent nations use their bilateral and multilateral financial assistance programs to capture and control the markets of the Third World for their own agricultural firms. They point out, for example, that aid for agricultural development may be granted on the condition that seeds, fertilizer, farm machinery, and so forth, be purchased from the donor nation. In the case of food aid, the aid itself is tied to an agreement to purchase certain commodities in the future. The authors also show how the trade regulations of the First World are linked to the interests of the landed elite and the multinational corporations. By imposing tariffs and quotas, governments can effectively bar agricultural imports from the Third World that might compete with commodities produced in the First World.

3. The Third World as locus of the problem's solution. Although Lappé and Collins believe that the primary source of the Third World's hunger problem lies in the affluent world, they contend that the solution to the problem ultimately rests with the Third World. They believe that even if production could be increased in the Third World and trade could be liberalized and aid could be increased, the only group to benefit would be the elite that currently controls the world's agricultural resources. Lappé and Collins contend that the poor must be given control over their own agricultural resources and production so that they may become self-reliant in food: "People will escape from hunger only when policies are pursued that allow them to grow food and to eat the food they grow."[29] The "development" policies of the Third World must enable people to become self-reliant in food first. Agricultural production in the Third World in other words must be geared to produce food for domestic consumption first. Only after the Third World's domestic nutritional needs have been met should it be possible to export any crops. As Lappé and Collins point out, "self-reliance starts with the nutritional needs of all the people and translates them into a national agricultural plan."[30] So the governments of the Third World must pursue policies that enable people, particularly the landless poor, to take control of the production and distribution of their own food. Agricultural production in the Third World should be controlled by "local, self-provisioning units, democratically organized."[31] The experience of countries like China, Cuba, Japan, Taiwan, and North Vietnam has proven that when people are given control over their own agricultural resources, they can and will produce enough food to feed themselves:

> People who own their own land, either privately or collectively, naturally invest more time, labor, and money in it than do nonowners. Only the redistribution of control of the land can create a new kind of farmer, one willing to face up to difficult challenges, no longer afraid of bosses, moneylenders, and landlords.[32]

We in the affluent nations of the world, Lappé and Collins hold, can contribute to the self-reliance of the hungry in the Third World by removing the obstacles imposed by our government that prevent the poor from controlling their own agricultural production and feeding themselves. The program that Lappé and Collins propose is worth quoting here:

> —Outlaw government assistance through AID and OPIC and, indirectly, through the World Bank to U.S. private corporations investing in underdeveloped countries.
> —Remove all tax laws that encourage American corporations to be abroad to escape environmental and wage laws and taxes here.
> —Outlaw the export or sale abroad by a U.S.-based corporation of any additive, pesticide, or drug that is prohibited in the United States.
> —Outlaw the importation for food from those countries in which the priority is not food for local people. At least 40 percent of all imported food that directly competes with United States farm production comes from underdeveloped countries.
> —End economic assistance to any country that is not actively redistributing control over food-producing resources to the people (includes in-rhetoric-only land-reform countries like the Philippines and Pakistan).
> —Promote foreign assistance to countries where steps are being taken to democratize control over agricultural resources.
> —Supply food aid only where it directly contributes to creating the preconditions for food self-reliance.[33]

Because the forces that contribute to the monopolization of our own food industry are the same forces that keep the Third World from feeding itself, Lappé and Collins believe that by working to democratize our own food system we are indirectly helping the hungry to feed themselves. Lappé and Collins suggest that we work, for example, for land reform in the United States and for decent income for all family farmers. We should try to keep corporations with nonfarm investments out of agriculture, we need to reform the inheritance tax laws that force families to sell their land in order to pay inheritance taxes at the inflated prices of farmland; and we need to bring about changes in corporate food-advertising techniques.[34]

Let us now take up the concepts developed by Susan George, another expert on world hunger, whose analysis of world hunger and proposed solutions are similar to those of Lappé and Collins.

1. The inability of the poor to grow or buy their own food. In *How the Other Half Dies* George argues that people are hungry because they are poor. The poor lack the agricultural resources to grow their own food or the capital to purchase food or both. Like Lappé and Collins, George believes that food is not scarce; it has simply been priced out of the reach of the poorest segment of society. The people who starved during the food crisis were those who could not afford the artificially inflated price of food.

2. The role of the landed gentry. George's position is that the vast majority in the Third World are poor because they have been kept poor by the landed elite in their own societies and by the world economic system, which effectively discriminates against their products. Although the majority of the poor in the Third World live in rural areas and earn their living through agriculture, few own enough land to be able to accumulate sufficient capital to support themselves and their families. The vast majority of the rural poor are tenant farmers, sharecroppers, landless laborers, serfs, or squatters. She points out that the land tenure system reflects the inequality that exists in many Third World countries:

> In South America overall, 17 per cent of the landowners control 90 per cent of the land. The situation is not quite so dramatically skewed in Asia where there are a lot more farms in the five- to fifty-hectare category. But even here, the top fifth of landowners control three fifths of the arable land (and are gaining control over more every day . . .). To describe the same situation from the opposite angle, in Latin America, over a third of the rural population must make do with just *1 per cent* of the cropland; in Africa, three quarters of the people have access to not quite 4 per cent of the land. World Bank figures for 22 UDCs [underdeveloped countries] show that, on the average, fully a third of the "active agricultural population" has *no land at all*.[35]

3. The role of the West in reinforcing inequities. George further shows that the West has played a significant role in reinforcing the inequities that exist within the Third World. Many of the economic elite in the Third World have been educated or trained in western educational, commercial, and military establishments. The West, she affirms, deliberately cultivates and tries to maintain a lasting relationship with the elite so that the elite will be receptive to western forms of development and hence western influence. Friendship with the elite in the Third World has paid off for both parties. George holds that basically the so-called development programs in the Third World have primarily benefited the elite in the Third World, while securing the West's economic, political, and military interests in those countries. The Green Revolution is for her a typical example of how western "development" aids the rich in the Third World and the West's own commercial interests. The miracle grains, she points out, require large amounts of fertilizer, pesticides, high-pressure sprayers, motorized equipment, and irrigation—all not commonly available to small subsistence farmers. The larger farmers who have access to these inputs profit most from this technological innovation. So too do the western multinational corporations that are the main suppliers of these inputs. As for the overall effects of the Green Revolution, Susan George tries to weigh the good and the bad:

> It would be foolish and inaccurate to pretend the Green Revolution has had no good effects in UDCs [underdeveloped countries]: its role in increasing the *marketable* surplus, thus in helping to feed urban consumers, has been very important. Unfortunately, it has also seriously increased inequalities between farmers who can afford it and those who cannot, as well as between more and less favored areas in the same countries. . . . There seems little doubt, however, that aside from its contributions to the profit side of MNC [multinational corporation] business ledgers it has also been viewed by various American interests pushing it as an *alternative to land reform* and to the social change reform would require. Since land reform is the only *other* way to increase food production, these experts are willing to settle for the lesser of two evils.[36]

4. Discrimination against products of the Third World. As mentioned, George contends that the vast majority of the poor in the Third World have been kept poor not only by the elite within their own societies but by a world economic system that discriminates against their products. She says that agricultural production in the Third World is dominated by cash or export cropping. This type of land use employs not only the best land in the Third World but also scarce fertilizer, technology, pesticides, research, and credit. Because it is more profitable to grow crops for export, more and more land is being taken out of production for domestic consumption and used instead for export cropping. In the Philippines 55 percent of the land goes for export cropping; in Mauritius, 80 percent; and in Senegal 50 percent of all cultivated land is used for groundnuts that will be exported.[37]

George's position is that the world trade system is controlled by the affluent West and is structured against the interests of the Third World. Although the Third World's production and export value have increased, the price it receives for its products has declined. The reason for the decline in price is due to the inability of the Third World to control the prices it receives for its products, the distribution circuits, or the technology that might add value to the goods produced. She points out that the prices the Third World receives for its raw materials are kept artificially low by the terms of trade set by the affluent nations. Moreover, products other than its raw materials and cash crops are effectively barred from western markets through the imposition of protectionist measures. The processing of the Third World's products, furthermore, is handled by foreign-based multinational corporations.

According to George, Brazil's coffee and soybeans are for the most part processed by American multinationals. Much of the Third World's oil, tea, timber, rubber, fish, and fruit are also processed by foreign-based multinationals.[38] Thus not only are the Third World's valuable land and resources used for producing crops for export rather than for domestic consumption but the prices it receives for its exports do not provide enough revenue for the Third World to purchase food to stave off hunger.

5. The need for structural change in the Third World. The solution to the problem of hunger, in George's view, is dependent upon fundamental structural change within the societies of the Third World and a change on their side of the relationship with the affluent nations of the world:

> So long as thoroughgoing land reform, regrouping and distribution of resources to the poorest, bottom half of the population does not take place, Third World countries can go on increasing their production until hell freezes and hunger will remain, for the production will go to those who already have plenty—to the developed world or to the wealthy in the Third World itself.[39]

Like Lappé and Collins, George contends that the Third World must reduce its dependency on western trade and aid and build its own self-reliance.

6. The need to restructure systems and transform values in the First World. As for what we in the affluent world can do about hunger, George does not propose, as I would, a radical restructuring of the systems and transformation of the values that govern the relationship of rich and poor, but an almost total termination of the relationship:

> Stay out of other peoples' affairs. Stop sending out your experts whose training suits them only for proposing Western-oriented "solutions." Stop forcing your unadapted and usually unadaptable technology on radically different societies. Stop shaping their environments to suit your needs. Stop educating people to think that yours is the only road to "progress." Stop sending the kind of aid which will aid *you*, in the form of myriad commercial advantages, a hundred times more than it will ever help the poor. Stop running the multilateral agencies and the U.N. Stop giving aid and comfort, political and material support to repressive local elites that have no intention of changing the lot of their people, and give the people a chance. Put a leash on your corporations, your foundations, your universities, your bureaucracies and your banks.[40]

Needless to say, George does not expect this to happen.

In my judgment, Lappé, Collins, and George correctly link the problem of world hunger with the problem of poverty in the Third World. While overpopulation, bad weather, and a growing scarcity of natural resources certainly place a strain on the world's food supply, people are hungry principally because they are poor. As we learned from the food crisis of 1972–75, people who could afford to pay the price of food did eat; those who could not, starved. Thus hunger and poverty are inextricably related.

The work of Lappé, Collins, and George is important because it exposes the political and economic dimensions of world hunger. When the poor are denied access to land to grow their own food; when the best land is concentrated in the hands of a few and is used for export cropping rather than for producing food for domestic consumption; when governments pattern their development after that of the industrialized First World; when foreign governments structure their trade and aid policies to protect and foster the economic interest of their own industries in the Third World; and when giant multinational firms gobble up land, exploit laborers, and prey on the victims of poverty—when all the conditions described above occur, then we must expect hunger as a result.

Finally, the work of Lappé, Collins, and George is important for implicating the free market system in the problem of world hunger. Lappé and Collins write:

> The heaviest constraint on food production and distribution turns out to be the inequality generated by our type of economic system—the system now being exported to the underdeveloped countries as the supposed answer to their food problems.[41]

All three authors call on us to challenge the basic assumptions of our own economic system.

Lappé, Collins, and George have clearly broken new ground in our understanding of the causes of world hunger. As important as their contributions are, however, I believe that their approach to the problem may be somewhat misleading. The problem, as I see it, is not really hunger but underdevelopment, that is, the structural relationship between the First and Third Worlds. World hunger is only one of the effects, although one of the more visible effects, of the unequal development generated by the aid, trade, and investment policies of the First World. The priorities governing the First World's food aid, food trade, and food investment in the Third World, I believe, are the same priorities that govern the First World's aid, trade, and investment policies with the Third World in general. These policies, as I will show, are the inevitable outcome of an economic system based on the profit motive.

Lappé, Collins, and also George maintain that a solution to the problem of hunger lies ultimately with the Third World. While fundamental structural changes are needed in the Third World, I hold these changes alone will not bring an end to the exploitation of the Third World. Since the poverty and hunger of the Third World are a by-product of our own economic system, we cannot expect poverty and hunger to be alleviated without a fundamental transformation of this system. Denis Goulet, the development ethicist, expresses well the need for this transformation:

> As long as privileged classes or nations continue to regard the emancipation of the world's poor as the fruit of productivity gains alone or mere increases in GNP [gross national product], without altering present arrangements governing access to resources or shattering the nexus between productive capacity and purchasing power, rapid worldwide development remains impossible. . . . Only massive restructuring of production priorities, allied to major changes in the distributive norms governing wealth, skills, and access to resources, can produce universal development. These major changes in the world's economic, political, and cultural systems are prerequisites of development.[42]

I wish to propose another modification in the approach of these authors. Lappé, Collins, and George treat world hunger as a political and economic problem. Hunger, I believe, is not merely a political and economic problem; it is also a moral problem. As we shall see in the following pages, the policy decisions of the First World toward the Third World reflect the choice of certain goods or values over others. For example, the withholding of grain from Bangladesh in the midst of the food crisis because of trade arrangements existing between Bangladesh and Cuba, President Nixon's decision to withhold farmland from production despite warnings of impending drought from the United Nations, and the decision of multinational corporations to sell infant formula to illiterate peasants in the Third World—all these decision are ethical choices.

In the pages that follow we will see how these and other decisions clearly reflect a choice of the economic and political good over the human good. If hunger and poverty are ever to be eliminated, I believe that a fundamental change is needed not only in our political and economic systems but also in the values upon which those systems are based.[43] Until nations and individuals give priority to meeting human needs over private materialistic gain, poverty and hunger will continue to plague our world.

Thus far I have distinguished between the factors that triggered the food crisis of 1972–75 and what some leading experts in the field believe to be the underlying or more deeprooted causes of hunger. I have highlighted the main points of their theories and also pointed out some of the weaknesses in their arguments.

Hunger is not just a result of overpopulation and overconsumption. It is rather one of the more visible effects of the situation of underdevelopment for which our own economic system is to a large extent responsible.

Thus if poverty and hunger are ever to be alleviated, far-reaching changes will be needed in the economic, political, and social systems and values that have produced underdevelopment for two thirds of the world's population. Now let us turn to a fuller explanation of the roots of hunger.

Chapter 2

ROOTS OF THE
THIRD WORLD'S POVERTY

It is important to point out from the start that the Third World has not always been poor. It was made poor. In fact, many believe that the very process that produced wealth for the countries of the Northern Hemisphere produced poverty for those in the Southern Hemisphere. While some debate exists today as to whether the European colonization of the Third World in the fifteenth, sixteenth, and seventeenth centuries could be termed a capitalist undertaking, it is safe to say that the colonizers paved the way for what could properly be called the "capitalist exploitation" of the Third World that was to come with the Industrial Revolution.

PHASE OF COLONIAL DEPENDENCE (1400–1850)

Theotonio Dos Santos, the Brazilian economist, has argued that there have been three phases in the relationship between the rich nations and poor nations. He appropriately refers to these phases as "phases of dependence."[1] The first phase was the phase of colonial dependence. It began during the late fifteenth century and lasted until about the middle of the nineteenth century. This was the period of the great discoveries by Portugal, Spain, Holland, Britain, and France. The initial motive for establishing colonies was to secure existing trade routes. But under the protection of the absolute monarchs of feudal states, the conquerors seized the lands of local peasant farmers and extracted precious metals and stones as well as tropical produce. The colonies thus became an invaluable source of wealth and power for the mother countries.

PHASE OF FINANCIAL INDUSTRIAL DEPENDENCE (1850–1940)

According to Dos Santos, next came the phase of financial industrial dependence. It began in the second half of the nineteenth century with the second Industrial Revolution and lasted until about the Second World War.

Most Marxist analysts describe this development as the beginning of capitalist imperialism in the Third World. Economist James O'Connor lists five characteristics that distinguish this period from the precapitalist period that preceded it:

> First, in pre-capitalist societies, economic expansion was irregular, unsystematic, not integral to normal economic activity. In capitalist societies, foreign trade and investment are rightly considered to be "engines of growth." Expansion is necessary to maintain the rhythm of economic activity in the home, or metropolitan economy, and has an orderly, methodical, permanent character. Second, in pre-capitalist society, the economic gains from expansion were windfall gains, frequently taking the form of sporadic plunder. In capitalist societies, profits from overseas trade and investment are an integral part of national income, and considered in a matter-of-fact manner.
>
> Third, in pre-capitalist societies, plunder acquired in the course of expansion was often consumed in the field by the conquering armies, leaving the home economy relatively unaffected. In capitalist societies, exploited territories are fragmented and integrated into the structure of the metropolitan economy. . . . Fourth, in precapitalist societies, debates within the ruling class ordinarily revolved around the issue whether or not to expand. In capitalist societies, ruling class debates normally turn on the question of what is the best way to expand.
>
> Last, in relation to colonialism, pre-capitalist and capitalist societies also differ in this fundamental way. In the former, colonialism (land seizure, colonist settlement, or both) was the only mode of control which the metropolitan power could effectively exercise over the satellite region. . . . Capitalist societies have developed alternative, indirect, and more complex forms of control.[2]

The advances in technology and transportation brought on by the Industrial Revolution made it necessary for the industrial powers to locate and control new sources of raw materials. They also needed new outlets for capital investment and markets for their manufactured goods. Thus the territories already seized between the fifteenth and eighteenth centuries assumed new importance for the industrial nations. As a result, a mad scramble began among the European powers for the acquisition of more and more territories.

The effects of western capitalist expansion into Asia, Africa, and Latin America are of particular interest to us. Under European domination, the economic, political, and social systems of what has come to be called the Third World were virtually uprooted and restructured to meet the needs of the mother countries. Their once sufficient or semisufficient economies collapsed. Their agricultural systems were restructured to produce so-called marketable commodities. Indigenous capital was diverted into commerce or money lending, and even rural artisans whose crafts were exposed to foreign competition suffered ruin. From the nineteenth century on, the Third World was integrated into the international market system. Its role in that system would be to provide resources for the economic expansion of the Northern Hemisphere as well as outlets for its surplus production. Comparing the colonial to the industrial phase of capitalism, Michael Harrington comments:

> In a development that was less dramatic and more important than that often bloody process of capital accumulation, the capitalist economies deepened and institutionalized their original advantage by means of the world market of the nineteenth century.[3]

With its incorporation into the world market, the Third World became a mere apendage of the First World. In some writings you will see the term "periphery" applied to the Third World and "center" applied to the First World. Both terms capture the relationship that has existed between these two worlds.

PHASE OF NEW DEPENDENCE (1945–PRESENT)

Dos Santos refers to the third phase of the relationship between the First and Third Worlds as the phase of new dependence. The end of the Second World War may have signaled the end of the colonial era, but it also marked the rise of a new international institution, the multinational corporation, which in certain respects is richer and more powerful than some nation states. The dismantling of the colonial system and the rise of the multinational corporation brought about new structures of domination. While most of the colonies gained independence by the end of the Second World War, their relationship with their former masters has not changed very much. In fact, it merely assumed a more subtle and rational form.

As mentioned previously, the colonies were an invaluable asset to the industrialized capitalist nations. The capitalist economies could not prosper without their resources and markets. Therefore, after the colonies finally gained independence, the industrialized capitalist nations were faced with the problem of retaining economic benefits from their former colonies. They solved this problem quite effectively by structuring the international systems of trade and aid to their own advantage. The multinational corporations contributed further to the Third World's recolonization. As we shall see, under the protective arm of the advanced industrialized capitalist nations multinational corporations have been able to exploit the resources, labor, and savings of the Third World, leaving the economies of countries in the Third World more dependent on foreign input than in the past. The systematic subjugation of the Third World just described is sometimes referred to as "neocolonialism," a term coined by French Marxists in 1950 and taken up by the nonaligned Asian and African ex-colonies in the 1960s.[4] The term "neocolonialism" suggests that the new nations, while no longer colonies in theory, function as colonies in fact. This dynamic will be examined in detail in the analysis that follows.

To summarize briefly, the Third World has not always been poor. It was made poor by the mercantilist powers of Europe seeking trade advantages, precious stones and metals, and tropical produce. Later the industrial capitalist nations sought new sources of raw materials and markets to feed their own economic development. After the Second World War those same powers institutionalized their own advantages by controlling and manipulating the international systems of trade and aid to their own advantage. Finally, multinational corporations have joined in the exploitation of the Third World. Thus it is possible to say that the poverty of the Third World is inextricably linked to the economic growth of the First World. Underdevelopment is nothing less than a by-product of development. It is a by-product of the very process that produced wealth for the First World. Karl Marx argued in the nineteenth century that capitalism is an economic system that makes exploitation of individuals and nations necessary. At this point let us review Marx's theory of labor and capitalist expansion to see if it sheds any light on our problem.

MARX'S CRITIQUE OF CAPITALISM

The Role of Labor

According to Marx, labor is the only property that commodities have in common.[5] It is, therefore, the only standard for determining the value of a commodity. The more labor that goes into producing a commodity, the greater its value should be. Marx pointed out that in a capitalist system where profit is the overriding motive for production, the relationshship between the laborer and the value of his or her product becomes distorted. This is because laborers in a capitalist system sell their labor to an employer in exchange for wages. Since employers derive their profit from the difference between the wages they pay employees and the exchange or true market value of the laborers' products, they cannot pay laborers the true value of their labor. In fact, Marx argued, there is little relationship between wages and the real value of the laborers' own labor. Wages are merely the price employers choose to pay to keep laborers alive and producing. Thus, in a capitalist system, profit is always derived by exploiting laborers, that is, by depriving laborers of the true value of their labor.

Capitalist Expansion

Marx's criticism of capitalism did not stop with his explanation of the exploitation of individual laborers. Whole nations might become victims of a profit-oriented system. And this part of Marx's analysis is of particular interest to us as we try to understand the roots of hunger.

Marx holds that in a system in which the overriding concern is the maximization of profit, it is necessary for capitalists to find new sources of raw materials and new outlets for production. Expansion, therefore, is a necessary component of the capitalist system. Here is how Marx described the process of capitalist expansion.

> The need for constantly expanding outlets for its products drives the bourgeoisie over the entire globe. It must plant itself everywhere, build everywhere, produce interconnections everywhere. The bourgeoisie has formed the consumption and production of all lands in a cosmopolitan way by the exploitation of the world market. To the great sorrow of the reactionaries, it has pulled the national basis of industry from under their feet. Ancient national industries are annihilated and are daily still being annihilated. They are forced by new industries, whose introduction becomes a matter of life and death for all civilized countries, by industries which no longer use the raw materials of their own land but raw materials that come from the most distant places and whose products are no longer consumed within the nation itself but at the same time in every part of the world. In place of the old needs, which were satisfied by products within the nation itself, there are now new needs which require the products of the most distant lands and climates for their satisfaction. . . . The cheap prices of their commodities are the heavy artillery with which the bourgeoisie destroys all the Chinese walls, with which it forces the most stiff-necked and xenophobic barbarians to capitulate. . . . *In a word, it creates for itself a world in its own image* [emphasis added].[6]

Now that we have looked at Marx's theory of labor and capitalist expansion it might be helpful to briefly examine some of the differences between a capitalist and a socialist system.

Differences between a Capitalist and a Socialist System

There are a number of characteristics that distinguish a capitalist from a socialist or planned system. For our purposes it might be best to focus on just two of the primary characteristics. In a socialist system neither the means of production nor the value derived from production are privately owned. All the forces of production are organized according to a national economic plan to meet certain consciously felt social needs. The goal of socialists is not to maximize their private profits but rather to carry out the tasks assigned to them by the national economic plan.[7] A capitalist system, on the other hand, operates on different principles and has different goals. In a capitalist system, the means of production and the profits that accrue from production are privately held. Unlike a socialist system, where production is organized according to a national economic plan, in a capitalist system capitalists act in their own interests and independently of each other. Their overriding goal is the goal of the system itself: the maximization of profit. Thus in a capitalist society production is structured not to meet social needs but rather to accumulate private profit.

The Role of the State in a Capitalist System

Capitalism is not just an economic system. Economic systems are always intertwined with political and cultural systems. In a capitalist society the state plays a critical role in insuring the growth and stability of the economic system. This is because of the "boom-and-bust" nature of the capitalist economic system itself.

As mentioned previously, in a capitalist system capitalists produce goods and services independently of each other and for their own interest. Production in such a system is geared primarily for profit rather than for use. In a system such as this where individual capitalists are constantly producing to increase their own profits without reference to the final market, overproduction is bound to occur. This results in a surplus of unsold goods, a drop in profits, a stagnation in production, and an increase in the rate of unemployment. Eventually, however, stocks will be sold, goods will wear out, new materials will be needed, and production will pick up again[8].

In a capitalist system, therefore, state intervention in the economy becomes increasingly necessary to ease the shock of the "boom-and-bust" cycle. As Harrington points out, the state must intervene, if for no other reason than to insure its own survival:

> Its [the state's] funds, its power, its political survival, depend on private-sector performance. So do the jobs of most workers. The state's interest in perpetuating its own rule is thus, in economic fact, identified with the health of the capitalist economy.[9]

State intervention in the economy assumes a number of forms. The most obvious of which are state spending (welfare, military spending, space exploration, etc.), taxation, and regulation of the supply of money. While there is a direct link between military spending and the problem of hunger, it would take us too far afield to go into the subject here. I would like to refer you, however, to *Hunger for Justice,* a book by Jack A. Nelson of Clergy and Laity Concerned which treats the subject in detail.[10]

What is of particular interest to us here, however, are the more subtle ways in which the state protects and promotes the interest of the capitalist system at the expense of increased poverty and hunger in the Third World. We shall examine these problems in more detail in Chapters 3, 4, and 5.

Chapter 3

THE STRUCTURE OF WORLD TRADE
AND ITS EFFECTS ON
THE THIRD WORLD

At the outset it was stated that the roots of the problem of hunger lie in our own economic system. As Marx pointed out, our economic system is inherently expansionist. It is also a system that, if left to its own devices, experiences periods of "boom and bust." Thus the state in our economic system assumes an increasingly important role in mitigating economic crises. One of the more subtle ways in which the state fulfills this role is by protecting and promoting the interest of its system abroad. We shall now examine the various mechanisms employed by the state. The overall effect of such mechanisms on the Third World has been to increase its poverty and hunger.

To illustrate how these mechanisms contribute to poverty and hunger in the Third World, let us focus on some trade and aid decisions of the United States during the food crisis of 1972–75. I have chosen to concentrate on the United States because the United States, as one of the most influential capitalist nations in the world, has played a major role in structuring the international systems of world trade and aid. It is responsible therefore to a large extent for the present world economic order. In addition, our country is one of the world's largest producers of grain and it supplies most of the world's food aid. An examination of American food trade and food aid during the food crisis of 1972–75 illustrates how the mechanisms of trade and aid work to the detriment of the Third World. Our analysis of American food trade and aid also shows that the motives behind the trade and aid in food are no different from the motives that guide our trade and aid with the Third World in general. If our observations are correct, it should become clear that hunger is not an isolated problem but is one of the more visible effects of policies structured to protect and promote the interest of our own economic system.

In sum, if hunger is ever to be eliminated from our world, change cannot be brought about simply by liberalizing trade or aid with the Third World. It will take a fundamental change in the relationship of the state to the capitalist system and ultimately will require transformation of the capitalist system itself. Let us now turn to an analysis of the present systems of international trade, aid, and investment.

DETERIORATING TERMS OF TRADE

Exports are an important source of foreign exchange for the Third World. Unlike rich nations that transact most of their trade among themselves, the bulk of the Third World nations' trade (80 percent) flows between themselves and the industrial capitalist nations of the world. It is important, therefore, for the Third World to have access to the markets of the First World and also receive a fair price for its products.

With the exception of the OPEC nations, the Third World has experienced a marked deterioration in the rate of exchange for its products. Although its export volume has increased by more than 30 percent over the last two decades, its export earnings have risen by only 4 percent.[1] The Secretariat of the United Nations Council on Trade and Development (UNCTAD) estimates in fact that the Third World actually loses an average of $2.5 billion per year because of its deteriorating terms of trade. In other words, the price of goods the Third World must import from the First World has risen disproportionately to the price of goods that the Third World exports. In 1950, for example, 55 pounds of bananas from the Third World could buy a ton of steel. In 1974, however, 140 pounds were needed. In 1954, 6,000 kilograms of tea could buy 100 tons of steel. In 1974 it could buy only 50 tons. One final example, 25 tons of natural rubber could buy 6 tractors in 1960 while in 1975 they could buy only 2.[2]

THEORIES OF UNEQUAL TRADE

What accounts for the Third World's deteriorating terms of trade? There are a number of theories that explain unequal exchange. For our purposes, however, it might be best to briefly describe the three that are most widely held.

1. Composition of trade. One very common theory states that the Third World must produce more in order to purchase the same amount or less on the world market because of the composition of its trade. The colonial system, it argues, left many Third World countries with economies that specialize in the production of a few agricultural commodities and raw materials. The First World, however, produces primarily manufactured goods. According to this theory, the demand and the price for primary products on the world market have steadily declined while the demand and the price for manufactured goods have steadily increased. Moreover, the price of primary products tends to fluctuate on the world market while the price of manufactured goods has climbed steadily. Thus the Third World finds itself in the position of having to export a greater quantity of its primary products in order to purchase the manufactured goods it needs for its own development.

2. Exchange of unequal labor. Another theory of unequal exchange espoused by analysts such as Arghiri Emmanuel and Samir Amin takes issue with this easy identification of primary products with the Third World and manufactured goods with the First World.[3] The poor nations, they hold, do not have a monopoly on raw materials any more than the rich on manufactured goods. They point out, for example, that over the last decade the Third World has steadily increased its manufacture export sector as well as its imports of grain and fuel. The First World, they point out, is also an exporter of agriculture and raw materials. The United States, for example, is the world's major exporter of grain. Canada and Australia both have significant mineral exports. Emmanuel clarifies the misleading identification of the products of the Third World as "primary":

> The copper of Zambia or the Congo and the gold of South Africa are no more primary than coal, which was only yesterday one of the chief exports of Great Britain; sugar is about as much "manufactured" as soap or margarine and certainly more "manufactured" than Scotch whisky or the great wines of France; before they are exported, coffee, cocoa, and cotton (especially cotton) have to undergo a machine processing no less considerable, if not more so, than in the case of Swedish or Canadian timber; petroleum necessitates installations just as expensive as steel; bananas and spices are no more primary than meat or dairy products. And yet the prices of the former decline while those of the latter rise, and *the only common characteristic in each case is that they are, respectively, the products of poor countries and the products of rich countries* [emphasis added].[4]

Both Emmanuel and Amin argue that unequal exchange is due to the value the multinational corporations and the local wholesale trade assign to labor in the Third World rather than to the declining world-market price for primary goods.

Samir Amin contends that the rate of productivity in the Third World is comparable to and in some cases greater than the rate of productivity of the same sector in the advanced capitalistic nations. The rewards for productivity, however, are not the same. To cite three examples, the wages United Fruit pays in Central America, Unilever in Malaysia, and Firestone in Africa average between 4 and 15 percent of the wages paid by the same corporations in the United States.[5] According to this theory, the multinational corporations, foreign firms, and wholesale firms control the modern productive sectors in the Third World and keep the rewards of productivity artificially low to increase their own profits.

Even more disturbing is the fact that the profits that accrue from the Third World's cheap labor are not invested in the Third World's economy. They are transferred instead to the industrial capitalist nations in the form of investment or purchases of technology or luxury goods.[6]

Amin and Emmanuel maintain that because the rewards for labor are low and because the bulk of the Third World's trade is conducted with the First World, when the Third World trades with the First World, it actually exchanges a larger quantity of its labor for a smaller quantity of the First World's labor. The result is an unequal exchange.[7] Amin illustrates this point:

> Altogether then if exports from the periphery amount to about $35 billion, their value, if the rewards of labor were equivalent to what they are at the center, with equal productivity, would be about $57 billion. The hidden transfers of value from the periphery to the center, due to the mechanisms of unequal exchange, are of the order of $22 billion— twice the amount of the "aid," both public and private, received by the periphery.[8]

3. Inability to sell products that compete with First World products. There is yet another theory for unequal exchange that falls somewhere between the two theories just cited. In my judgment it is the most plausable of the three. According to this theory, it is inaccurate to claim that raw materials come from the Third World and manufactured goods from the First World. In 1975 alone, for example, the First World exported 66.1 percent of the world's total primary products.[9] It is, however, more accurate to say that while the Third World is not the world's largest exporter of primary products, it nevertheless is dependent on the earnings from its export of primary products for a major portion of its foreign exchange.[10] This theory also corrects the other common misconception that on the world market the prices of primary products tend to fluctuate in comparison with the prices of processed or manufactured goods. Political scientist Cheryl Payer points out that this may be true for certain commodities, but not for all:

> For those [commodities] which are produced at one end of an integrated structure of production which includes several stages of processing under a single corporate control, the statement does not hold true. The price will not be determined by short-term supply/demand relationships, but by a decision taken within the planning structure of the firm. This "transfer price" is a sort of accounting fiction made necessary by the corresponding fiction that the firm's affiliate in the producing country is "exporting" the commodity to the processing plant in another country, and is not likely to vary more sharply than the price of the finished goods.[11]

The price fluctuation associated with primary goods is more typical of goods traded on commodity exchanges where the market price is based on supply and demand.[12] If these generalizations are inaccurate, what can we say then about the Third World's export sector that might account for its deteriorating rate of exchange? Payer provides a valuable clue. She claims that the feature that the nations of the Third World share in their trade with the First World is their inability to sell products on the world market that compete significantly with those of the First World. Consequently, the exports of the Third World are limited to foodstuffs and raw materials that the rich nations cannot economically produce themselves or in great enough quantity to satisfy their markets as well as labor-intensive, low-wage manufactured goods. Payer describes the situation of the Third World well in these words:

> The poor countries are accurately enough described as raw materials exporting economies, but even within this realm the products they export fall within this narrow range of "leftovers" which the developed countries cannot, or do not find it profitable to produce.[13]

DISCRIMINATORY TRADE PRACTICES

1.GATT. The soundness of this last theory can be demonstrated by a brief look at how one of the institutions that regulates international trade, the General Agreement on Tariffs and Trade (GATT), operates. Toward the end of World War II, representatives of the world's nations met in Bretton Woods, New Hampshire, for the purpose of normalizing post-war international economic relations. Out of that meeting emerged the International Monetary Fund (IMF), the International Bank for Reconstruction and Development (IBRD, or World Bank), and the General Agreement on Tariffs and Trade.The primary concern of these institutions was the rehabilitation of western European capitalism, the restructuring of the international monetary system, and the expansion of international trade and investment.[14] It is important to point out that these institutions were and continue to be dominated by the First World, particularly the United States, as their structures reflect.

The General Agreement on Tariffs and Trade provides a good illustration of this point. It was founded for the express purpose of dismantling some of the barriers such as tariffs and quotas that restrict the flow of trade among nations. Members of GATT include nearly all the rich, free-market nations, some eastern European nations, and a number of Third World nations. Representatives of GATT meet periodically to negotiate trade barriers. Negotiations are conducted on the basis of reciprocity, that is, each nation concedes no more than it will receive in return. This places the nations of the Third World at a serious disadvantage. Because its markets are not very large, the Third World has little to bargain with. Moreover, the Third World lacks the organization needed to negotiate effectively with the large powers. It is safe to say that the concessions that have been won at GATT are, for the most part, for products of particular interest to the major capitalist nations that dominate the institution. Products of interest to the Third World are generally not included in the general tariff cuts.[15] This is what happened at the Kennedy Round of GATT negotiations in the 1960s. Duties on products from the First World were cut in half while there was virtually no reduction in duties on products from the Third World.[16] In the 1973–79 Tokyo Round of

GATT negotiations the Third World again did not fare as well as the rest of the world. Tax reductions on Third World products averaged about 25 percent compared to worldwide tax reductions of 33 percent.[17]

One final point should be kept in mind about trade concessions. All concessions won in GATT negotiations are to be applied across the board to all GATT members—rich and poor alike. This is called the Most Favored Nation (MFN) principle. It is not unusual, however, for some of the major powers to deny MFN treatment to Third World nations or to impose quotas on them that the major powers do not impose on each other.[18]

2. Tariffs. Rich nations discriminate against poor nations in other ways. It is common knowledge that real profits are made in processing goods. By levying tariffs proportionate to the degree of processing of raw materials or manufactured goods, the First World has made it virtually impossible for the Third World to reap the full benefits of its own production. It is estimated that the Third World receives a mere $30 billion of the $200 billion that consumers pay for products that originate in the Third World.[19] Most favored nation tariff reductions on products of interest to the Third World averaged 60 percent on raw materials, 27 percent on semimanufactures, and 24 percent on finished manufactures at the conclusion of the Tokyo Round.[20] Such discrimination against Third World semimanufactured and manufactured products impedes the Third World's attempt to increase its production in these high growth, high profit areas.

As we might expect, the protection on manufactures from the Third World is significantly higher than the protection on manufactures from the First World. In 1967, for example, the effective protection on all manufactures into the First World was 19.2 percent while the effective protection on manufactures from the Third World was 33.4 percent—or 84 percent higher than the overall protection on manufactured imports into the First World. The same was true in 1972. The effective protection on manufactures into the First World was 11.1 percent, but 22.6 percent on Third World manufactures. This represents a protection 109 percent higher on Third World manufactures.[21] The effect the Tokyo Round will have on these figures remains to be seen.

3. Non-tariff barriers. Nontariff barriers represent another, and in many ways, a more debilitating form of discrimination against exports from the Third World. One GATT document lists over 800 nontariff restrictions.[22] Nontariff restrictions include quotas, packaging and labeling requirements, health and safety standards, customs regulations, and others. These restrictions can increase the effective tariff on an item by more than 200 percent. Take peanuts, for example. In the United States in 1968, peanuts were subjected to a 69 percent tariff, but the effective protection that includes the various nontariff restrictions amounted to 204 percent.[23]

4. Trade reform frustrated. The nations of the Third World are attempting to address the problem of discrimination against their products in the United Nations Council on Trade and Development (UNCTAD), which was founded in 1964 to provide a forum for discussing economic arrangements between the First and Third Worlds. One of the main developments that has emerged out of UNCTAD is the General System of Preferences (GSP), which provides for the nonreciprocal abolition or reduction of tariffs on Third World exports. While the GSP appears impressive on paper, its implementation has been less so. To begin with, the rich nations have not been able to reach a consensus on a single preference scheme. Consequently, each nation has tended to develop its own preference scheme that differs on the coverage a product receives and the method of preference given.[24] The GSP, moreover, does not provide any legal guarantee that the rich nations will follow through on their individual schemes. In fact, the rich nations have become very adept at getting around their own schemes.

The U.S. Trade Act of 1974, which authorized the implementation of the GSP, for example, has a number of loopholes. In accord with its stipulations, OPEC nations and other nations that join cartels, nations that do not observe the proper procedures for nationalizing foreign industries, and nations that do not cooperate with the American government in drug control are excluded from GSP benefits. The GSP scheme, moreover, excludes textiles, footwear, and petroleum—all important Third World exports. It also stipulates that preferential treatment be denied to countries whose exports of a certain product to the United States exceed $25 million or 50 percent of our total imports of that product from all sources.[25] Finally, one of the most disappointing features of the GSP is the fact that it does not cover nontariff barriers.

In sum, by imposing heavier than average tariff and nontariff restrictions on Third World products that compete with its own, or by lifting or simply not imposing those restrictions, the First World can regulate the flow of trade between itself and the Third World to its own advantage. The Third World, therefore, must adjust its own production to meet the market requirements of the First World. Its concentration on the production and export of food stuffs, raw materials, and labor-intensive, low-wage manufactures is not merely the result of their colonial past or of their comparative advantage. It is rather a product of a system that has been rigged by the First World to its own advantage.

The Third World is hungry because it is poor. Since trade is one of the primary sources of foreign exchange, trade restrictions on the Third World pose a major obstacle to growing and/or purchasing enough food to feed itself. Had the Third World been earning enough capital from its exports when the food crisis of 1972–75 struck, it would have been in a position to compete with other nations for scarce commodities.

STATE INTERVENTION IN PRODUCTION AND EXPORT SECTORS: AMERICAN GRAIN EXPORTS

If the First World goes to such lengths to protect its industries from Third World imports, it goes without saying that it is just as involved in protecting its own export sector. Instead of examining the topic of state involvement in the export sector in general, we might gain a better perspective for understanding the problem of world hunger if we focus our attention on our own nation's involvement in regulating the production and export of grain, one of its major exports. We shall limit our analysis to decisions made during the food crisis years of 1972-75 in order to demonstrate how closely our nation identifies with the interests of the capitalist system. There is little doubt that even when massive human suffering is involved, economic and political interests take precedence over human interests in our system.

Effects of American Policy on the World Food Supply (1972-75)

The American economic crisis. The Third World depends on the United States for most of its grain. Thus any change in American policy regarding grain production or export is bound to affect the Third World. Two policy decisions in 1972 virtually cut off the food supply to the poorest nations of the Third World. The first was the continued withholding of farmland from production; the second was the virtual elimination of American grain reserves through export sales.[26] The important question for us is why these decisions were made.

In his book *Hunger for Justice,* Jack Nelson points out that by 1971 the American economy was in rather bad shape. For the first time in this century, the United States experienced a trade deficit. More and more American dollars were being sent abroad. The following figures give some idea of the increase in American spending on foreign imports, especially in the area of high-technology items such as chemicals, nonelectrical machinery, electrical apparatus, and transport equipment:

> In 1960 the U.S. imported $807 million in chemicals; ten years later it imported $1.45 billion, a 79.6 percent increase. In nonelectrical machinery the 1960 import bill was $438 million; by 1970 that figure had jumped to $3.1 billion, a 608.2 percent increase. In the area of electrical apparatuses, the import bill jumped from $286 million in 1960 to $2.27 billion in 1970, a 694.4 percent increase. And in the area of transport equipment, the import bill jumped from $742 million in 1960 to $5.79 million in 1970, a 681.3 percent increase.[27]

In 1971-72 the U.S. trade deficit tripled from $2.2 billion to more than $6.6 billion.[28] To add to the nation's economic woes, inflation reached a new high as a result of spending for the war in Vietnam.

In an effort to come to terms with the mounting economic crisis, the Nixon Administration commissioned in 1970 a study of American trade and investment policy. The study was chaired by Albert Williams of International Business Machines (IBM). In its report the Williams Commission recommended a number of measures to restore vitality to the economy, one of the most important of which was to launch a vigorous export drive in high-technology goods and agriculture. Nelson points out that this recommendation took two forms: a campaign to sell military hardware abroad and a campaign to increase food sales in a world experiencing food shortages.[29] The latter recommendation is of particular interest to us here.

Reduction in the world food supply. At the time when the U.S. was experiencing its economic crisis, dramatic developments were taking place in the world's food supply.[30] Since 1966 the industrialized countries, particularly the United States, were cutting back on grain production in an effort to raise farm prices. This left the world with a reserve of less than 10 percent of its annual grain needs in 1972. Japan, Australia, western Europe, and the Soviet Union were making a concerted effort during this same period to upgrade their countries' diets, and as a result more grain was needed to feed livestock. The effect of this change in diet was reflected in the fact that the Soviet Union, which had been a net exporter of grain, became a net importer by 1970. The decline in the world's fish catch around 1969 forced nations dependent on fish as a major source of protein in their diets or as a feed supplement for livestock to import more grain. As early as 1969 there were forecasts of an impending drought in West Africa. And by 1971, the political repression in Bangladesh that drove millions into exile had created a catastrophic food shortage. The United States was warned by the United Nations and other agencies that the world's food supply was reaching a dangerously low level. It was clear that the United States as the world's largest supplier of grain would be called upon to meet these commercial and humanitarian needs.

Idling of farm land. The year 1972 was also an election year in the United States, and farm income became an important election issue. Author Hal Sheets points out that despite the unmistakable evidence of impending international food shortages, the Nixon administration decided to idle 62 million acres of farmland—the most farmland held idle in years. As compensation, farmers received $4 billion—double the previous year's payment for withholding land from production.

The Russian grain deal. In July and August of 1972, the Soviet Union contracted for the sale of 18 million tons of grain from the United States. This is sometimes referred to as the "Russian grain deal." While its mechanics are fascinating, it would take us too far afield from our study to go into them here. While the public and the American farm community were uninformed of the transactions taking place between the major American grain corporations and the Soviet Union, CIA reports that have been disclosed in the meantime indicate that the government knew of the deals and did nothing to stop them.[31] The Soviet Union's total purchase of grain worldwide that year amounted to 28 million tons—the largest grain purchase in history.

Removal of grain subsidies and devaluation of the dollar. Most people blamed the Soviet Union for the spiralling cost of grain and the shortages that followed. What in fact happened was that word of the Soviet Grain Deal set off panic buying worldwide, which in turn bid up the price of grain on the world market.[32] As Sheets points out, two events further intensified the mad scramble for grain. In September 1972 the United States government removed its subsidies on grain, and a rush ensued to buy whatever subsidized grain was left. And in February 1973 President Nixon devalued the dollar for the second time in fifteen months, which, of course, increased foreign buying power. The price of grain skyrocketed. In just a year the price of wheat, for example, climbed 300 percent from less than $60 to $180 per ton.[33]

Additional acreage idled. Finally, Sheets points out another factor that contributed to the shortages. In September 1972 when the presidential election was two months away, President Nixon, who had full knowledge of the world food situation, decided to idle an additional 5 million acres of farmland. It has been estimated that the grain lost in that year alone was sufficient to have met all the food needs that occurred over the next few years.

Effects of American Policy Decisions on the Third World

The commercial sale of grain to the Soviet Union as well as the decision of the Nixon administration to idle land despite growing food shortages had a devastating effect on the poor in the Third World. Because of the commodity-availability constraints of Public Law 480 (which specify that "commodities can only be made available for shipment under PL 480 when supplies have been assured for domestic consumption, adequate carryover stocks, and expected commercial exports"), the United States cut back its shipment of food aid to the Third World. United States food-aid shipments of wheat in 1973, for example, were reduced to less than 30 percent of the assistance given in 1971. Rice and vegetables were below even half of the 1971 levels, and feed-grain shipments were cut in half.[34] The PL 480 Report for 1974 shows that food aid was at its lowest level since the beginning of the program.

This drastic reduction in food aid consequently forced the food-deficit countries to compete for scarce commercial commodities with rich nations like Japan, Germany, and Britain. Between 1973 and 1974, thirty-two of the poorest nations classified as "Most Seriously Affected" by the United Nations were forced to triple their commercial imports from the United States.[35] The tragedy of the situation is demonstrated by Bangladesh, which at the height of the famine in 1974 was forced to purchase 80 percent of its farm imports on commercial terms. In the summer of that year, when it could no longer pay the going commercial rate for grain or purchase grain on credit, its people starved.[36]

To summarize briefly, the capitalist, or free-market, system is inherently expansionist. It requires a constant supply of raw materials, cheap labor, and outlets for its production in order to survive and prosper. In societies with such an economic system the state has come to play a key role in insuring the stability of the capitalist system. The advanced capitalist nations have dominated and structured world trade to maintain the stability of their own economic, political, and social systems. By rigging the system of trade to its own advantage, the First World has been able to exclude products from the Third World that might compete with its own products. It has been able for all practical purposes to gear the production and export sectors of the Third World to meet its own economic needs. And finally, the First World has been able to create artificial shortages that raise the price of products like grain out of the reach of the majority of people in the Third World.

Because the terms of trade are weighted in favor of the First World, the Third World cannot accumulate enough capital from its export earnings to meet its balance-of-payments deficit. It is forced, therefore, to turn to the First World for aid.

Chapter 4

THE STRUCTURE OF AID AND
ITS EFFECTS ON THE THIRD WORLD

The capitalist system needs markets to survive and prosper. Without outlets for its production, the economy of the first World would collapse. It is in the interest of the First World, therefore, to find new markets, or if it cannot find them, it must create them with whatever means it has at its disposal. Aid, as I will show, is one of the mechanisms by which the First World expands its markets in the Third World.

Although it is not widely acknowledged, the First World actually needs the Third World to sustain its own economic growth and high standard of living. Former Secretary of State Cyrus R. Vance for example, testified that in 1977, the Third World bought over one third of all American exports.[1] United States AID (Agency for International Development) figures also tell us that our nation is dependent on exports to the Third World for two million jobs.[2] In sum, the system of aid, like that of trade, is structured by the First World to protect and promote its own economic and political interests in the Third World. Thus aid has effectively tied the Third World to the purse strings of the industrial capitalist nations.

More than half the aid that the Third World receives from the First World is in the form of loans and not grants. These loans are repayable to the donor at interest. But because of its heavy indebtedness for previous loans, very little of the aid received by the Third World is actually used for development purposes. In fact, it is estimated that of every dollar that the Third World receives in aid, 87 cents are returned almost immediately to the donor to repay previous loans.[3] As previously noted, the terms under which aid is transferred to the Third World are structured to maintain the economic interests of the donor nation in the Third World.

MULTILATERAL AID

Aid can flow through multilateral channels, that is, through international lending agencies; it can flow bilaterally, that is, directly from country to country, through private lending institutions or charitable organizations.

38

For our purposes we will concentrate on multilateral and bilateral agencies. An examination of some of the practices of the World Bank Group (the major multilateral aid agency) and the United States Agency for International Development (AID), a bilateral lending agency, will show the extent to which the First World's aid programs are motivated by economic self-interest.

The World Bank Group consists of the International Monetary Fund (IMF), the International Bank for Reconstruction and Development (IBRD, or the World Bank), the International Finance Corporation (IFC), and the International Development Association (IDA). As stated in Chapter 3, both the IMF and the World Bank were founded in 1944 at Bretton Woods, New Hampshire. Although they were established for different purposes and continue to perform different tasks, the effect of their policies on the economies of the Third World is very similar. Resources for both the IMF and the World Bank come from subscriptions of their member nations, which are based on quotas initially negotiated at Bretton Woods. The size of each member's quota determines its voting power in the IMF and the World Bank. Consequently, the largest contributors to the IMF and the World Bank wield the most power. At present, the industrial capitalist nations control two-thirds of the votes of both institutions.[4] As Payer points out in her book *The Debt Trap,* the IMF is one of the most powerful international institutions in the world. It not only controls vast economic resources but it also has the power to interfere in the internal affairs of nations that borrow from the Fund.[5]

The International Monetary Fund (IMF)

The IMF was founded for the purpose of providing stability through short-term loans to member nations experiencing a temporary balance-of-payments crisis. Loans are made to save members from the necessity of having to curtail imports or impose trade restrictions to deal with a payment crisis.[6]

Conditions for loans. To qualify for a loan from the IMF, an applicant must agree to a program negotiated with the IMF, which outlines specific measures that must be taken to remedy the payments problem. Measures include:

1. Abolition or liberalization of foreign exchange and import controls.
2. Devaluation of the exchange rate.
3. Domestic anti-inflationary programs, including:
   a. control of bank credit; higher interest rates and perhaps higher reserve requirements;
   b. control of the government deficit; curbs on spending; increases in taxes and in prices charged by public enterprises; abolition of consumer subsidies;
   c. control of wage rises, so far as within the government's power;
   d. dismantling of price controls.
4. Greater hospitality to foreign investment.[7]

Failure to adhere to the IMF's development program by a recipient of IMF aid may jeopardize future opportunities to borrow not only from the IMF but from almost every public or private multilateral or bilateral lending agency in the capitalist world.

Effects on borrowing nations. Although the IMF loan provides temporary financial relief for an ailing economy, the conditions under which the loan is granted in the long run may do more harm to the economic growth of the borrowing nation. Payer maintains that the IMF program does more to pave the way for the growth of foreign industries in the borrowing nation than to restore health to an ailing economy. Take the devaluation of the borrowing nation's currency, for example. Payer holds that the devaluation of local currency makes it more difficult for domestic firms in the borrowing nation to purchase materials needed to carry on their operations. It also makes it more difficult for them to pay back past loans. When the firms try to borrow the money to keep their businesses going, they run into another IMF-caused obstacle in higher interest rates. The IMF's abolition or liberalization of foreign exchange and import controls, Payer points out, is also geared to benefit the industries of the donor nation. It enables foreign industries to gain greater access to the products and raw materials of the borrowing nation. Both the IMF measures just described, Payer holds, have a serious effect on the production and consumption of products such as food in a borrowing nation. Here is how. The liberalization of imports stimulates foreign consumption which, in turn, creates a scarcity of goods. When goods are scarce, prices rise. Moreover, because their currency has been devalued, fewer people can afford the inflated prices of domestically produced goods.[8] This is just one example of how aid can actually be geared to benefit the donor more than the recipient.

The International Bank for Reconstruction and Development (The World Bank)

The World Bank, unlike the IMF, finances and guarantees long-term (fifteen-to-twenty-year) development projects. To qualify for World Bank aid, applicants must have their general economic policies approved by the Bank and also their specific development projects.

A development project of the World Bank serves a purpose similar to the program of the IMF. It enables the donor nations to exert leverage on the economies of borrowing nations. Let us look at how a development project works. One of the most subtle forms of leverage is the selection of one development project over another. In making its selection, the World Bank can actually shape the type of development and the speed at which development takes place in the Third World. In the past, the projects selected by the World Bank have tended to be those particularly advantageous to the industries of the advanced capitalist nations. For example, western corporations need highways, ports, and transportation, electric, and communications systems to carry on their operations in the Third World. All these systems, however, tend to be expensive and also unprofitable for a corporation to build. Moreover, governments in the Third World tend to be rather slow to provide these services. The World Bank projects, in the past, provided an obvious solution to this dilemma. A survey of World Bank projects through 1970 shows that of the $14.3 billion allocated for Third World development projects, $9 billion were in the areas of electrical power and transportation.[9]

In addition to selecting certain projects, member nations of the World Bank also exercise leverage by specifying where a project is to be located, how it is to be managed, the type of equipment to be used, and where the equipment is to be purchased. The last requirement has proven particularly costly for the Third World. Under the conditions of aid, a recipient may be required to import equipment and also personnel for the project rather than use cheaper equipment or local personnel. For example, because of these stipulations, a country may be forced to use aid-financed imported earth-moving equipment rather than domestic manual labor for a project or aid-financed imported cement when the country's own cement works may be working at below capacity.[10] It is important to emphasize the fact that World Bank projects and the terms under which they are approved are designed to provide new markets and revenue for the industries of the donor nations.

The International Finance Corporation (IFC)

The IFC and the IDA are more recent additions to the World Bank group. Although both institutions have the same membership and structure as the World Bank, they perform different functions and have less capital. The IFC makes loans to private enterprises without a government guarantee, something that the World Bank is prevented from doing because of a statutory limitation. The IFC, Bruce Nissen argues, is in fact the "institutional embodiment of one of the Bank's basic priorities."[11]

The International Development Association (The IDA)

The IDA, on the other hand, makes long-term (fifty-year) loans to the poorest Third World countries at a .75 percent service charge. The IDA was created because certain Third World nations that had had a close relationship with the West could no longer afford loans from the World Bank. Such an institution was needed, therefore, to protect the First World's outstanding loans to the Third World and to maintain a favorable climate for investments in that area. IDA loans are used for purposes similar to World Bank loans, but the economic situation of a country and its credit-servicing ability, rather than a particular project, are the determining factors in granting IDA loans. It is not unusual for an IDA loan to be made to a country for the purpose of making payment on a previous loan. IDA loans are sometimes the only way the First World can insure payment of World Bank loans.[12] The First World's overall concern for the poorest nations of the world—those that are of little economic or military importance to the industrial capitalist nations—is reflected in the fact that each year there is some question as to whether the IDA will receive sufficient replenishments from its member nations to continue to make loans. Using the United States as an example, existing legislation authorizes the United States to contribute $1.5 billion to the IDA over a period of four years, beginning with FY 1976. For the first two years of its pledge to the IDA, the United States fell short of its commitment by $55 million.[13] Because funding for the IDA is so difficult to obtain from member nations, there is some speculation that the association may have to be dissolved.

BILATERAL AID

Bilateral lending agencies are no less self-serving than multilateral agencies. Since the policies of our own nation are of particular interest to us, it might be best to focus on the United States for our discussion of bilateral aid.

The Agency for International Development (AID)

A significant amount of our bilateral aid is transferred to the Third World through the Agency for International Development (AID). AID was set up in 1963 by the Kennedy administration for the purpose of administering American foreign bilateral aid programs. AID's position papers clearly state that its purpose from its inception has been to assist United States industry and commerce, the United States balance of payments, and United States strategic goals. Congress has only recently taken steps to insure that bilateral aid be used to meet the basic needs of the poor in the Third World. But as James Morrell of the Center for International Policy has pointed out in his 1977 study of foreign aid, a significant amount of multilateral and bilateral aid that is transferred to the Third World escapes congressional approval. Although the aid may be authorized by Congress, it does not necessarily come under congressional control. In FY 1976, for example, only $7.7 billion of the $24.9 billion of Third World mutilateral and bilateral aid received congressional approval. The rest was distributed through self-sustaining government corporations or international banks.[14]

Military Spending

Most people are unaware of the fact that a sizeable amount of American economic assistance is in the form of military aid. In 1971, for example, half of American aid was used to support existing governments either directly through the transfer of arms or personnel or indirectly through economic assistance.[15] Congress has recently also taken steps to separate military assistance from economic assistance. However, "security-supporting assistance," which was established to provide support for governments with particularly high defense budgets because of a threat from our common enemies, is still officially classified as development assistance.[16] This is particularly confusing to the public, which for the most part is under the impression that all American aid goes to the poor. Ann Crittenden of the *New York Times* reports that security assistance to countries like Egypt and Israel is the largest component of American bilateral aid.[17]

AID Development Program

Like the IMF and the World Bank, AID exercises leverage through its development program. Although AID does not approve specific projects for which its assistance will be used, it does approve a program in which the conditions for the transfer of aid are stated. The aid program contains economic and political policies that the recipient nation must adopt as a condition of aid. These may include a liberalization of trade for certain goods, the guarantee of a safe investment climate for United States companies, special treatment for a particular United States corporation in the aid-recipient country, and other stipulations. The program may also specify the quantities of goods and services to be purchased, where they are to be purchased, and how they are to be shipped. The practice of tying aid to the conditions of purchase and shipment of goods and services has been a boon to American industry and commerce. It is estimated that 75 percent of United States aid to the Third World is spent in the United States. Moreover, the Third World actually spends $2 in the United States for every $1 that the United States contributes to international financial institutions.[18]

FOOD FOR PEACE: AN EXAMPLE OF BILATERAL AID

Let us turn now to a more detailed study of one United States bilateral aid program, the Food for Peace Program. It goes without saying that United States food aid, like its other forms of bilateral aid, serves the economic and political interest of the United States. United States food aid is available through the Agricultural Trade Development and Assistance Act, commonly known as PL 480, or the Food for Peace Act.

Evolution of Public Law 480

The history of PL 480 reveals that the purpose of United States food aid has been primarily to stabilize the price of domestic grain and to assure United States interest in markets and politics abroad rather than to feed hungry people.[19] PL 480 is administered by the United States Department of Agriculture and AID. In 1954 the act was passed by Congress specifically to dispose of price-depressing surpluses that were accumulating in domestic siloes and warehouses at high government expense and to increase the dollar-purchasing power of foreign nations in need of United States farm commodities.[20] The expressed purposes of PL 480 were to:

(1) expand international trade among the United States and friendly nations, (2) facilitate the convertibility of currency, (3) promote the economic stability of American agriculture, and (4) further U.S. foreign policy.[21]

Not until 1961 was the act amended to include the awarding of agricultural commodities to friendly countries for development purposes, and the phrase "to combat hunger and malnutrition and to encourage economic development in developing countries" was added to its statement of purpose. This change of focus from a mechanism for disposing of surpluses to a means of using food for development purposes was due largely to the effort of the late Senator Hubert H. Humphrey. Humphrey conceived the idea that food assistance could serve the dual purpose of insuring United States Cold War objectives while meeting humanitarian needs. This point was made by Humphrey in his comments before a Senate Committee on Agriculture and Forestry in 1957:

> I have heard . . . that people may become dependent on us for food. I know that was not supposed to be good news. To me that was good news because before people can do anything they have got to eat. And if you're looking for a way to get people to lean on you and be dependent on you, in terms of their cooperation with you, it seems to me that food dependence would be terrific.[22]

In 1966 PL 480 was again amended. This time reference to "grain surplus" was deleted and more emphasis was placed on the use of United States grain to combat malnutrition and initiate self-help and family-planning projects in developing countries.[23] This amendment was occasioned by the decision to send food to India during the 1966 famine despite low stocks in the United States. Although grain available through PL 480 no longer had to be surplus grain, Section 401 of the Act provides that "commodities can only be made available for shipment under Public Law 480 when supplies have been assured for domestic consumption, adequate domestic carryover stocks, and expected commercial exports."[24] Thus PL 480 has evolved from a mechanism to dispose of surplus stocks, to a means of using food as a tool of foreign policy, to a method of using food for development and humanitarian purposes. The humanitarian objectives of PL 480, however, particularly during the food crisis years, have been subordinated to the economic and political objectives of the act.

Title I—Concessional sales. Unlike the European community, which distributes its food aid entirely in the form of grants, the United States makes food aid available either through concessional sales or through grants. Title I, the concessional sales section of PL 480, comprises 75 percent of United States food aid, while Title II, the grant section, makes up the remaining 25 percent. The word "concessional" refers simply to the favorable terms—low interest, long payment periods, and occasional forgiveness of repayment requirements—under which the sale is contracted.

Title I of the 1974 PL 480 Annual Report states that "the Commodity Credit Corporation finances the sale and export of commodities . . . [while] actual sales are made by private U.S. suppliers to foreign importers, government agencies, or private trade entities."[25] The commodities are then resold on the foreign country's domestic market. Thus more food is made available and additional revenue generated through the sale of Title I commodities. There is no stipulation in Title I that the commodities or proceeds from the sale of the commodities go to feed hungry people.[26] In fact, until July 1974 foreign currencies generated from the sale of Title I commodities could be used by the recipient government for common defense. This was the case in 1973. Under an agreement with the South Vietnamese government all proceeds from the sale of Title I commodities could go into its military budget. In Cambodia 80 percent was approved for defense purposes.[27]

Title II—Grants. Under Title II, commodities are provided to nonprofit United States relief agencies and intergovernmental organizations, friendly governments operating under bilateral agreements with the United States, and the World Food Program, a joint undertaking of the United Nations and the Food and Agriculture Organization (FAO). These commodities are used to feed the more nutritionally vulnerable, such as mothers, infants, and school children, as well as for food-for-work projects and emergency relief.

Allocation Decisions

Food-aid allocations for both Titles I and II are decided by the Interagency Staff Committee (ISC). This committee is chaired by the Department of Agriculture and draws its members from officers below the level of assistant secretary from the Departments of Treasury, State (AID), Defense, Commerce, and the Office of Management and Budget.[28] All the aid-allocation decisions by the ISC are made on the basis of consensus. A study of the distribution of United States food aid in the past, particularly during the food crisis years 1972–75, clearly shows the degree to which our nation will go to protect and promote its own economic and political concerns.

Food aid for military purposes. The bulk of United States food aid has not gone to countries most in need of food but rather to countries of economic and political importance to us. Since PL 480 began in 1954, reporter Emma Rothschild points out:

> Most food aid . . . has gone to countries that were also military friends, such as Israel and Turkey in the 1950s, South Korea and Pakistan throughout, South Vietnam in the 1960s, and 1970s. (Ten countries, including these, account for more than half of all P.L. 480 shipments. The others are India, Egypt, Yugoslavia, Indonesia and Brazil.)[29]

The priority given to the use of food aid to support military activity is reflected in the fact that during the food crisis years, in spite of a budget cut in food aid from 9.9 million metric tons in 1972 to 3.3 million metric tons in 1974, South Korea received the largest shipment of food aid in 1972 and South Vietnam in 1973 and 1974.[30] As a study in contrasts, compare the fact that in 1973 Cambodia, South Vietnam, and South Korea received 67 percent of all Title I aid with the fact that Bangladesh received a meager 5 percent.[31]

Disturbed by the blatant use of food aid for military purposes, Congress tried to put an end to this practice. In 1973 it approved the Foreign Assistance Act that curtailed the use of foreign currencies from the sale of Title I commodities for common defense at the conclusion of FY 1974. The following year Congress passed the Foreign Assistance Act of 1974, which directed that at least 70 percent of all Title I food aid be distributed to nations designated by the United Nations as "most seriously affected." Congress made further revisions in the Act in 1975, specifying that 75 percent of United States food aid go to countries with per capita Gross National Products of $300 or less. To stop the fluctuations in the amount of commodities allocated to Title II, Congress also stipulated that at least 1.3 million metric tons in food grants must be provided annually. This congressional action, it must be pointed out, shows that public policy can at times be governed by moral considerations.

Despite these major legislative revisions in the PL 480 program a number of abuses still occur. In its testimony before the Senate and House, the Interreligious Taskforce on U.S. Food Policy reported on these abuses. The following are just a few of its findings:

> Less needy but politically favored countries have continued to receive priority consideration. For example:
> —The Republic of Korea, a "semi-industrialized" developing country with a rapidly increasing GNP of $400 per capita in 1973 and with the growing capacity to purchase its food imports commercially, received $134.9 million in Title I food aid in FY 76 and the transition quarter, or 12 percent of the Title I program for that period. It is scheduled to receive $145 million in FY 77, making it the second largest recipient of Title I food aid after Egypt.
> —Chile, one of the more wealthy Latin American countries with a per capita GNP of $720 in 1973, received nearly 85 percent of all Title I shipments to the region in FY 76 and the transition quarter, and is scheduled to receive fully two-thirds of the shipments to Latin America in FY 77, although 1976 congressional limits placed on aid to Chile because of continuing human rights violations will probably reduce this portion somewhat.
> —. . . Total food aid shipments (Titles I and II) to the entire African continent, with the largest number of needy countries of any continent (though not the largest number of hungry people), declined from $89 million FY 75 to $67 million FY 76, with FY 77 programming rising only to $80 million.[32]

Food aid for political purposes. Besides its use to support military interests, food aid has also been used to persuade borrowing nations into positions politically more advantageous to the United States. Two cases will serve to illustrate my point. During the Allende administration, Chile received only small amounts of Title II commodities: $7.2 million in FY 1970, $7.3 million in FY 1971, $5.9 million in FY 1973.[33] When severe food shortages occurred in 1973, the Allende government tried to purchase wheat from the United States on credit. Its request was denied. Yet one month after the coup, the United States government approved a credit sale to the new regime, a sale eight times the total commodity credit extended to Chile during Allende's years in office.[34] Since the coup, the military government received $33.1 million in PL 480 commodities in 1975 and 85 percent of all Title I shipments to Latin America in FY 1976 and the transition quarter.[35]

A similar situation occurred in Bangladesh. Our food-aid legislation stipulates that countries receiving food aid must certify that they are not trading with Cuba or North Vietnam. At the height of the food crisis, Bangladesh was refused its request for Title I commodities because of a $3 million sale of jute that it had made with Cuba in the spring of 1974. It was not until October when the last shipment of jute to Cuba had been made that the United States signed a food-sales agreement with Bangladesh. The food was finally loaded for shipment in mid-November. It was too late, however, to stave off the tragic famine.[36]

These are but a few examples of the use of food aid for military and political purposes. The fact that military and political concerns continued to dominate our food aid during the food crisis—a time of immense suffering—suggests that the alleviation of human suffering is of secondary importance to maintaining our economic and political interests.

Food aid for economic purposes. The conditions attached to receiving Title I aid raise questions about the priority that the United States gives to its own economic expansion. Food aid, no less than other types of United States aid, is tied to certain conditions. As stated in the PL 480 Annual Report for 1974, requests for food aid are forwarded to the Department of Agriculture, which in turn "develops a program which provides for suitable commodity quantities, establishes levels of required commercial imports from the United States and friendly countries (usual marketing requirements), and includes self-help measures suitable to the needs of the requesting country."[37]

It should be obvious by now that the "suitable commodity quantities" and "required commercial imports" provisions are there to insure that the borrowing nation will expand its imports of United States agricultural commodities. Needless to say, the conditions of food aid are structured to satisfy our own market needs more than the needs of the food-deficit countries. As we will see, the amount of those "suitable quantities" and the timing of their shipment often has more to do with the need to dispose of price-depressing surpluses on our own market than with meeting the needs of the food-deficit country.[38]

Two blatant examples of this practice were reported by the Interreligious Taskforce on United States Food Policy in its congressional testimony:

—In 1976, although large quantities of grains (including PL 480 commodities) were known to be spoiling in warehouses and in open storage in Bangladesh, a PL 480 shipment of 50,000 metric tons of rice was made anyway, pushed through in response to pressures from rice producers by USDA over AID's opposition. Bangladesh, a country with less than $300 per capita GNP, was forced to take more food than it could handle, in part to justify PL 480 purchases in U.S. markets and in part to make possible additional shipments to countries with more than $300 GNP per capita. . . .

—Dry powdered milk was reintroduced into the PL 480 program after an interlude of several years, but without Vitamin A fortification, an essential safety precaution. (Consumption of unfortified rich protein can stimulate Vitamin A deficiency diseases in malnourished people, which in turn frequently result in blindness. Milk fortification had formerly been assured under PL 480, but dry milk shipments were phased out almost entirely in Fiscal Years 73–75 due to shrinking commodity availability. Renewed domestic stockpiles brought dry milk back into the food aid program but without fortification. While all milk used in Title II food aid programs is now again being fortified, the pattern of dry milk programming and fortification in recent years suggests that commodity availability rather than human need is the controlling factor.[39]

The second part of the Department of Agriculture program, the right to establish "levels of required commercial imports from the United States and friendly countries," likewise places the interest of our own market before the satisfaction of human needs. To qualify for food aid, requesting countries must agree to increase their imports of United States commercial agricultural commodities as their own markets expand.[40] Susan DeMarco and Susan Sechler of the Agribusiness Accountability Project point out, for example, that Egypt a few years ago had to agree to purchase 2,144,000 tons of wheat from the United States to qualify for PL 480 aid. The same was true for South Korea, which agreed to purchase 150,000 tons of rice.[41] The effect of this provision, economist Michael Hudson argues, is that:

. . . the aid-borrower's deficit on food account *must* widen over the years as a *precondition* for obtaining food aid: it must increase its aggregate farm imports from the United States in accordance with its domestic market growth while its farm exports must not increase (on the ground that they might potentially displace U.S. commercial exports.)

. . . neither the farm sector nor the balance-of-payments position of the aid-borrower is helped. The aid client is contractually obliged *not* to implement policies of domestic agricultural self-sufficiency, but to enter into agreements similar to that which the United States signed with Britain in 1968 assuring it a "guaranteed marketshare."[42]

Part of the Food for Peace Act also stipulates that commodities sold under Public Law 480 will not "displace usual commercial markets for U.S. agricultural commodities, nor unduly disrupt normal patterns of commercial trade with countries friendly to the United States."[43] A recent example of the effects of this policy occurred in 1976. Bangladesh farmers could not sell their surplus wheat from an exceptionally good experimental harvest to a country like Indonesia, which was receiving United States food aid. The Bangladesh farmers were thus forced to sell their wheat at a loss to private traders. Because of this provision in our PL 480 Program, Bangladesh lost out on two accounts. Its farmers lost their incentive to experiment with another crop and the country itself lost out on much needed foreign exchange.

Besides protecting our own markets, PL 480 has also strengthened the United States balance of payments, funded development of commercial markets, and provided revenue for the United States shipping industry. PL 480 has helped strengthen the United States balance of payments by enabling United States government agencies to pay the expenses they have incurred overseas with foreign currency generated from the sale of PL 480 commodities. As Michael Hudson explains:

> U.S. government agencies are thus saved from having to throw dollars onto world foreign exchange markets to purchase the client countries' currencies (which could set up potential claims on the U.S. gold stock).[44]

This practice has resulted in a considerable saving to the United States. The PL 480 1974 Annual Report states that "the total balance of payments benefits in 1974, including payments made on long term credit loans, were $324 million."[45]

PL 480 is also used to develop dollar markets for United States commodities. Since the program began, $153 million of PL 480 funds has been spent on market development alone.[46] As stated in the Food for Peace 1974 Report:

> . . . market development activities encompass virtually every U.S. farm commodity entering world trade and include advertising, trade servicing, training and educational programs, seminars, demonstrations, international trade exhibits, and trade missions to and from the United States.[47]

These activities are aimed at developing a preference for American agricultural commodities and eating habits in the Third World. It goes without saying that the ultimate goal of these market development activities is to turn short-term aid recipients into long-term commercial importers of United States agricultural commodities.

One of the other ways that our food aid helps business is through the Private Trade Entity Program.[48] Under this program private corporations may request PL 480 commodities, which they then can sell. Proceeds from such a sale are considered a loan from the government to finance company projects in the Third World. The only stipulation that the government makes regarding the project is that it contribute to the sale of United States agricultural commodities for dollars or to the development of future commercial markets. DeMarco and Sechler have pointed out some of the problems with this program. They argue, first of all, that there is no stipulation in the Private Trade Entity Program Agreement that PL 480 commodities must be sold in countries that have the most need of food. Moreover, when corporations select a project, their overriding concern is not human need but commercial advantage. DeMarco and Sechler also argue that the proceeds that come from the sale of PL 480 commodities may even go to finance projects that are not in keeping with the development plans of a particular country. Or the proceeds may go for projects that compete with local businesses or local food needs.[49]

PL 480 also benefits the United States shipping industry. By law, half of the commodities distributed under PL 480 must be transported in ships flying the United States flag. Because of this requirement, the United States government pays our country's shipping industry an additional charge beyond what the importing country would pay a non-United States shipper. This additional charge amounts to a sizeable subsidy for the United States shipping industry—$229 million between 1970 and 1974.[50] Besides the subsidy, United States shipping firms have admitted that by using PL 480 cargoes as their basic cargo they have been able to service more remote ports and, therefore, increase their profits.[51]

To summarize, PL 480 funds—besides their use for military and political purposes—have been used to expand our own markets, strengthen our own currency, and provide business for our own industries. Food aid, in other words, has been used as a tool by our government to strengthen our own economy.

The tragedy of the situation is that the hungry must pay the price of our economic expansion. The Central Intelligence Agency report on United States food power clearly states that the expansion of our political and economic power through food aid is still a primary motive behind our aid:

> It seems clear that the world of the poor, at least, will experience continued food shortages and occasional famine over the coming decades. . . . The disparity between the rich and poor is likely to get even wider. And the world's dependence on North American agriculture will continue to increase. . . . Ability to provide relief food in periods of short-

age or famine will enhance U.S. influence in the recipient countries. . . . (If the cooling trend in the world's climate predicted by climatologists) continues for several decades there would almost certainly be an absolute shortage of food. . . . In a cooler and therefore hungrier world, the U.S. near-monopoly position as food exporter . . . could give the U.S. a measure of power it never had before—possibly an economic and political dominance greater than that of the immediate post-World War II years. . . . Washington would acquire virtual life and death power over the fate of multitudes of the needy.[52]

Thus food aid has been an important means, like other types of aid, for promoting our own economic well-being at the expense of the primary needs of hungry people.

There are other institutions responsible for transferring aid to the Third World that have not been covered here. The multinational commercial banks, for example, account for an increasing amount of Third World aid. Their operations have been detailed in a study by Howard M. Wachtel of the Transnational Institute entitled *The New Gnomes: Multinational Banks in the Third World*. Voluntary agencies, such as the Cooperative for American Relief to Everywhere (CARE), Catholic Relief, Church World Service, and others also distribute a significant amount of American aid in the Third World. John G. Sommer of the Overseas Development Council has completed a fine study of their operations entitled *Beyond Charity*. In each of these studies you will find examples of how the interest of the donor enters into the aid-distribution process.

Chapter 5

MULTINATIONAL CORPORATIONS
AND THE THIRD WORLD

Up to this point, we have been looking at how the nations of the First World maintain the prosperity of their own economic, political, and social systems at the expense of the Third World. Let us now discuss a capitalist institution that is probably the most representative of the latest phase in the expansion and accumulation of capital—the multinational corporation. In discussing multinational corporations, we shall focus especially on how they have used the Third World for their own economic expansion. As was the case for trade and aid, we shall discover how multinationals have contributed specifically to hunger in the Third World.

THE RISE OF MULTINATIONAL CORPORATIONS

Monthly Review editor Paul Sweezy has argued that since its beginning capitalism has gone through a number of technological and organizational transformations.[1] It has gone through a manufacturing phase, an industrial phase, and is now in the phase of monopoly capital. Each phase of capitalist development, Sweezy holds, brought with it an expansion of the unit of production and, with the exception of the latest phase, an intensification of competition.

The phase of monopoly capital is very different from the preceding phases. Its organizational form, for example, is no longer a proprietor or partner but a corporation, which in Sweezy's words "permits an unlimited concentration and centralization of capital."[2] In earlier phases of capitalism, the proprietor or partners competed by selling their products at or below the market price. In the monopoly capital phase, however, the unit of production—the corporation—has become so large and the competition so significantly reduced that the corporation must take the effect its own production will have on the market price into account in the process of production. In other words, with competition so greatly reduced, the corporation itself must regulate the expansion of its own production in order to insure profitable growth.

The result, Sweezy argues, is "an irresistible drive on the part of the monopolistic firm to move outside of and beyond its historical field of operation, to penetrate new industries and new markets."[3] Thus in the latest phase of capitalism the typical unit of production, according to Sweezy, is the multinational corporation. It is a conglomerate by virtue of the fact that it operates in many industries and it is multinational because it has operations in almost every country.[4]

EFFECTS OF MULTINATIONALS ON DEVELOPMENT

The influence of multinational corporations on the economy of Third World countries is a problem of increasing concern to those countries. The abundant resources, cheap labor, weak or nonexistent labor unions, ineffective environmental laws, and tax concessions of the Third World provide a fertile climate for corporate growth. A growing number of development experts argue, however, that corporate success in the Third World has been achieved at the expense of the Third World, thus compounding the poverty and dependence of its countries. The multinational—or transnational, as they are called by the United Nations—companies claim that they contribute necessary financial, technological, and employment benefits to the economies of the Third World. Their claim merits investigation.

Finance Capital

Do multinational corporations contribute capital to the Third World? Richard J. Barnet and Roland E. Müller maintain in their major study of multinationals that multinationals reap greater financial benefits than they contribute to the Third World. Let us begin with a look at finance capital—the capital used to finance new multinational operations in the Third World. Where does it come from? Barnet and Müller report that the bulk of finance capital surprisingly is supplied not by foreign firms but rather by local Third World sources. Two reputable studies have borne this statement out. One study done for the United Nations by Fernando Fajnzylber has found that between 1957 and 1965 United States-based corporations alone financed 83 percent of their Latin American operations from local Third World savings.[5] The other United Nations study by Aldo Ferrer confirmed Fajnzylber's findings. Ferrer reports that between 1960 and 1970, 78 percent of United States multinational manufacturing operations in Latin America were financed with local capital.[6]

Some may argue that this large initial outlay on the part of the Third World is justifiable inasmuch as foreign corporations can be expected not only to stimulate new business activity but also to promote the growth of old local businesses. Expectations for new businesses will be examined in more detail shortly, but it is sufficient to point out here that old or local industries in the Third World have not fared well as a result of the presence of multinationals.

To begin with, much of the capital that comes from local sources is used by multinationals to buy out or absorb local firms. Barnet and Müller, for example, report that "of the 717 new manufacturing subsidiaries established in Latin America by the top 187 U.S.-based global corporations, 331, or 46 percent, were established by the buying out of existing local firms."[7] This practice is especially injurious to the Third World economy because local industries are an important source of goods and services for domestic consumption and local savings. More often than not, products made by local industries are consumed by local people. And the profits that local industries make are reinvested in the Third World economy. To make the situation even worse for local industries, firms that are not bought out or absorbed by multinationals find themselves in the very difficult position of having to compete with the multinationals for scarce local credit and sales.

Finally, a study by Robert J. Ledogar of United States food and drug multinational corporations in Latin America reports that multinationals are gaining increasing control over the major "growth" industries in the Third World. He cites the example of multinational corporations in Brazil that, as early as 1971, controlled 70 percent of the total net profits of the five major sectors of Brazil's economy: rubber, automobiles, machinery, household appliances, and mining.[8]

Trade

Multinational corporations claim that they contribute to the Third World's total trade. While it is true that multinationals do conduct a significant amount of the Third World's trade (for example, in 1968 more than 40 percent of all of Latin America's manufacturing exports and over one third of its imports from the United States were transacted by United States-based multinational corporations),[9] it is important to determine whether that trade has helped strengthen the Third World's balance of payments. If we were to examine those transactions a little more closely, however, we would soon see that the bulk of the activity, especially export activity from the United States, is conducted by the United States-based multinational parent company with its subsidiary in the Third World. Barnet and Müller estimate that more than half of all United States' exports are exports from United States' parent companies to their subsidiaries overseas.[10] The problem with these in-house transactions is that they actually hurt the Third World's economy. Why is this so?

We need to keep in mind that multinationals trading with their Third World subsidiaries can manipulate the price of the goods exchanged to the advantage of the multinationals through a mechanism known as "transfer pricing." This means that a multinational can adjust the price of goods exchanged between the parent company and its subsidiary according to the rate of taxation of the countries involved in the exchange . Barnet and Müller give a good explanation of how one form of transfer pricing works:

If an automobile manufacturer with operations in many countries wishes to export from a manufacturing subsidiary it owns in one country to a distributing company it owns in another country, it is often advantageous for tax reasons to direct the exporting subsidiary to undervalue its exports. One common reason for this is that the the taxes in the manufacturing country may be higher than the taxes in the importing country. Thus the artficial price charged on the export minimizes total taxes for the world corporation and increases its global profits, but the result in the manufacturing country is that it loses foreign exchange (not to mention tax revenues) it would have received had there been an arm's-length transaction between independent buyers and sellers.[11]

Barnet and Müller found transfer pricing to be a rather common practice. They point out that an Andean Common Market study found that in Chile overpricing ranges from 30 percent to more than 700 percent. According to another study, overpricing in Peru ranges from 50 percent to 300 percent, and in Ecuador from 75 percent to 200 percent.[12] United Nations studies have found the same to be true for other Third World countries. Because the Third World is dependent on foreign exchange and tax revenues for its own economic development, transfer pricing has an especially debilitating effect on its economy. It deprives the Third World of revenue that could be generated from the sale of export commodities as well as from taxes and tariffs, and it also deprives the Third World of the advantages that come from managing its own market.

Policy on the Use of Profits

Multinational corporations claim that they contribute to the growth of the Third World's economy. Let us examine this claim. Barnet and Müller state that multinationals treat profits from their Latin American operations differently from profits derived through their western European operations. The corporations tend to reinvest western European profits in the western European economies, while the Latin American profits tend to be taken out of the country almost as quickly as they are made.

The Fajnzylber United Nations' study reports, for example, that between 1960 and 1968 United States-based corporations took an average of 79 percent of their net profits out of Latin America. [13] In manufacturing—one of the most rapid areas of growth for Latin America—Barnet and Müller found that United States manufacturing firms repatriated 52 percent of all profits between 1965 and 1968. The irony of the situation, according to Barnet and Müller is that although 78 percent of the capital used to finance those operations originally came from Third World sources, 52 percent of all profits wound up leaving the Third World. The situation is not better for the mining, petroleum, and smelting industries in Latin America. Barnet and Müller state that in these industries 83 percent of the finance capital came from local sources and only 21 percent remained in the local economy.[14]

Technology

The claim that multinational corporations contribute valuable technology to the Third World, without which it could not develop, can also be challenged. Multinational corporations certainly have introduced new technology into the Third World, particularly in the mining and manufacturing industries, where their activities are concentrated. It is important to point out, however, that the technology introduced is more suited to the needs of the multinationals than to the needs of the countries in which they operate. That technology is largely capital-intensive, that is, geared for the type of production that uses as little labor as possible. In countries in which unemployment has reached a crisis proportion, capital-intensive technology only aggravates the problem.

Multinational corporations use less labor than local firms do. Moreover, since multinational corporations tend to buy out or absorb local firms, they intensify the rampant unemployment problem in the Third World.[15] In his study of the effects of multinational corporation technology on unemployment in Latin America, Müller asserts:

> Between 1925 and 1960 the manufacturing sector was able to absorb only 5 million of the 23 million people who migrated into urban centers from the countryside, and while the total output of modern manufacturing industries expanded relative to other activities so that it increased its share of the national product from 11 percent in 1925 to 25 percent in 1970, the percent of the Latin American work force which it employed actually decreased from 14.4 to 13.8 over the same time period. This, then, is the employment contribution of the technology of the multinational corporations to Third World countries: MNCs are eliminating many more jobs than they are creating.[16]

In addition, Barnet and Müller maintain that the capital-intensive technology of multinational corporations has intensified the class divisions and disparity of income in the Third World. Because it is the rich who enter into partnership with the multinationals or who own the technology itself, capital produced by the new technology increases the profits of the rich.[17]

Advertising

Finally, multinational corporations affect the societies of the Third World in more subtle ways. Their advertising campaigns, for example, exert a significant influence in those countries. Such campaigns create new needs among rich and poor alike—needs that the rich can satisfy mostly through imports or needs that for the poor must either go unmet or be met at exorbitant costs. Barnet and Müller point out that multinational advertising in the Third World has had a negative effect on traditional values and cultures. TV, radio, newspaper, and magazine advertisements bombard the Third World with the message "West is best," thus creating and reinforcing a sense of inferiority about the indigenous culture, values, and products of the Third World.[18]

MULTINATIONALS AND HUNGER IN THE THIRD WORLD

Besides expropriating profits that rightfully belong to the Third World, eliminating jobs through capital-intensive technology, and extracting the labor of those who hold jobs at below-subsistence wages, global corporations have contributed to hunger in the Third World principally in two ways: (1) they have diverted land that would ordinarily be used to meet the domestic food needs of the Third World for their own commercial use; and (2) they have helped alter the dietary patterns of the poor.

Diversion of Land for Cash Cropping

Colombia. In *Hungry for Profits* Robert Ledogar documents the effects of multinational or cash cropping on the economies and nutritional status of Colombia and the Dominican Republic. The United States-based firm Ralston Purina is one of the largest producers of feed in the world. The feed industry can thrive only when there also exists a thriving industry that consumes the feed. So when Ralston Purina came to Colombia in 1958 (using a loan from the sale of United States PL 480 commodities), it set out to build a feed industry along with a broiler industry that would consume the feed produced. Let us consider how Ralston Purina went about establishing these two industries in Colombia.

To encourage Colombian farmers to go into feed and broiler businesses, Ralston Purina provided farmers with the necessary credit and technology to set up such operations. It then sold the farmers feed as well as baby chicks with the understanding that the poultry would be sold back to Ralston Purina after it had been fattened up. The corporation has done well for itself in Colombia. Ledogar reports that the annual broiler production doubled between 1966 and 1971, while the annual egg production jumped from 1.1 billion to 2.0 billion between 1970 and 1973.[19] The real question, however, is whether the vast majority of Colombians have done well because Purina is there. Ledogar thinks not. He points out that the per capita income in Colombia in 1969 was $335 per year, while 27 percent of the population earned less than $75 per year. With a kilogram of chicken costing 84 cents and a dozen eggs costing 40 cents, only the rich can afford such luxuries.[20] The poor, in fact, cannot afford to buy the products they help produce. According to

Ledogar, the poor lose out in yet another way. Because of the expansion of feed and broiler industries, more and more land formerly used to grow pulses (an inexpensive source of protein) was converted to feed and poultry farming. Thus the influence of Ralston Purina in Colombia has been the reduction of the toal amount of protein available in the country.[21]

> In 1960, when the country's population was 15.4 million, domestic protein production in Colombia fell short of the nation's protein requirements by 40,000 metric tons. By 1970, the population had increased about one third (to 21.1 million), but the protein deficit had almost tripled, to 115,000 metric tons. At present, population is estimated at 23 million, and the protein deficit somewhere between 130,000 and 150,000 metric tons.[22]

The Dominican Republic. The situation of the poor is very similar in the Dominican Republic. Sugar is this country's major export, accounting for over two thirds of the export earnings.[23] Much of the Dominican Republic's sugar-producing operations, however, are owned by a United States-based multinational corporation, Gulf & Western Industries, which came to the Dominican Republic in 1967 by buying out the Southern Puerto Rican Sugar Company. Since that time the company's control of the Dominican Republic's sugar industry has grown immensely. By 1975 it controlled more than 8 percent of the arable land and 30 percent of the Dominican Republic's sugar crop exports.[24]

Ledogar points out that much of Gulf & Western's expansion in the Dominican Republic has been through the "colonia." This is a system whereby the corporation contracts with farmers owning land near sugar mills or loading docks to grow sugarcane on their land. Gulf & Western advances the resources that the farmers need to convert their land into growing sugarcane. It also tells them when to plant as well as when to harvest the cane. In return for their labor, the farmers receive a percentage of the value of the crop agreed upon before planting. As of October 1973 Gulf & Western had 49,362 acres planted with sugarcane under the colonia system in addition to the corporation's own 109,642 acres.[25] The problem with Gulf & Western in general and with the colonia system in particular is that more and more land is being taken over for growing sugar rather than food for local consumption. In short, because more sugarcane is being raised for export, less food is available for purchase at the local market. This has hurt the vast majority of people in the Dominican Republic. While two-thirds of its agriculture is exported, the price of food for domestic consumption has skyrocketed. Between 1969 and 1974, Ledogar points out, food prices in the Dominican Republic doubled.[26] The effect of the increasing food prices is reflected in the nutritional status of the people of the Dominican Republic. According to a 1969 study of the nutritional status of people in the Dominican Republic by W. Henry Sebrell of Columbia University, of the 5,000 people tested, more than half were anemic and suffering from chronic malnutrition since birth. In surveying their diets, Sebrell found that the average caloric intake was 79 percent and their protein intake 62 percent of the amount recommended by the Institute of Nutrition of Central America and Panama.[27] These are but two examples of how multinationals affect the production and distribution of food in the Third World. Many more cases are reported by Frances Moore Lappé and Joseph Collins, whose writings are cited in Chapter 1.

Effects of Multinationals on Eating Habits

Let us now consider what the effects are of the increased control exercised by multinationals over the domestic food industry of the Third World. Ledogar reports that in Mexico alone Coca-Cola, Pepsi, and Crush supply three fourths of the soft-drink market; Gerber products, 80 percent of the baby food; Carnation, 85 percent of the evaporated milk; and Kellogg Company, 95 percent of the breakfast cereal.[28] Lured by corporate advertising that promises the nutritional value, convenience, and prestige associated with First World products, people in the Third World have become hooked on an assortment of prepackaged, canned products from western companies. They trade their domestic foods for nutritionally inferior imported products.

Although Coca-Cola and Pepsi are far from nutritious drinks, their association with youth and the "good life" of the First World makes them highly marketable commodities. Ledogar points out that the bottling industries have capitalized on this appeal, and have adapted their advertising to local themes. For example, in Brazil, Pepsi has changed its slogan from the "Pepsi Generation" to the "Pepsi Revolution." The unattainable revolution Pepsi pushes, however, is the revolution of western consumption.[29] The effectiveness of soft-drink advertising is reflected by the increase in soft-drink consumption. In Mexico, for example, per capita soft-drink consumption is about 220 bottles per year or four bottles per week.[30] The irony of the situation is that people who spend more than 80 percent of their income on food are increasingly spending more of it on worthless calories.

Probably the best documented and most tragic example of the effects that advertising can have on eating patterns in the Third World is the marketing of infant formula by some major First World pharmaceutical companies. A number of fine studies on this problem have been reported in the Ledogar book and the *Agribusiness Manual*, a publication of the Interfaith Center on Corporate Responsibility. Let us briefly review this situation.

As the rate of population growth declines in the First World—a well-established development—fewer babies require products such as infant formula that are produced and marketed by the major pharmaceutical firms. As a result, corporations like Abbott Laboratories, American Home Products, Bristol-Myers, and Nestlé have found it necessary to seek new markets for their products. The Third World with its growing population is an obvious solution to this problem. The corporations have mounted massive advertising campaigns employing nurses or women dressed as nurses to promote their formula in hospitals and clinics. Combined with ads in magazines and on radio and billboards, the corporations have lured an increasing number of new mothers to abandon breast-feeding for bottle-feeding. It is important to point out that breast-feeding, even in the case of malnourished mothers, usually provides enough nutrients and antibodies to protect newborn infants during the first four to six months of life.[31]

For bottle feeding to be safe and effective, the following five conditions must be met:

> 1) the cost of the product must fit into the budget of the recipient so that other nutritional foods, etc., are not neglected; 2) medical personnel must be available for proper guidance to the user; 3) sanitary water must be readily available; 4) the water must be heated for sterilization purposes and the formula must be refrigerated after opening; and 5) the user must be able to follow the directions on the label.[32]

Henry J. Frundt and Douglas Clement of the Interfaith Center on Corporate Responsibility have tried to determine whether it is possible to meet such conditions for safe bottle-feeding in countries where Bristol-Myers markets its infant formula. Here are their findings:

1. The cost of the product must fit into the budget of the recipient. The average cost of feeding an infant formula per month is approximately $17.60, which equals about 40 percent of the per capita GNP of countries of the Third World. Frundt and Clement observe that the lower the average per capita GNP is for a country, the less safe water there is for individual households; the fewer sewage systems there are; the greater is the incidence of infant parasitic diseases and infant mortalities; and the less protein is consumed. When the infant's formula consumes such a large portion of a family's income, the chances are the formula itself will have to be diluted to stretch over not just four days but four weeks.

2. Physicians, nurses, midwives, and pharmacists are needed to help new mothers use the infant formula properly. Frundt and Clement report that as the GNP for a country declines, we tend to find fewer medical personnel. For example:

> In countries where Bristol-Myers apparently is involved, there is one doctor, on the average, for every 4,463 people. In Indonesia, one doctor is available for 25,847 people; in the Sudan there is one for 13,056. Even when a physician is available for each 1,800 persons, which is true in a number of the developing countries, it is unlikely that a young mother can get to see the doctor more than once a year.[33]

3. Clean water is needed to mix the infant formula. Frundt and Clement have discovered that two-thirds of the people in countries where Bristol-

Myers operates do not have easy access to water. Moreover, only half the people are assured that their water supply is safe.

4. The unused portion of the formula must be refrigerated to avoid contamination. In countries where Bristol-Myers operates, 55 percent of the people do not even have electricity.

5. To prepare the formula, people must follow explicitly the directions on the product. Yet Frundt and Clement report that in those countries 31 percent of the women cannot read. In rural areas the rate of illiteracy is over 50 percent. Even where the women who use the formula can read, Frundt and Clement point out there is no guarantee that the directions on the package will be written in their native language. Leah Margulies of the Interfaith Center on Corporate Responsibility reports that in Haiti, where 84 percent of the women cannot read, the labels on the Mead-Johnson infant formula are written in Spanish and English although most of the Haitians speak either French or Creole.[34]

We need to keep in mind the fact that when one or more of the conditions outlined above are not met, the formula cannot be used without the danger of causing harm to infants. Needless to say, there has been a dramatic increase in infant diseases and mortality rates as a result of bottle-feeding, especially among the rural poor in the Third World. Mike Muller, a British writer who has done much to bring the infant-formula problem to public attention, reports that in Chile in 1973 there were three times as many deaths among bottle-fed infants before three months of age than among infants who were totally breast fed.[35]

To summarize, world hunger is a problem that cannot be understood apart from the larger problem of underdevelopment. It is but one of the more visible products of a world economic order dominated and structured by the advanced capitalist nations for the purpose of maintaining the stability of their own economic, political, and social systems.

As we have seen in Chapters 2 through 5, the economic arrangements governing the relationship between the First World and the Third World are neither "natural" nor "inevitable." They have been determined by nation-states more concerned with protecting and promoting the capitalist system than meeting basic human needs or relieving human suffering. This is a clear indication that our own nation and the nations of the First World are experiencing a profound crisis in values.

Chapter 6

PLANTING THE SEEDS OF CHANGE

TYPES OF CHANGE

In his book *The Cruel Choice,* Denis Goulet talks about two types of incremental change.[1] The first he calls "palliative" incremental change, and the second "creative" incremental change. Because the two types of change are very different, we need to learn how to distinguish them.

Palliative change, Goulet argues, is change that merely tinkers with the symptoms of a problem without attacking its root. And for this reason palliative change actually worsens the problem by allowing it to fester until it becomes virtually incurable.

Creative incremental change, on the other hand, seeks out the root of a problem without ever losing sight of it. Each act of change, no matter how incidental, is directed toward attacking the very root of the problem. As such, it "breed[s] new possibilities for subsequent radical change. . . . Such measures contain a latent dynamism, however, which propels society beyond immediate problem-solving toward new possible futures."[2]

Most of the solutions proposed to rid the world of hunger, in my judgment, are palliative measures. They are palliative insofar as they do not identify the root of the problem—the capitalist, or market, system—and work for its change. Let's consider, for example, the United Nations Declaration on the Establishment of a New International Economic Order of 1974. It calls for adjusting the mechanisms of world trade, aid, and investment to make them more responsive to the needs of the Third World. Seeking to change these mechanisms without seeking to change the system that produced them, in my judgment, would be just tinkering with the symptoms of the disease. Like Michael Harrington, I believe the point is not to perfect the market system but to transform it.[3]

Change on behalf of the hungry is creative, I believe, when it acknowledges the fact that the root of the problem lies in our own economic system and when actions are directed to transform that system. Because the roots of the Third World's poverty and hunger ultimately lie in the capitalist system—a

62

system that necessitates and legitimates the exploitation of the Third World—nothing less than a fundamental change in that system is required. In Harrington's words, "There is no possibility that the mechanisms that were designed to produce that inequality will provide the means for ending it."[4]

HUNGER AS A CRISIS IN VALUES

Hunger, as we have already seen, is a moral problem. The policies and practices of nations reflect not only political and economic choices but moral choices as well. They reflect the choice of certain goods or values over others. The choice by the First World to structure the world economic order to its own advantage, despite the poverty and hunger that this decision produces in the Third World, is a moral choice. Moreover, the choices made by our own nation during the food crisis of 1972–75 were moral choices as well. They are good indicators of where our national values and priorities lie.

My own reading of the trade, aid, and investment policies and practices of the First World, especially those that affected the hungry during the food crisis, indicates that the First World is in a state of moral crisis. I say this because I believe that those decisions show how economic and political values have become ends in themselves. Whenever financial and political gains are to be made, the human good inevitably becomes subordinate to the economic and political good. In the international economic and political arena normative judgments seem to have no bearing on decisions. For this reason the increasing poverty and hunger in the Third World are clearest signals of our crisis in values.

It is not just the governments of the First World that are to blame, however. This moral crisis is reflected in our individual and collective lives as well. We cannot escape our personal responsibility for poverty and hunger in the Third World. For the policies of our government and corporations are what keeps the Third World dependent and poor. Without our approval or silence these policies could not be carried out.

We are responsible for the poverty and hunger of the Third World in yet another more subtle way. We members of the middle and upper classes enjoy the rewards of the favorable terms of trade, aid, and investment. Our food, clothing, and jobs have been won at a very high price. To the extent that we never question whether it is morally right for us to enjoy wealth when millions suffer from lack of the basic goods needed for survival, we personally are in a state of moral crisis.

This crisis in values is also reflected in a mass rationalization and justification of our unbridled pursuit of affluence in spite of the dire need of other human beings. The tolerance of poverty and hunger by societies that have the means to alleviate them must lead us to the conclusion that either we have lost the capacity to make moral choices or that we have ignored or suppressed them for so long that we are blinded to them. An essential human quality—the capacity to respond to human suffering—has been lost or dulled.

It is precisely this inability to respond that has led Denis Goulet to question the very "development" that has been achieved by the First World and to call it "antidevelopment." Development, for Goulet, is the process by which a society moves from less human patterns of life to those that are more human.[5] But the development achieved by First World societies is far from human; it is rather a form of alienation that expresses itself in a relentless need to consume. Paulo Freire terms this attitude an "oppressor consciousness":

> [This attitude] tends to transform everything surrounding it into an object of its domination. The earth, property, production, the creations of men, men themselves, time—everything is reduced to the status of objects at its disposal.
>
> In their unrestrained eagnerness to possess, the oppressors develop the conviction that it is possible for them to transform everything into objects of their purchasing power; hence their strictly materialistic concept of existence. Money is the measure of all things, and profit the primary goal. For the oppressors, what is worthwhile is to have more— always more—even at the cost of the oppressed having less or having nothing. For them, *to be is to have* and to be the class of the "haves."[6]

In accommodating our own lives and values to the logic of the market system, we not only make the exploitation of the Third World both possible and necessary but also lose our freedom, that is, we lose our capacity to make authentic human choices.

Goulet has pointed out that for there to be any change in the attitude of the First World we shall have to undergo a revolution in values as profound as the revolutionary changes that are needed in the Third World.[7] Only by freeing ourselves from the determinism of the market system can we reclaim our humanity and become free to work to change that system. Ironically, the liberation of the Third World and our own human liberation are interrelated.

In sum, the alleviation of poverty and hunger in our world, I believe, depends on at least two interrelated factors: a radical transformation of the market system and a transformation of the values that are produced by that market system and that, in turn, reproduce it.

SUMMARY OF PART I

We began by analyzing the factors that led directly to the food crisis of 1972-75, and then took up various explanations for world hunger advanced by scholars in the field. Paddock and Paddock see hunger as a problem caused by overpopulation in the Third World; Lester Brown blames it on overpopulation in the Third World and overconsumption in the First World; Georg Borgstrom is concerned with overpopulation defined in ecological and economic terms; and Frances Moore Lappé, Joseph Collins, and Susan

George see world hunger as a problem caused by economic and political systems.

In Chapter 2 we traced the roots of poverty in the Third World from the establishment of the colonial system by the European powers in the fifteenth century to the present day. There is a discussion of Karl Marx's analysis of capitalism. Chapters 3 and 4 are concerned with the effects of world trade and western aid on the Third World.

The role of multinational corporations is described in Chapter 5, and a relationship is established between their policies and the poverty of people in the Third World. Finally, the theories of Denis Goulet are examined. In his model different types of change in the world are outlined, including "palliative" change and "creative" change. World hunger is then posited as a crisis in the moral values of the First World.

PART II

THE PUBLIC AND POLITICAL RESPONSIBILITY OF CHRISTIANS

As we have seen in Part I, the First World has done everything in its power to integrate the economies of the Third World into the free-market system and to keep the Third World in a state of dependency. Because the fate of the Third World at present is so closely tied to the systems and policies of the First World, change in the situation of people in the Third World is integrally related to change in the First World. In other words, the alleviation of the Third World's poverty and hunger depends to a large extent on whether we who live in the First World can change our systems and values so that we respond to the human good rather than devote ourselves to the accumulation of material goods.

Our religious tradition, I believe, can be a force for changing our systems and values. Within this tradition lies the potential to make us more conscious of the contradictions in our personal lives and in the policies and actions of our nation. Our religious tradition also has the potential to challenge us to accept the responsibility to work for political, economic, and social changes.

Part II will explore the crisis of values in our society in more detail. It will examine why we should act in the interest of the poor and hungry on rational grounds alone. It will show how much more binding is the responsibility of Christians to the poor and hungry. Finally, it will examine the public and political nature of our responsibility as Christians to the poor and hungry of the Third World.

Chapter 7

RECOVERING OUR RELIGIOUS TRADITION

THE PURSUIT OF PRIVATE MATERIAL GAIN

"The best and the worst in a society or an individual," the American sociologist of religion Robert Bellah writes, "are often closely related."[1] The unbridled pursuit of economic gain on the part of our nation and of multinational corporations, which we examined in Chapters 5 and 6, has its parallel on the individual and societal level. In *The Broken Covenant* Bellah argues that one of the dominant characteristics of American society today is the lack of a sense of obligation to anyone other than ourselves and our immediate families. The pursuit of private material interest has become the end toward which we as individuals strive and the standard against which we measure all actions. Thus we judge the worth of policies and programs increasingly on the basis of whether they enhance our or our families' private interests.

Bellah traces the roots of our lack of a sense of general obligation and our obsession with private material gain to two related factors: the rise of the industrial capitalist economic system and the disengagement of our national ideals from a moral and religious context. Let us stop for a moment and look at this statement more closely. If we were to challenge the right to pursue private material interest in this country, most Americans would argue that that right is God-given. It is one of the ideals upon which our nation was founded; it is a right guaranteed by the Constitution. Many might say that it is a primary right that must not be infringed upon, regardless of the human or ecological costs at which it may be achieved. This tendency to equate freedom to pursue private material interests with our national ideals regardless of the consequences is nothing less than a perversion of those ideals.

SOURCES OF OUR NATIONAL IDEALS

The ideals on which our nation was founded emerged out of the New England Puritan vision of the good society. That vision was shaped by the

Old and New Testaments and the classical vision of the Greek polis. All of these sources presented a highly social and communal picture of men and women in their relationship with one another and with the society at large. Bellah comments:

> That collective emphasis, that understanding of man as fundamentally social, was derived from the classical conception of the *polis* as responsible for the education and virtue of its citizens, from the Old Testament notion of the Covenant between God and a people held collectively responsible for its actions, and from the New Testament notion of a community based on charity or love and expressed in brotherly affection and fellow membership in one common body. This collective emphasis did not mean a denigration of the individual because the Calvinist synthesis of the older traditions maintained a strong sense of the dignity and responsibility of the individual and especially stressed voluntaristic individual action. But Calvinist "individualism" only made sense within the collective context. Individual action outside the bounds of religious and moral norms was seen in Augustinian terms as the very archetype of sin.[2]

The experience of conversion was central to the religious life of New England Protestants. Conversion was viewed not merely as an act of private piety; it brought with it new social obligations. To walk in the way of the Lord implied a new relationship with God, oneself, one's fellow human beings, and one's environment. That new relationship was grounded in the Puritan understanding of the biblical concept of convenant. Thus charity, brotherhood, responsibility for the common good, and voluntary restraint from excess were central ideals that governed the lives of the converted. The communal nature of conversion is reflected in the following extract from a sermon by an eighteenth-century Baptist preacher, Isaac Backus:

> The true liberty of man is, to know, obey and enjoy his creator, and to do all the good unto, and enjoy all the happiness with and in his fellow creatures that he is capable of; in order to which the law of love was written in his heart, which carries in it's nature union and benevolence to Being in general, and to each being in particular, according to it's nature and excellency, and to it's relation and connection with the supreme Being, and ourselves. *Each rational soul, as he is part of the whole system of rational beings, so it was and is, both his duty and his liberty, to regard the good of the whole in all his actions* [emphasis added].[3]

Our national ideals of life, liberty, and the pursuit of happiness, therefore, emerged out of a religious framework in which the biblical notion of covenant was central. Thus the rights of an individual were always balanced by the rights of the larger society. Even freedom was never reduced to its negative form alone. While the founders of our nation believed that individuals should be free from incursions (negative freedom), they also believed that it was the responsibility of the individual and society to create conditions in which all would be able to participate fully and to reach their full human potential. In Bellah's words:

> The defense of negative freedom, of civil rights and liberties, while ignoring massive injustice, poverty, and despair will be self-defeating. Negative freedom only defends the individual against incursions, whereas positive freedom actually creates the conditions for the full participation of all. Positive freedom, what Jefferson called public freedom, has always been an element in American political life, even though its meaning has changed over time. *That larger freedom that not only defends self-interest, as negative freedom does, but fulfills it in the common good, is the essence of inward or internal covenant* [emphasis added].[4]

THE DISTORTION OF OUR NATIONAL IDEALS

It is Bellah's belief that with the rise of industrial capitalism, the perception of the ideals of justice, liberty, and equality changed dramatically. Our ideals were separated from their moral and religious context and eventually came to serve the ends of the economic system. Let us take the ideal of freedom, for example. Freedom in the seventeenth and eighteenth centuries was practically a virtue. It meant freedom to do good. Today when we think of freedom we think of it primarily in terms of freedom to do our own thing, that is, freedom to pursue our private material interests until our freedom is limited by someone or something. The ideal of freedom consequently has come to serve as a cover for a number of unscrupulous practices, such as the freedom to amass great wealth in the midst of great need, the freedom to produce products harmful to ourselves and our environment, the freedom to exploit the labor of others such as farm and textile workers, the freedom to interfere with another nation's internal affairs—the list could go on. In short, the ideal of freedom, once associated with an obligation to the common good, has come to serve as a justification for a way of life that is largely individualistic, materialistic, and competitive.

We tend to see ourselves as independent of everyone and responsible to no one and for no one. We have lost our sense of responsibility to the community and the world at large. In short, the communal dimension that was once an integral part of our national ideals has been lost to consciousness. Like Bellah, I question whether a society for which private material interests is so central can long survive.

At one time in our history, being a good citizen was fairly equivalent to being a good person or a good Christian. Today, however, one might have to become a bad citizen in order to be a good Christian and vice versa. The crisis facing us today is the increasing inability not only of nations but also of individuals and society to make profound value choices. The need to satisfy our private material interests keeps us from seeing and responding to the real and pressing needs of others, especially the poor and hungry in our own society and in the world at large. The pursuit of goods has substituted itself for the pursuit of the good life in the moral sense of the term. And in a mad pursuit of more and more goods we have practically lost the capacity to choose the human good over the accumulation of goods.[5] In Bellah's words:

> Is it not possible that our punishment for breaking the covenant is to be the most developed, progressive, and modern society in the world? What those adjectives point to is utter devastation—of the natural world in which we live, of the ties that bind us to others, of the innerness of spiritually sensitive personality. . . . Our punishment, ironically, lies in our "success," and that too not for the first time in history.[6]

Dorothy Day of the *Catholic Worker* once said that we in America need great liberators to liberate us from our wealth. Could it be that the poor and hungry of the Third World might just be our liberators? We shall address this question later in this part, but here we need only deal with the question of whether there is any way of getting out of our own skins.

THE POSSIBILITY FOR TRANSFORMATION

Bellah believes that hope for our society lies in recovering a transcendent vision of humankind:

> The history of modern nations shows that segmentary rational politics is not enough. No one has changed a great nation without appealing to its soul, without stimulating a national idealism, as even those who call themselves materialists have discovered. Culture is the key to revolution; religion is the key to culture. If we win the political struggle, we will not even know what we want unless we have a new vision of man, a new sense of human possibility, and a new conception of the ordering of liberty, the constitution of freedom. Without that, political victory, even were it attainable, could have no lasting result.[7]

I believe that the religious tradition of Christians may provide them with the vision to which Bellah is referring.

This tradition "does not confirm simply the fact that there are hungry people in the world; it interprets the hungry to be our brethren whom we are allowing to starve."[8] In the pages that follow we will take a closer look at the potential of our religious tradition to liberate us from our oppression and our need to oppress others.

Chapter 8

OUR RESPONSIBILITY TO THE POOR AND HUNGRY: A NONRELIGIOUS PERSPECTIVE

Before proceeding with our discussion of the Christian's responsibility to the poor and hungry it is important to show how arguing on reason alone one can make a strong case for the moral responsibility of the First World to alleviate the poverty and hunger of the Third World. While the purpose of Part II is to examine religious grounds for acting in the interest of the least well-off, Christian educators and teachers in public schools or state colleges should be aware of some of the persuasive ethical arguments offered by contemporary philosophers for acting on behalf of the poor and hungry. After considering those arguments and comparing them with the demands imposed by the Christian tradition on Christians, we shall see how much more binding and radical is the obligation of Christians to respond to the needs of the poor and hungry in the Third World.

The philosophers whose positions are examined here were chosen because, while each of them approaches the problem from a different philosophical perspective, they all offer convincing arguments for acting in the interest of the poor and hungry. We all need to become familiar with such philosophical arguments because we live in a pluralistic society where people hold a variety of religious beliefs and some people hold none at all. In such a society, appeals to reason rather than to religious teachings may provide more persuasive arguments for changing our economic, political, and social policies toward the Third World.

DENIS GOULET AND THE ETHICS OF DEVELOPMENT

The most significant work in the ethics of development has been done by Denis Goulet. In his study *The Cruel Choice* Goulet argues that there are certain cultural universals or values that all people (regardless of their concept of human nature or society) hold in common. All human beings identify certain conditions as inhuman or unworthy of human life. Because we do indeed recognize this concept, according to Goulet, this suggests that "different qualities of human life can be observed and that some visible signs point to what 'human' ought to be."[1]

The Components of the Good Life

At least three values, Goulet says, are desired by people in all societies, although the form and mode of these values may vary from time to time and from place to place. They are the values of life sustenance, esteem, and freedom.

Life sustenance. All sane human beings value human life. Even in societies in which human life was sacrificed to the gods, Goulet points out, the human sacrifice was performed for the purpose of increasing the overall vitality of the life of the family or the community. Nevertheless, to live full human lives or to live at all, human beings require certain goods. Goods, Goulet argues, are so important for human existence that without a minimum amount of some goods, we cannot exist. It is not necessary to own the goods that we need for our existence, but it is necessary to have access to them in order to "assimilate [them] for vital inner purposes."[2]

Goods can be classified, Goulet thinks, according to whether they are needed for purposes of survival, enhancement, or luxury. Survival goods are just what the term implies—food, clothing, shelter, and also goods needed for our security and protection, such as storage facilities to protect crops between harvests, farm implements, and even basic training or education. Enhancement goods enable people to actualize their potentialities—to invent, explore, and bring their capacities to fulfillment. He writes:

> Men and societies need to go beyond what they already are in the hope of achieving what they can become. Because they are simultaneously individual organisms and social beings, men need physical objects to test their possibilities. They require goods—freely provided by nature or created by men's economic activity—to give material support to their actualizing and transcending activities. . . . Beyond subsistence, survival, and all useful functions, man in society has an endless range of enhancement needs, the satisfaction of which perfects him, actualizes his potentialities, thrusts him beyond perceived limits and into new environments he himself creates.[3]

Finally, luxury goods are goods that are not needed either for purposes of survival or of enhancement. While they may contribute to the enrichment of civilization, such goods can be a source of destruction and alienation for individuals and societies.

According to Goulet, individuals and societies should give as a rule their priority to satisfying the life-sustenance and enhancement needs of all human beings before satisfying their own luxury needs. In fact, he goes so far as to state that when masses of humanity lack the basic goods needed to survive or to develop their human potential, it is "morally reprehensible" for individuals or societies to pursue luxury goods.

Esteem. All societies value not only life sustenance but also esteem. Individuals as well as collectives need a sense of worth and dignity. The problem of a loss of self-worth or dignity, Goulet points out, is particularly acute in an age in which worth is increasingly measured in monetary terms. Thus the world's poor suffer most from a lack of self-worth.

Freedom. Finally, all people seek freedom—freedom from the oppressive constraints of nature, ignorance, other people, institutions, and beliefs. Goulet defines freedom as:

> at the very least . . . an expanded range of choices for societies and their members, together with the minimization of constraints (external, though not necessarily internal) in the pursuit of some perceived good.[4]

All people desire to be free from servitude and free for the possibility of self-actualization.

The values of life sustenance, esteem, and freedom, Goulet maintains, are essential components of the good life. No one of the values is more important than the other or has priority over the other. Moreover, the absence of any one of these values from the life of an individual or society diminishes the very quality of life. He states:

> Life is clearly not worth sustaining unless it can be lived with some measure of dignity. And genuine freedom is impossible if esteem is totally lacking or if one's livelihood is too precarious. It is no tautology to say that life exists so that men can give meaning to life; life is both a precondition for the realization of all human values and itself the term of those values. To live *well* is the ultimate reason for living at all. Hence, all other values are instrumental to the good life.[5]

Criteria for Evaluating the Acts of Individuals and Society

It is against these values—life sustenance, esteem, and freedom—that the moral goodness or value of the acts of individuals and societies must be judged. These values, according to Goulet, constitute the good life. Therefore, if we place the process of development within a normative framework, development becomes not an end in itself but a means to an end: the good life. In other words, the goal toward which development is pursued as well as the standard against which it must be judged is the good life, that is, the ability to attain life sustenance, esteem, and freedom.

Two questions immediately arise: Do the programs and policies of the First World toward the Third World promote life sustenance, freedom, and esteem, and has our own development enhanced the life sustenance, freedom, and esteem of rich and poor alike in our own society?

Goulet maintains that on balance the development programs and policies pursued by the First World in the Third World have done more to hinder the life sustenance, esteem, and freedom of the vast majority of people in the Third World. The programs and policies of the First World have increased the vulnerability of the Third World economically, politically, and culturally. For example, instead of increasing the Third World's strength to bargain effectively on an international level, the programs and the policies of the First World have forced the Third World into the unenviable position of always having to react to the decisions of the capitalist powers. The Third World experiences economic vulnerability not only in its weak bargaining position on the world market but also in its dependence on foreign assistance and its inability to sustain self-reliant economic measures. As a consequence, it cannot meet the basic life sustenance and enhancement needs of the majority of its people. The Third World has been made politically vulnerable by the ideological position forced on it by the First World. Moreover, the Third World has become the battleground on which the Communist and capitalist powers are waging a cold war. The Third World experiences cultural vulnerability in the steady erosion of its traditional values as a result of the influence the West has over its economic, political, and social life. Measured against the standards of life sustenance, esteem, and freedom, Goulet argues that the so-called development policies and programs of the First World are morally irresponsible.

The moral value of the development achieved by the First World must also be questioned. If development is a process by which a society moves from patterns of life that are less human to those that are more human, has the First World achieved genuine development? Goulet says that it has not. The development achieved by the First World, he holds, is a form of antidevelopment or alienation. The alienation expresses itself in the subordination of all values to the economic value. He describes the priority system that operates in the First World:

> The theory of needs operative here declares that those goods and services will enjoy priority whose provision is most profitable. But long-term profitability depends on sustained demand. As a result, demand has to be induced. Within the market system, need priorities are simply those demands which effectively motivate suppliers to keep supplying. . . . In practice, it becomes the prime function of consumption to assure continued production, which is itself justified on the grounds that it is necessary in order to keep employment high. High employment, in turn, is assumed to be a requisite of high levels of material living which are, to close the circle, equated with high levels of consumption. Normative judgments about priority needs are meaningless because the system obeys patterns of response which tend to absolutize economic functions.[6]

Apart from the ecological devastation and exploitation of the Third World, the development pursued by the First World has bred alienation in its own societies. "Having more" has become a substitute for "being more." The mass pursuit of wealth and the excessive attachment to goods, he thinks, has had the effect of rendering the societies of the First World incapable of perceiving the human good and choosing it.

The Responsibility of the First World toward the Third World

The alleviation of the poverty and hunger of the Third World, Goulet holds, is at once a moral responsibility of the First World and a challenge to its own humanity:

> The rich are now "responsible" for abolishing absolute want in others even if they have not been "guilty" of producing it in the past. The distinction between responsibility and guilt is crucial. Responsibility concerns the present and the future; it presupposes freedom—that is, the possibility of responding to an exigency which is perceived and accepted. Responsibility is founded on the belief that human agents are not always subject to absolute determinisms, but rather that they can respond to the solicitation of goals perceived by them as humanly worthy. Precisely because they are human, men are "responsible" for creating conditions which optimize the humanization of life.[7]

In sum, if the goal of development is the good life, the First World clearly has a responsibility, according to Goulet, to maximize life sustenance, freedom, and esteem in the Third World and in its own society. To refuse to do so is an admission of the loss of both our freedom and our humanity.

JOHN RAWLS AND THE DIFFERENCE PRINCIPLE

It is possible to make a case for an initial obligation on the part of rich nations to prevent or alleviate world hunger on the basis of the "original position" proposed by John Rawls, the American philosopher of ethics. In his monumental work *A Theory of Justice* Rawls argues that the justice of a social system can be determined on the basis of its distribution of the primary social goods according to a correct moral precept.[8] Primary social goods are simply goods necessary for fulfilling one's life plan—goods such as freedom, income and wealth, opportunity and self-respect. The question is, therefore, what is the moral precept according to which the primary goods of society ought to be distributed?

Because we are all unequal, Rawls argues, it is very difficult for us to arrive at a moral precept or principle of justice. The biases that accompany our social positions prevent us from arriving at a principle that would be fair to all. But suppose it were possible to create a situation of genuine equality, what principle of justice would rational people choose?

Rawls tries to answer this question by constructing a hypothetical scenario, which he calls the "original position." The "original position" is a situation of genuine equality. It is a situation in which rational people would for a period of time be kept in a veil of ignorance about their own social position, wealth, power, intelligence, and education. If we were in this situation and were given the task of devising a principle that would govern the distribution of primary goods, and if we at the same time were told that whatever principle we agreed to would govern the distribution of primary goods in our society after the veil of ignorance was lifted, what principle would we decide on?

Through lengthy argument Rawls shows that in a situation of genuine equality, people will unanimously prefer what he calls the "difference principle." In Rawls's words:

> Assuming the framework of institutions required by equal liberty and fair equality of opportunity, *the higher expectations of those better situated are just if and only if they work as part of a scheme which improves the expectations of the least advantaged members of society.* The intuitive idea is that *the social order is not to establish and secure the more attractive prospects of those better off unless doing so is to the advantage of those less fortunate* [emphasis added].[9]

In simpler terms the difference principle says that "all primary social goods ought to be distributed equally unless an unequal distribution is to the advantage of the least well-off person in society."[10] People in a situation of equality will choose the difference principle primarily because in situations of uncertainty, such as the situation of the "original position," it is rationally in their own interest to see that the least well-off are taken care of in case they may find themselves among the least well-off when the veil of ignorance is lifted. Here is a good illustration of how the difference principle would work:

> Robinson does not know whether he is caucasian or not. Nor does he know the ratio of caucasians to non-caucasians in society. He desires as much money as he can get, knows that certain jobs pay the best salaries, and that discrimination against non-caucasians will increase the chances of caucasians getting those jobs. He is cautious. Therefore, Robinson votes against a law excluding non-caucasians from the jobs in question.[11]

It must be pointed out that Rawls's theory of justice is not an egalitarian theory; inequality may be justified.[12] If we were to apply Rawls's line of argument to the problem of world hunger, we would reason that were we ignorant of the nation to which we belonged, it would be in our interest to do whatever we could do to prevent or alleviate hunger, in the event that we might find ourselves citizens of a food-deficit nation when the veil of ignorance is lifted.[13]

WILLIAM K. FRANKENA AND THE PRINCIPLES
OF BENEFICENCE AND JUSTICE

The American philosopher William K. Frankena has argued in his important work *Ethics* that we cannot derive a theory of moral obligation from the
principle of utility. To spell this idea out a little, this means that we cannot
come up with a theory—solely on the basis of the principle of utility—to the
effect that we ought to do acts that will bring about the greatest possible
balance of good over evil. This is because the principle of utility presupposes
a more fundamental principle, namely, the principle of beneficence. What is
this principle? Simply stated, the principle of beneficence states that it is right
for us to do good and to prevent or avoid doing harm. Beneficence implies
that (1) we ought not to inflict evil or harm; (2) we ought to prevent evil or
harm; (3) we ought to remove evil; and (4) we ought to do or promote good.[14]
Although beneficence precedes utility, Frankena points out that beneficence
is not always sufficient for us to determine what our moral obligation might
be in a given situation. Beneficence simply tells us that we ought to do good
and not how to distribute that good.

How do we learn how to distribute what is good? According to Frankena, a
second principle—the principle of justice—is needed for that purpose. Justice and beneficence together enable us to know our moral obligation.
Frankena is concerned with the following question: Should we distribute
what is good on the basis of merit, on the basis of equality, or on the basis of
need and/or ability? Frankena replies that if we decide to distribute what is
good on the basis of people's merit, ability, or virtue, then we are presup-
posing that all people have an equal opportunity to realize their potential.
For this reason he believes that equality is a better basis for distributing what
is good than merit, ability, or virtue. Equality means that we ought "prima
facie to make proportionally the same contribution to the goodness of [peo-
ple's] lives, once a certain minimum has been achieved by all."[15] In sum,
Frankena argues that the principles of beneficence and justice, understood as
equal treatment, provide a basis for determining moral obligation. Beneficence, however, may take precedence over justice if beneficence promotes
greater equality in the long run. Along with these two principles, Frankena
maintains that good will, clarity of thought, and knowledge of the relevant
facts are essential for determining moral obligation.[16]

In a 1977 essay Frankena argued that the principles of beneficence and
justice may not be sufficient to meet the demands of the food crisis.[17] If we are
to be realistic about human nature, he says, a solution to the problem of
world hunger cannot be left solely to private conscience; some sort of positive
morality is also required. He thinks that our global society needs a publicly
promoted ethic that would praise or blame human beings and institutions on
the basis of how well they meet the requirements of beneficence and justice.

More important than the need for a public ethic in Frankena's opinion is
the need to create or modify national and international institutions according

to the principles of beneficence and justice. If the institutions of our society are restructured according to these principles, Frankena holds that this would result in greater beneficence and justice in society at large. He writes:

> Given such a system, individuals and other moral agents could and should determine what to do, not by themselves appealing directly to basic moral principles, but by looking to the rules of the system.[18]

Assuming that institutions do function properly and that citizens follow the rules, all people would ultimately be fed:

> It might be that the institution of national states is calculated, when functioning ideally, to solve or to obviate problems about beneficence and justice across boundaries. At any rate, one may suppose that there is some possible system of institutions that would do so, one which would then also dispose of the problem of WH [world hunger], at least if natural resources permitted.[19]

Until these institutions do materialize, Frankena believes that we all have a moral responsibility to apply the principles of beneficence and justice directly to the hunger crisis. This would entail at least that (1) we engage in activity that will bring about the creation of beneficent and just institutions and (2) we act directly to do whatever we can to insure that everyone is at least minimally or adequately fed.

Finally, to the question of whether affluent nations are obligated to prevent or alleviate hunger only when it entails no sacrifice on their own part, Frankena replies,

> Morality may require sacrifices, and . . . we should sometimes help people in other countries even if it involves giving something up, whether we do it by direct action or by indirect means.[20]

Thus we have here three different philosophical perspectives that argue the moral obligation of the rich to respond to the needs of the poor and hungry on the basis of reason alone. While a number of other philosophers might make just as strong a case as the three chosen here, we have limited the discussion to those three in order to show that on the basis of reason alone we are all morally responsible for helping the poor and hungry of the world. Those interested in pursuing the philosophical arguments further are referred to William Aiken and Hugh LaFollette's fine anthology *World Hunger and Moral Obligation* (see note 17 to this chapter).

THE NEED FOR SOMETHING BEYOND REASON

While philosophers like Goulet, Rawls, and Frankena provide a rational basis for acting in the interest of the least well-off, we are left with the question of whether reason alone can provide the motivation needed to bring an end to global poverty and hunger. The British educator Brian Wren states the issue well in his criticism of Rawls's *Theory of Justice*:

> In the real world, it is doubtful whether that degree of commitment will do much to achieve justice. . . . To have a passion for justice or sacrifice oneself for justice's sake is not rational. Yet it is sometimes necessary if justice is to be attained.[21]

Can reason alone enable us to enter into the suffering of others and make it our own? Given the fact that our own needs always seem so much more pressing and real than the needs of others, is there any way that the needs of others can be made more immediate for us?[22] While reason provides a justification for acting in the interest of the hungry, our religious tradition can provide much stronger grounds for doing so.

The Christian theological tradition places a more binding and radical obligation on the person of faith to alleviate and prevent hunger than does the moral philosophical tradition. From a Christian perspective, self-sacrifice is not an option but a requirement where human suffering is concerned.

THE RELATIONSHIP OF AGAPE TO BENEFICENCE

It might be wise at this point to try to clarify the relationship between the Christian ethical norm of agape (love) and the philosophical norms of beneficence and benevolence.

One of the moot questions for ethicists today is whether the Christian ideal of agape is the same as the principle of beneficence or the virtue of benevolence. Frankena argues that the way Thomas Aquinas and the twentieth-century Protestant theologians Reinhold Niebuhr and Emil Brunner define agape is not all that different from the way he himself does. Their understanding of agape, he claims, is essentially beneficence supplemented by the principle of distributive justice or equality.[23] He points out, however, that only the second of the two great Christian commandments—the obligation to love one's neighbor as oneself—can be designated as beneficence supplemented by justice. The first commandment—the obligation to love God with one's whole heart—cannot be so interpreted. While the second commandment may be regarded as a moral obligation, the first may be regarded as a religious obligation.[24]

The famous Yale ethicist Gene Outka, on the other hand, holds that a rational justification for agape must be left open. He argues that while Frankena's principle of beneficence may certainly overlap that of agape, it does not exhaust the meaning of agape as it functions within the religious context.[25] Outka maintains that the Christian tradition significantly shapes the meaning as well as the specific implications of the principle of loving one's neighbor.[26] He then points out some of the most characteristic features of the concept as expressed historically in the Christian tradition. This tradition has spoken of agape in terms of enjoining Christians to consider the needs and interests of others as much as their own. Specifically, they must try to enter imaginatively into the lives of others and their points of view. We must actively identify with the needs and interests of our neighbors. Active identification with our neighbors' interests must be unconditional, that is, we are enjoined to love our neighbors regardless of their merit or attractiveness as well as of any benefits that may result to ourselves. Nothing that our neighbors do should be a condition for our being concerned with their well-being. Finally, because of our neighbors' irreducible value and dignity before God, we Christians are bound to acknowledge the claim that the neighbors make on us.

Outka points out the three characteristics that appear frequently in the Christian tradition with respect to our responsibility for our neighbors. The first is that all people are equally related to God. Our lives, therefore, should reflect that fact. Second, the physical as well as the social needs of our neighbors are to be met, that is, we Christians are obliged to attend to their need for food, clothing, shelter, health, liberty, respect, and affection. In addition, according to Outka, we need to be concerned with their "need to be heard."[27] Finally, because God does not interfere with his creatures' freedom, in loving our neighbors, we must respect them as free moral agents.

Outka points out further that there are also certain biases built into the concept of agape. The tradition emphasizes, for example, the fact that needs have precedence over merits. It deemphasizes the differences between persons and maintains that privileges must always be justified.

This brief summary of the arguments of Goulet, Rawls, and Frankena is intended to show that on rational, nonreligious grounds alone we can make a convincing case for the responsibility of the rich to alleviate the suffering of the poor and hungry of our world. The moral responsibility of Christians, as demonstrated in Outka's study of agape, is much more radical and binding than that defined by the philosophers. The two great commandments of the Christian faith, in short, require persons of faith to view unconditionally the needs of their neighbors as their own.

In the following chapter we shall try to spell out more specifically just what the responsibility of Christians in the First World might be toward the poor and hungry of the Third World.

Chapter 9

POLITICAL THEOLOGY AND LIBERATION THEOLOGY

In this chapter we shall explore the insights of two relatively new schools of theology that may help broaden and deepen our understanding of our religious tradition and faith as well as our understanding of the mission of the church.

THE PRIVATIZATION OF FAITH

If we wish to respond as Christians to the problem of world hunger, we must learn to think about faith in less individualistic and private terms. For most of us Christians of the First World, faith has become simply a private matter between ourselves and God. We tend to think of it primarily in terms of obtaining comfort and strength in time of need. As the German theologian Dietrich Bonhoeffer points out, we use God as a stopgap—a source of answers to questions we cannot answer on our own. We turn to God when we are sad or depressed or in need of help. God is useful as a convenient explanation for the tragedy and mystery of life. And we look to God as a source of immortality when our natural life is ended. Bonhoeffer's criticism that we have pushed God away from the center to the fringe of life is no less true than when he formulated it in the prisons of Nazi Germany.

The tendency to privatize faith is responsible to a large extent for the general apathy among First World Christians regarding problems of poverty and hunger. Something is drastically wrong when Christians, whose very religion is based on the command to feed the hungry and clothe the naked, ignore the suffering of the poor and hungry of the world. Even more disturbing is the widespread rationalization and justification by Christians of our own wealth and our pursuit of private comfort in the face of absolute human need. The sight of massive suffering from poverty and hunger has become normal and acceptable—even justifiable.

One of the Latin American liberation theologians, Juan Luis Segundo, has said that Christians in the First World are undisturbed by human suffering because they have molded their image of God in their own likeness. In other words, we who live in affluent nations have fashioned a God who no longer disturbs us. It is a God who condones our way of life, our exploitative systems, and our hopes and dreams for private material gain. In Segundo's words, our God is a God "whom we accommodate to our easy world of convenience and habit."[1] This God dispenses us from the task of being human.[2] Segundo asks the right question in these words:

> Do we ever realize that we may be operating with a distorted notion of God? Do we ever realize that we may be injecting into our God the base, egotistical values that rule our lives and that are not God at all? Is it not possible that when we say, "I believe," we are making an act of faith in capitalism, injustice, suffering, and egotism?[3]

The image of God that so many of us operate with is a far cry from the biblical God who summons the people to solidarity with the poor and who calls us to become a holy people—a people who loves mercy, does justice, and feeds and clothes the hungry and the poor.

Can it be true that the reason that we are so complacent about human suffering is that we have read the gospels selectively?[4] Can the Protestant theologian Robert McAfee Brown's criticism be true that "we read what we can bear to read, we hear what is tolerable to hear, and we evade (or 'spiritualize') those parts which leave us uncomfortable, if not outraged."[5]

CHALLENGE OF POLITICAL AND LIBERATION THEOLOGIANS

Over the last two decades two schools of theology have emerged—one in western Europe and the other in Latin America. Theologians of the former school are sometimes referred to as political theologians. Those who belong to the latter school are called liberation theologians. Both schools provide a fresh approach to theological reflection, and what is even more important, they have forced us in North America to reevaluate our interpretation of faith and our understanding of what it means to be Christians in a world plagued by poverty and hunger.

In many ways the political and liberation theologians challenge us to move from the faith of our childhood to the faith of adulthood. As social scientists who study moral and religious development have told us, moral and religious growth generally takes place through a process in which individuals gradually come to perceive themselves as part of something larger—the group, the society, or certain principles and ends. Moral and religious growth requires the development of the ability to think more abstractly, to enter imaginatively into another's situation, and to develop critical awareness of the institutions, laws, and customs of our society.

Disequilibrium, the social scientists tell us, is crucial for movement through the various stages of moral and religious growth. It is only when the old ways of thinking are no longer adequate for interpreting our new situation and when we are forced to reconsider or reevaluate what we hold to be true that growth can take place.

I believe that the political and liberation theologians may, in fact, be catalysts of our moral development. If we take what they say seriously, they will surely create a considerable amount of disequilibrium for us. No longer can we be certain that our received understanding of faith is true to the spirit of the gospel. No longer can we be sure that charity is all that is required of us as Christians. We can ignore the challenge that the political and liberation theologians make for us and continue to live the faith of our childhood, or we can accept their challenge and begin the difficult process of rethinking the meaning of our faith and the responsibility it carries for the poor and hungry.

Among the Latin American liberation theologians whose work is extremely helpful in rethinking the meaning of faith and our responsibility to the poor and hungry are Gustavo Gutiérrez, Hugo Assmann, Juan Luis Segundo, Antonio Pérez-Esclarín, and José Míguez Bonino. Among the European political theologians the same is true of Johannes Metz and Dorothee Sölle. While the liberation and political theologians do not attempt or pretend to address our specific situation as Christians in North America and while their theologies cannot be simply applied to our own situation, their work nevertheless provides a basis from which we can reflect ethically about our moral responsibility to the poor and hungry of the Third World.

At this point we shall review briefly the background of the two types of theology by highlighting some of their major thrusts and differences.[6]

DIFFERENCES BETWEEN THE TWO SCHOOLS OF THEOLOGY

Political theologians have a different starting point, goal, presupposition, and method from those of liberation theologians. Political theologians take as their starting point the western European experience of secularization, specifically the challenge to live responsibly in a world in which God's presence is neither presupposed nor necessary for its normal existence.

Political theology essentially tries to fill the gap left by existentialist and personalist theologies by providing a new hermeneutic that illumines the public dimensions of the gospel and tries to work out the relationship between faith and society. In short:

> Existential theology asks, "What meaning does this Gospel text have for my individual life?" Political theology asks, "What is the meaning of the Gospel text for the life of all men, not for the individual person alone but for the life of every one, for the society of persons that constitute the whole world?"[7]

For political theologians, faith cannot be reduced to personal or individual piety but must be lived responsibly in the social and public realms. Thus political theology primarily serves as a corrective to the relegation of faith to the private sphere. It is important to point out that the term "political" as used by political theologians, "is contrasted with private and individual, and is nearly equivalent to social or public."[8]

While political theologians try to respond to the challenge posed to faith by nonbelievers, liberation theologians try to respond to the challenge posed by nonpersons. Gustavo Gutiérrez writes:

> This challenge in a continent like Latin America does not come primarily from the man who does not believe, but from the *man who is not a man*, who is not recognized as such by the existing social order: he is in the ranks of the poor, the exploited; he is the man who is systematically and legally despoiled of his being as a man, who scarcely knows that he *is* a man. His challenge is not aimed first at our religious world, but at our *economic, social, political and cultural world.* . . . The question is not therefore how to speak of God in an adult world, but how to proclaim him as a Father in a world that is not human.[9]

The theology of liberation has emerged out of the experience of poverty and exploitation in Latin America and is addressed to that situation. Unlike traditional theology, which takes revelation and tradition as its starting point, liberation theology begins with the concrete historical experience of oppression and the struggle for liberation in Latin America. Theological reflection is a second step for liberation theologians. It is critical reflection on the practice of liberation in the light of faith.

Unlike traditional theology, liberation theology does not limit its task to interpreting the Christian tradition. It attempts to be part of the process of social transformation itself. Liberation theology asks not only "what does the tradition say, but what does the tradition tell us to do in the struggle for liberation?"[10]

Liberation theology differs from traditional theology in yet another way. Unlike traditional theology, which separates itself from the secular sciences, the theology of liberation freely draws on the analysis of the social sciences, including Marxist analysis, to understand the oppression of the Third World and its struggle for liberation. For liberation theologians the economic, political and social analysis of an oppressive situation is a necessary and integral step in doing theology.

Finally, the theology of liberation is a committed theology; it is partisan and even militant.[11] Liberation theologians contend that to remain neutral in the struggle for liberation is equivalent to being a collaborator in the oppression of the poor.

If we understand the criticism that liberation theologians raise against political theology, we shall grasp the main difference between the two types of theology. Liberation theologians maintain that political theologians assume too easily that the problem of faith is universal. Liberation theologians point out that in Latin America, where the practice of faith and the activity of the church are still very public, the problem is not the privatization of faith but the church's support of unjust and oppressive systems.[12] Liberation theologians also criticize political theology for its abstractness and for its lack of economic, political, and social analysis. Finally, they argue that political theology does not lend itself immediately to action.[13]

From this brief overview, it should be clear that the two schools of theology have emerged from different cultural settings and are addressed to very different problems. In suggesting that their insights may provide a basis upon which we can begin our own ethical reflection, I am by no means suggesting that we should ignore the differences between their situations and our own, or that we should simply apply their theologies to our situation. Rather I am suggesting that both schools provide valuable insights regarding the public and political nature of both our religious tradition and our theological methodology. We in the First World cannot afford to ignore such insights.

POLITICAL THEOLOGY AND THE PUBLIC NATURE OF THE CHRISTIAN MESSAGE

We are indebted to the political theologians for exposing the public nature of the Christian tradition. They have called our attention to the fact that the gospel is not simply a biography of a private individual but rather a public summons and a promise made to a society. The freedom, peace, justice, and love that Jesus preached and came to establish are not abstract ideals. They are public realities that must be embodied in concrete historical relationships, institutions and among individuals and societies. If we take this insight to its logical conclusion, then we have to conclude that the countries of the Third World are not free if they cannot break out of the cycle of debt because of the financial aid policies of the First World. When nations in the First World budget huge sums each year for military research and the development of weapons, they are not working for peace. When we in the First World discriminate against the products of the Third World, we are not being just. And when we ignore the problems of the poor and hungry, we are not displaying love.

The freedom, peace, justice, and love that Jesus spoke of are concrete realities. We must not fool ourselves into believing that the message of the gospel is merely a spiritual message. To be sure, freedom, peace, justice, and love are all inner virtues, but they also have social and public manifestations. How can we know what freedom, peace, justice, and love are except by observing them in our economic, political, and social relationships?

As Johannes Metz points out, one of the clearest indications that the gospel message is indeed public is the fact that Jesus' proclamation of that message of salvation led him into conflict with the public authorities of his day. His trial and death have to be interpreted as a public response to a public message.[14]

Because the gospel is a public summons, faith cannot be reduced to a private matter. It is not simply a private relationship between individuals and God. Faith is the acceptance of Jesus' summons to live out publicly the promise of freedom, justice, love, and peace in concrete historical situations. Acceptance of the gospel summons must be reflected in our posture toward others and our environment. Of course, the particular meaning of that summons will vary from epoch to epoch, and it is our responsibility to determine the precise meaning of that summons for our own day.

The mission of the church, according to the political theologians, is also public. The church must become an institution of free social criticism. It must act as an institutional reminder to society of our ultimate end and of the provisional character of all human efforts. It must:

> . . . constantly use this liberating power of criticism with regard to all political systems; it must stress that history as a whole is subject to God's eschatological proviso.[15]

If the church fails to assume its public responsibility, according to the political theologians, it is failing in its mission. By denying its own public role the church is denying the very reason for its existence.

LIBERATION THEOLOGY AND THE POLITICAL NATURE OF THE JUDEO-CHRISTIAN TRADITION

Liberation theologians have helped us see not only the public but also the political character of the Judeo-Christian tradition, which speaks of God's political actions in history. God's intervention in history has been primarily political insofar as it has challenged the status quo and paved the way for the establishment of a radically different new order. Liberation theologians point to the liberation of the Israelites from Egypt in the Exodus as an example of the political nature of God's action. In Egypt the Jews lived a life of slavery in which they were exploited and kept in a state of misery. By leading them out of Egypt and into the Promised Land, God freed the Jews from political, economic, and social injustice in order that they might build a more just and humane social order. Gutiérrez explains God's liberating actions as follows:

> Yahweh liberates the Jewish people politically in order to make them a holy nation: "You have seen with your own eyes what I did to Egypt. . . . If only you will now listen to me and keep my covenant, then out of all peoples you shall become my special possession; for the whole earth is mine. You shall become my kingdom of priests, my holy nation" (Ex. 19:4-6). The God of Exodus is the God of history and of political liberation more than he is the God of nature.[16]

The life and preaching of Jesus, liberation theologians hold, continues the political activity of God in history. Jesus announces the end of the old order—the end of all hatred and exploitation. He proclaims its replacement by the creation of a qualitatively new order based on the values of love, justice, peace, and freedom. The message of the gospel is by its very nature a subversive message:

> . . . it takes on Israel's hope: the Kingdom as "the end of domination of man over man; it is a Kingdom of contradiction to the established powers and on behalf of man." And the Gospel gives Israel's hope its deepest meaning; indeed it calls for a "new creation." The life and preaching of Jesus postulate the unceasing search for a new kind of man in a qualitatively different society.[17]

Thus the message of the gospel is not only a public but also a political message. Its purpose is to challenge the status quo and establish a new order in its place.

Next, liberation theologians see faith itself as a political activity. All human activity is performed within a particular political, economic, and social context. And because it cannot help but affect the context in which it is performed by either changing it or by maintaining it, our human activity is by its very nature political. Faith is a human activity, that is, it is lived within a specific political, economic, and social human context. As such it affects the context in which it is lived by maintaining or changing it. Thus faith in itself is political. Assmann goes so far as to state that it is incorrect to speak of the "political dimension" of faith or its "political implications," as if the political were something that could be added onto or subtracted from faith. This way of speaking, he says, "gives a false impression that it is possible to live a life of faith in isolation from daily life, but with the bonus of occasional political 'applications.' "[18] Liberation theologians prevent us from falling into the common error of thinking of faith in ahistorical or apolitical terms.

Finally, liberation theologians regard the church as a political institution with a political mission. Whether the church acknowledges this fact or not, it is structurally integrated into the present economic, political, and social order. Its activity as well as its inactivity, therefore, reinforces or challenges the existing order. Because the church is, as Assmann puts it, "in the world, and not merely facing the world, it will always be embodied in socio-cultural situations tied to historical projects."[19] The church, consequently, must come to terms with the fact that it really has no choice about using its influence in a particular situation. It always uses its influence even when it keeps silent. The real question for the church is how it will use its influence and for whom.[20]

The church can best serve humanity, liberation theologians think, by becoming a visible sign of liberation, that is, by becoming a place where justice, peace, and love are not just preached but also practiced. The church should not tolerate privilege, discrimination, or injustice of any kind within its structures or beyond them. It should become a place where new relationships are forged and where the rules and logic of the status quo do not hold.

To be faithful to its political mission, liberation theologians argue, the church must become an institution of social criticism. It must expose and denounce the injustice and inhumanity of the present order, and it must play an active part in the struggle for a qualitatively new order. The Roman Catholic bishops who met at Medellín, Colombia, in 1968, wrote:

> To us, the Pastors of the Church, belongs the duty . . . to denounce everything which, opposing justice, destroys peace. . . . The "duty of solidarity with the poor . . . means that we make ours their problems and their struggles. . . . This has to be concretized in criticism of injustice and oppression, in the struggle against the intolerable situation which a poor person has to tolerate.[21]

The church's mission, however, does not stop with denouncing the injustices of our present society. Liberation theologians argue that the church must also support those institutions and systems that are just. As the Peruvian bishops wrote:

> When governments arise which are trying to implant more just and human societies in their countries, we propose that the Church commit itself to giving them its backing; contributing to the elimination of prejudice; recognizing the aspirations they hold; and encouraging the search for their own road toward a socialist society.[22]

José María González-Ruiz summarizes the issue for the Church quite clearly:

> . . . the Church cannot have the same institutional relationship with a society in which personal gain is the guiding rule of social, economic, and political organization as it can with a society that tries to organize the distribution of goods in such a way as to level out differences between rich and poor.[23]

These, then, are but some of the presuppositions that underlie political theology and the theology of liberation. I have presented them here and will discuss some of their major themes not just for purposes of giving information but because those theologies offer the most promising perspective for rethinking the nature of our tradition and faith as well as the mission of the church today, especially as they bear on the problem of poverty and hunger.

Chapter 10

THE METHODOLOGY OF
LIBERATION THEOLOGY

As Christians living in the First World we not only can learn new insights from the political and liberation theologians about our religious tradition but we can also profit from the new methodology developed especially by liberation theologians. Let us first of all examine this methodology, and then see how its application can help us grasp better the problem of world hunger.

SIX STEPS IN THE METHODOLOGY

This methodology can be broken down into six steps:

1. First of all, we do not engage in theological reflection simply for intellectual reasons but rather out of a fundamental commitment to the poor and hungry. Unlike the other sciences and academic disciplines, theology cannot be neutral. It is committed to the cause of the poor and oppressed of the world.

2. Liberation theologians argue that theological reflection should not begin with revelation and tradition but rather with the concrete suffering of the poor and their struggle for liberation. We should break with the tradition of the past and no longer begin our theologizing with *a priori* principles, scripture, or the teaching of the church. Instead, we should take as our starting point the problems posed to us by the world, the struggle to overcome those problems, and our commitment to join in that struggle. As Hugo Assmann puts it:

> If the state of domination and dependence in which two-thirds of humanity live, with an annual toll of thirty million dead from starvation and malnutrition, does not become the starting-point for *any* Christian theology today, even in the affluent and powerful countries, then theology cannot begin to relate meaningfully to the real situation.[1]

3. The third step is crucial. Liberation theologians argue that we must become suspicious of the way the problem has ordinarily been interpreted, including the generally accepted analysis of its causitive factors and solutions. Suspicion is important, they claim, because the accepted analysis has at times contributed to masking the roots of the problem rather than to exposing them.

4. The fourth step is to analyze the problem. We must try to determine its causative factors, and for this we need the help of the social sciences. The social sciences, they argue, provide the analytical tools for uncovering the historical, systemic, and ideological roots of the problem as well as an understanding of their dynamics yesterday and today. Segundo has pointed out that we need to find a general theory of explanation for the problem so that we can place the problem within its proper context. It is also important, he claims, to be as specific as possible in our analysis. We must name the systems, people, and ideologies responsible for the problem and point out specific instances of exploitation. Here is how Segundo states this obligation:

We must find a theory of some general nature which will enable us to unmask the reality of oppression in general, and specifically its repercussions in theology. For oppression usually does not reveal itself in barefaced fashion; it hides and hallows itself behind ideologies that obscure what is really happening in concrete human reality.[2]

Thus for the liberation theologians, the analysis that the social sciences provide is a necessary and integral part of theological reflection. It is not something that is simply added on to theological reflection; it is inseparable from it. In sum, if theological reflection is to contribute to alleviating the suffering of the poor and hungry, it must expose the oppressive systems responsible for that suffering as well as the ideologies used to legitimate that suffering. Then it must confront them.

5. Liberation theologians maintain that only after we have analyzed the roots of a problem can we begin to interpret it in the light of faith. They remind us that God still speaks to us and acts in history by advising us to try to discern what God is saying to us through events, people, and institutions. We should try to discover what God is "telling us in and through what is going on and what we have already evaluated."[3] Then and only then can we go to Scripture and tradition and try to correlate what we believe God is saying to us today with how God has spoken at other times and through other means.

Raul Vidales stresses the fact that the methodology employed here, unlike the methodology of western European theology, is provisional in character. Liberation theologians realize that today's interpretation can easily become tomorrow's ideology. They argue therefore that their analysis and their interpretation of that analysis in the light of faith must be constantly analyzed, evaluated, and revised. The truth of their reflection can be tested only by living out its full implications. According to Vidales, theology "moves forward by proposing hypotheses that are verified, corrected, or rejected as it proceeds."[4]

6. Finally, the last methodological step of liberation theologians is to decide, on the basis of theological reflection, what specific action should be taken on behalf of the poor and hungry. At this point we must act.

APPLICATION OF THE METHODOLOGY
TO THE PROBLEM OF WORLD HUNGER

If we were to reflect theologically on the problem of world hunger using the methodology of the liberation theologians how might we go about it?

First we would have to make clear our reason for engaging in theological reflection, namely, our concern and commitment to the poor and hungry of the world. We would then start with the problem of world hunger itself, familiarizing ourselves with the so-called facts and figures as well as the various theories and proposed solutions to the problem. While doing this, it would be important to develop a sense of suspicion as we keep in mind Segundo's point that the accepted common interpretations of the problem often obsure the very roots of the problem.

While researching world hunger, we might want to keep in mind some very basic questions. Why does hunger exist today? What is its history? Why is hunger concentrated among the poor in the Third World? Why can't the hungry feed themselves? Are there any systems or ideologies that work against the interest of the poor and hungry or prevent us from seeing and responding to their problems? What are those ideological systems? What will happen if we do nothing about hunger?

We ought to rethink the meaning of terms like "underdevelopment" and "development." Most of us in the First World believe that "underdevelopment" is measured in terms of GNP. A country is underdeveloped if its GNP is significantly lower than our own. We believe that the way to become developed is to do what our own nation has supposedly done, namely, work hard and "pull itself up by its bootstraps." Many Third World scholars, however, reject the term "underdevelopment" to describe their situation. Underdevelopment rather means for them "being kept in a state of underdevelopment . . . 'a state of dependence,' rather than simply the situation of countries 'not yet developed' or 'in the development phase'."[5] The term "underdevelopment," Third World scholars argue, conveys neither the history of exploitation nor the assymetrical power relationships that exist in the world today.[6] In short the economic, political, and cultural vulnerability as well as the immeasurable human suffering of the poor in the Third World are obscured by the antiseptic term "underdevelopment."

For this reason the spokespersons for the Third World have chosen to call the process by which it will overcome its oppression "liberation" rather than "development." The Third World has no desire to imitate the institutions, values, or lifestyle of its oppressors. It understands its "liberation" in terms of freedom from the social restraints imposed on them by the First World as well as freedom to create a qualitatively new order, in Gutiérrez's words:

> The liberation of our continent means more than overcoming economic, social, and political dependence. It means, in a deeper sense, to see the becoming of mankind as a process of the emancipation of man in history. It is to see man in search of a qualitatively different society in which he will be free from all servitude, in which he will be an artisan of his own destiny.[7]

In his book *The Cruel Choice* Denis Goulet argues that it is important:

> to recognize the qualitative difference between freedom *from* wants and freedom *for* wants. The first exists when genuine human needs are adequately met, the latter when men control the dynamisms by which their wants are multiplied. The essential point is not how many wants can be met, but the degree of mastery men exercise over the forces by which their wants are generated.[8]

Goulet believes that the kind of development that our own society has achieved is distorted. In his words it "alienates even its beneficiaries in compulsive consumption, technological determinisms of various sorts, ecological pathology, and warlike policies."[9]

It is only after we become suspicious of some of the common assumptions about the problem of hunger that we can begin to analyze the roots of the problem by using the critical tools provided by the social sciences. In this connection I have found the work of American economists and political scientists like Paul Sweezy, Paul Baran, and Cheryl Payer and of Third World economists like Arghiri Emmanuel, Samir Amin, and Mahbub ul Haq extremely helpful.

As we analyze the roots of the problem of hunger, we should also formulate a general theory of how specific systems and ideologies involved work. We should try to identify specific instances of how those systems and ideologies actually contribute to the problem.

After we have analyzed the problem and clarified our views about its roots and our own involvement in it, we can then reflect on the situation and our response to it in the light of faith. This will be our task in the following chapter.

Chapter 11

WORLD HUNGER IN THE LIGHT OF FAITH

How are we to understand the problem of world hunger and our response to it in the light of faith? The political and liberation theologians, I believe, can provide valuable insights for this task.

Gustavo Gutiérrez argues that we should not fall into the trap of thinking about history on two levels—the supernatural and the temporal. For there is but one history. It is our history that God initiated at the moment of creation, our history in which God intervened, and our history that God will bring to fulfillment at the end of time. There is but one history, which is salvation history.

Moreover, all history is oriented toward only one goal—salvation—or the union of people with other people and of all humanity with God. For people of faith, salvation transforms and fulfills history and gives to history its fullest meaning.[1] Our own actions, Gutiérrez points out, have meaning in terms of salvation history. In fact, they may hinder or help usher in salvation.

In this chapter we will examine that thesis in greater detail and its implications for understanding and responding to the problem of world hunger.

THE MEANING OF HISTORY

What do liberation theologians like Gutiérrez mean when they say all history is salvation history? What should our role in history be?

Creation as a Call to Become a Community of Love

The first clue we have for understanding who we are and what God calls us to be is found in the message of creation. The story of creation tells us that we, above all creatures, were made in the image and likeness of God. But what does that mean? Quite simply, liberation theologians say, it means that we are called to be like the community of love that is God. Juan Luis Segundo points out that the God whom Jesus reveals in the New Testament is not a

God who is one person but a God who is a society.[2] The New Testament reveals the Father, Son, and Holy Spirit as distinct and equal, yet as acting in "a total and intimate collaboration in a history of love that is our own history."[3] In other words the God revealed by Jesus is the epitome of perfect unity in love and action. Segundo writes:

> God, the Christian God, is love. But not simply or not so much a love that unites two people and separates them from the world and time; that would be a false love. Rather, the love that fashions human society in history. The love which, ever since the first stages in the evolution of matter, has systematically broken up and broken through every simplistic synthesis in its quest for more costly but more total synthesis in which originality would be fully freed and a "We," such as all our "We's" on earth struggle and would like to be. Despite all our twisted and distorted images, the God that Jesus revealed to us is a *God who is a society*.[4]

Just as the three Persons of the Trinity are united in total and intimate collaboration in a history of love, so we who are fashioned in the image of God must be united with one another. Antonio Pérez-Esclarín states this well:

> The message of creation is tremendously positive. Humankind, as male and female, is meant to be a community of love. This community is loved by God in turn, and it is established here on earth to transform and humanize the world so that it will be a fitting place for the communal life of love.[5]

The Exodus as a Call to Overcome Obstacles to the Community of Love

The Scriptures reveal a God who is not only a community of love but a liberator as well. In fact, liberation theologians point out that all biblical thinking about God is rooted in the Exodus. The Israelites' idea of God was shaped by the way God was revealed to them, which was primarily through a series of salvific events. They knew a God who intervened in history through a series of events that freed them from the slavery and oppression of the Egyptians. In Pérez-Esclarín's words:

> Israel's faith in Yahweh is rooted in that series of events and constantly draws nourishment from it. Its whole history is organized around that saving action. When later writers talk about Yahweh, they constantly go back to the image of Yahweh as the liberator, the one who led Israel out of bondage in Egypt.[6]

By freeing the Israelites from Egypt, God made it known that God was against all forms of oppression and dehumanization—everything that separates people from one another and from God. By leading the Jews out of Egypt God made them free in order that they might build the community of love for which they were created.

After freeing the Israelites, God gave to them the Decalogue, which established rules that would govern their relationship with God and one another. The last seven commandments of the Decalogue, in particular, according to Pérez-Esclarín, "shore up the life of the community."[7] Just as creation teaches us that we are called to be a community of love, the Exodus teaches us that we must free ourselves from internal and external obstacles preventing us from creating that community of love.

The Incarnation as Salvation through Our Neighbor

Finally, the meaning of the history of salvation and our role in it is nowhere more fully revealed than in the person of Jesus the Christ. Liberation theologians point out that Jesus preached both the presence and the coming of a radically new order, the kingdom of God. The growth of the kingdom, he announced, was occurring in history and would come in all its fullness as a gift from God at the end of history. The kingdom of which Jesus spoke was one of peace, justice, and love. It meant the end of all hatred, oppression, and human misery, the end of all that separates people from other people and from God. The promise of the kingdom is the promise of salvation— communion with one another and with God. Jesus revealed that salvation is mediated through our neighbor, particularly through the poor, hungry, naked, and imprisoned as well as all who are oppressed and despised by this world. He taught that it is only by loving them that we can love God and thus be saved. Pérez-Esclarín captures this point beautifully:

> God went so far as to convert each and every human being into God himself. He became incarnate in Christ, and Christ identified himself with every human being, particularly with those who seem to be the most insignificant. . . . So true is this that we cannot love God if we despise human beings (1 John 4:20). Indeed if we despise our fellows, we cannot possibly know God; we are really murderers (1 John 3:14-15).[8]

OUR RESPONSIBILITY TO OUR NEIGHBOR

The crucial questions that we need to answer, however, are who is our neighbor? How do we love our neighbor? Both liberation and political theologians point out that biblically speaking the term "neighbor" refers not only to individuals but to collectives as well. Thus when we talk about loving our neighbor, we must broaden our understanding of "neighbor" to include nations, races, classes, and sexes, particularly those that are poor and oppressed. Liberation theologians also argue that our "neighbor" never exists "in general." Our neighbors are particular individuals, nations, and classes in concrete historical, political, economic, and social situations.

Most important, our "neighbors" are not simply individuals or collectives that approach me for help. Rather, as Gutiérrez says, the "neighbor" is the individual or collective "in *whose* path I deliberately place myself, the man 'distant' from me, the one whom I approach."[9] The neighbor is the specific individual or collective whom I seek out. Gutiérrez makes another very important point regarding the "neighbor." He says that as long as I continue to regard the "neighbor" simply as the individual who comes to me for help, my world will remain the same. However, if I am true to the biblical command to seek out my "neighbor" my world must change. In other words I will have to enter the world of the other and make it my own. Thus my world will have to become larger than my own egotistical self-interest and take on a radically different character.[10]

If we broaden the concept of neighbor, as the liberation theologians suggest, what then would it mean to "love our neighbor"? The radical demand of the gospel, both political and liberation theologians maintain, suffers today from being spiritualized and privatized. Dorothee Sölle, for example, says that today, especially in the affluent societies, the biblical injunction to love our neighbor has been reduced to "be nice to one another." As such, "it takes neither the victims nor the perpetrators of present conditions seriously."[11] If we reduce the radical demand of love to such social politeness, we in fact trivialize the gospel injunction and make it practically meaningless. This easy interpretation of the gospel is just another example of how we have accommodated the gospel to our world of convenience and habit.

Gutiérrez speaks of loving our neighbor in terms of a conversion. Conversion implies a radical change; it means assuming a new way of looking at things, a new way of living, and a new way of relating to people, institutions, and systems. How do we convert to our neighbor? According to Gutiérrez we must seek out oppressed individuals and collectives. We must enter into their suffering and make it our own. Conversion to our neighbor requires us to identify with our neighbor so that we see the economic, political, and social situation of the oppressed as they themselves see it.

To convert to our neighbors, finally, requires us to join in their struggle to overcome oppression; we must make their struggle our own. This identification with our neighbors must express itself not only in words but in action. Gutiérrez writes:

> We may talk about accepting the gift of divine sonship and making all people our brothers and sisters. But if we do not live that acceptance from day to day in the conflict-ridden reality of history, . . . [then] we are merely engaging in talk and allowing ourselves to indulge in the self-satisfaction of a noble ideal. This ideal must be translated into real-life identification with the interests of those human beings who actually are being subjected to oppression by other human beings. It must lead to identification with the struggles of the exploited classes.[12]

But what kind of action is called for? Liberation theologians answer very simply, action on behalf of justice. Referring again to Scriptures, liberation theologians point out that in the Hebraic-Christian tradition love of God cannot be separated from works of justice. The Old Testament, for example, speaks of knowing or loving God in terms of doing justice. Here is how Gutiérrez expresses this concept:

> To know Yahweh, which in Biblical language is equivalent to saying to love Yahweh, *is* to establish just relationships among men, it *is* to recognize the rights of the poor. The God of Biblical revelation is known through interhuman justice. When justice does not exist, God is not known; he is absent.[13]

In the Old Testament the great prophets—Amos, Hosea, Isaiah, Jeremiah, Micah, Zephaniah, and Malachi—constantly remind Israel that God does not simply want prayers and sacrifices but justice and the establishment of just social structures:[14]

> Why do we fast, and you do not see it? Afflict ourselves, and you take no note of it? Lo, on your fast day you carry out your own pursuits, and drive all your laborers. Yes, your fast ends in quarreling and fighting, striking with wicked claw. Would that today you might fast so as to make your voice heard on high! Is this the manner of fasting I wish, of keeping a day of penance: That a man bow his head like a reed, and lie in sackcloth and ashes? Do you call this a fast, a day acceptable to the Lord? This, rather, is the fasting that I wish: releasing those bound unjustly, untying the thongs of the yoke, setting free the oppressed, breaking every yoke, sharing your bread with the hungry, sheltering the oppressed and the homeless, clothing the naked when you see them, and not turning your back on your own. Then your light shall break forth like the dawn, and your wound shall quickly be healed. Your vindication shall go before you, and the glory of the Lord shall be your rear guard. Then you shall call, and the Lord will answer. You shall cry for help and he will say: Here I am! If you remove from your midst oppression, false accusation and malicious speech, if you bestow your bread on the hungry and satisfy the afflicted, then light shall rise for you in the darkness and the gloom shall become for you like midday [Isa. 58:3–10].

The theme that love must be expressed in just relationships and the establishment of just social structures is reechoed in the New Testament as well. Jesus talked about love in terms of feeding the hungry, clothing the naked, and visiting the imprisoned. The kingdom that he announced and called all people to be a part of is a radically new social order—one of peace, justice, and love in which there will be a union of people with other people and of humanity with God.

If we presume that it is possible to establish just relationships among people and to build a more equitable social order without changing our social systems, we are being naive. Acquiring profit or private material gain on a personal or institutional level can never be an end in itself for Christians. The worth or value of the institutions and systems of society can be measured only in terms of the kingdom, that is, in terms of whether they promote peace, justice, and love among people, communities, and nations. To refuse to evaluate our economic, political, and social systems against the kingdom and to strive to change them accordingly is tantamount to deifying them. Faithfulness to the gospel command to love our neighbor, therefore, requires us to act to change unjust systems and structures.

THE STRUGGLE FOR JUSTICE AND THE KINGDOM OF GOD

In the perspective of liberation theologians, the struggle to establish just relationships among people and to build a more equitable society *is* the struggle for the kingdom; it is a part of the growth of the kingdom. As Gutiérrez puts it:

> The historical, political liberating event *is* the growth of the Kingdom and *is* a salvific event; but it is not *the* coming of the Kingdom, not *all* of salvation.[15]

Without the struggle for justice there would be no kingdom.[16] Jesus proclaimed that the struggle for justice is not only a part of the growth of the kingdom but a precondition for its coming and a sign of it. Thus the vision of the kingdom impels Christians to work for justice and gives to their struggle for justice its fullest meaning.

One final point brought out by the political and liberation theologians needs to be mentioned. The presence of poverty and hunger in the world cannot be interpreted as anything but a fundamental break in our relationship with our neighbor and thus with God. It is a flat refusal to respond to our neighbor's needs and to make them our own. Poverty and hunger reflect a disturbance in the divinely willed union of people with other people and of humanity with God. In theological terminology this is sin. The political and liberation theologians have made us aware of the fact that we can no longer think of sin in ahistorical and abstract terms. Sin manifests itself in concrete political, economic, and social decisions, structures, and systems. Refusal to respond to a neighbor's needs is both visible and tangible. It can be seen in our ghettos, in unfair labor practices, in discrimination of all types, and in the trade, aid, and investment policies of the First World. Sin need not necessarily be a deed. The political and liberation theologians point out that it can be an atmosphere as well. Dorothee Sölle states:

> It is not our particular transgressions . . . but our whole way of life which is wrong. It is not so much our conscious deeds which make us

sinners as our half-conscious omissions. We are allowing capital to be our master, we are permitting the system to exploit third world countries. Our holistically understood sin is actually living in a culture of injustice.[17]

Let us return to our original question of how we should understand the problem of hunger in the light of faith. If we follow the methodology of the liberation theologians by beginning with the problem of hunger itself, analyzing its roots, and then trying to determine what God is saying to us now in light of God's statements in the past, we might come to the following conclusion. The Third World is today the supreme embodiment of our neighbor.[18] And because the Third World is our neighbor, love requires us to enter into its suffering. We must try to see the world as people in the Third World see it, and we must try to make their struggle for liberation our own.

The poverty and hunger of the Third World must be seen as a break in our relationship with our neighbor and with God. The Third World's poverty and hunger, therefore, are a sinful situation, and the causes of poverty and hunger can be characterized as sinful.

Love for our neighbor—the Third World—must be expressed not only in words but in actions. We must be willing to judge the systems, structures, and values responsible for the Third World's oppression in terms of the kingdom. And love requires us to work to change those systems, structures, and values to make them more just.

Therefore, Christians in the affluent world must join the Third World in its present struggle to change the present mechanisms of trade, aid, and investment. Since these mechanisms are rooted in the capitalist system, we must also participate in the more fundamental struggle to bring about an economic system that is more just and responsive to human needs.

Equally important is the need to work to change the values spawned by the capitalist system. By personally refusing to be caught up in the values of competition, individualism, materialism, and greed, we can begin to bring about the revolution in values that is so essential for any kind of radical change. Tarrou, one of the central characters in Camus's novel *The Plague,* remarks: "All I maintain is that on this earth there are pestilences and there are victims, and it's up to us, so far as possible, not to join forces with the pestilences."[19] Thus we must strive on a systemic and personal level to be on the side of the victims and not of the pestilences. For the struggle to change the systems and values oppressing the Third World is nothing less than the struggle for the kingdom. As such it is a work of salvation.

Chapter 12

THE SOCIAL TEACHINGS
OF THE CHRISTIAN CHURCHES

So far we have considered the responsibility of Christians with respect to the problem of world hunger in the light of the Judeo-Christian tradition of social justice. Let us now explore additional insights provided by the specific social teachings of various churches.

THE ROMAN CATHOLIC POSITION

Jesuit theologian David Hollenbach has provided a clear analysis of Roman Catholic teaching on social justice in a work entitled *Claims in Conflict*.[1] Much of the following discussion is based on this work. According to Hollenbach, one theme dominates the social encyclicals of the modern papacy from Leo XIII's *Rerum Novarum* to Paul VI's *Populorum Progressio*: the dignity of the human person. In the Catholic tradition, human beings are made in the image and likeness of God and for this reason have transcendent value. All humans are thus entitled to certain rights, and all societies, governments, and individuals are morally bound to respect these rights. While it is not possible here to examine in depth all the social encyclicals, we shall at least highlight some major themes that are important to our study.

Rerum Novarum *(On the Rights and Duties of Capital and Labor)*

Leo XIII considered the plight of workers in the first of the modern social encyclicals, *Rerum Novarum*, which was issued in 1891. One of the most important concepts to emerge from *Rerum Novarum* was the concept that humanity precedes the state. All human institutions are made to serve human beings and not vice versa. Laws, political systems, economic systems, and social institutions exist for the sole purpose of enhancing human dignity. When those systems use human beings for their own ends, they assault human dignity and thus offend the law of God. The standard set down by Leo

XIII for judging institutions and systems was human dignity. The moral value of a particular system or institution was to be evaluated on the basis of whether it contributes to the dignity and worth of human beings; this theme was repeated in many of the later encyclicals.

Quadragesimo Anno *(On the Reconstruction of the Social Order)*

Forty years later, in *Quadragesimo Anno*, Pius XI reaffirmed the basic principles laid down in *Rerum Novarum* and introduced a new element into Catholic social teaching: the concept of social justice. Pius XI was responsible for introducing the idea that the dignity that rightfully belongs to human beings is mediated not only through individuals but also through social institutions. In other words institutions, depending on how they are structured, can facilitate or hinder the growth and development of human beings. Let us consider the obvious issue of civil rights as an example. Discrimination is expressed not only by the actions of individuals; schools, churches, businesses, and landlords may also discriminate against minorities. In so doing they are depriving human beings of their inherent dignity and also of their right to realize the potential to which they are called by God. Pius XI stated clearly the moral duty of the state to insure that the institutions of society serve human dignity.

In *Quadragesimo Anno* Pius XI leveled heavy criticism against both capitalism and socialism. Of capitalism he writes:

> Just as the unity of human society cannot be built upon "class" conflict, so *the proper ordering of economic affairs cannot be left to the free play of rugged competition*. From this source, as from a polluted spring, have proceeded all the errors of the "individualistic" school. This school, forgetful or ignorant of the social and moral aspects of economic activities, regarded these as completely free and immune from any intervention by public authority, for they would have in the market place and in unregulated competition a principle of self-direction more suitable for guiding them than any created intellect which might intervene. *Free competition, however, though justified and quite useful within certain limits, cannot be an adequate controlling principle in economic affairs*. This has been abundantly proved by the consequences that have followed from the free rein given to these dangerous individualistic ideals. *It is therefore very necessary that economic affairs be once more subjected to and governed by a true and effective guiding principle*. Still less can this function be exercised by the economic supremacy which within recent times has taken the place of free competition: *for this is a headstrong and vehement power, which, if it is to prove beneficial to mankind, needs to be curbed strongly and ruled with prudence. It cannot, however, be curbed and*

governed by itself. More lofty and noble principles must therefore be sought in order to regulate this supremacy firmly and honestly: to wit, social justice and social charity [emphasis added].[2]

The pope goes on to say:

Unbridled ambition for domination has succeeded the desire for gain; the whole economic life has become hard, cruel and relentless in a ghastly measure. Furthermore, the intermingling and scandalous confusing of the duties and offices of civil authority and of the economy has produced grave evils, not the least of which has been a downgrading of the majesty of the State. *The State which should be the supreme arbiter, ruling in queenly fashion far above all party contention, intent only upon justice and the common good, has become instead a slave, bound over to the service of human passion and greed. As regards the relations of nations among themselves, a double stream has issued forth from this one fountainhead; on the one hand, economic "nationalism" or even economic "imperialism"; on the other, a no less noxious and detestable "internationalism" or "international imperialism" in financial affairs, which holds that where a man's fortune is, there is his country* [emphasis added].[3]

While Pius XI admitted that the principles of certain forms of socialism are not all that different from the principles of Christianity, he denounced socialism primarily on the grounds that it presents a materialistic concept of the person. In Hollenbach's words,

In its most radical form the theory of class struggle and the dictatorship of the proletariat is a denial of the relevance of the dignity of the persons of one social group to the strategies of another. Consequently, in order to defend transcendental personal worth he felt compelled to reject all forms of socialism including the more moderate revisionist versions.[4]

Summi Pontificatus *(On the Function of the State in the Modern World) and Addresses of 1939–1957*

In his writings and addresses Pius XII stressed the fact that government and legal institutions function primarily as moral agents. They play a critical role in promoting and guaranteeing human dignity. Government exists, according to Pius XII, to promote a community of morally responsible citizens—a community based on mutal respect and dignity for the rights of others. The purpose of legal institutions, on the other hand, is to support and insure the existence of such a community. Let us look at how this might work out in practice.

One of the ways the state serves as a moral agent is by promoting mutual respect and dignity for the rights of the poor in society. It does this in a number of ways: by giving priority politically and economically to civil rights, the generation of new jobs, fair housing, public health, and educational programs. Our legal system insures further the rights and dignity of the poor by providing a means by which their grievances can be addressed.

One of the other significant contributions of Pius XII to Catholic social teaching was his emphasis on human dignity, not just as an ideal to be striven for but as a reality that can be realized in personal, social, and institutional relationships. In other words, human dignity finds its expression in human relationships, institutions, and historical situations. Following the lead of Leo XIII and Pius XI, Pius XII reaffirmed the right of people to hold private property. He stipulated, however, that it was subordinate to the prior right of human beings to use material goods as a means to their own sustenance. That important point, as we shall see, was later discussed in greater detail by Paul VI.

Mater et Magistra *(On the Church and Social Progress)*
and Pacem in Terris *(On World Peace)*

During the brief pontificate of John XXIII, two major social encyclicals were issued: *Mater et Magistra* in 1961 and *Pacem in Terris* in 1963. Both documents stressed the interrelatedness of human beings in the technological age. John went beyond his predecessors in calling attention to our responsibility for the poor of the Third World in *Mater et Magistra*:

Perhaps the most pressing question of our day concerns the relationship between economically advanced commonwealths and those that are in process of development. The former enjoy the conveniences of life; the latter experience dire poverty. Yet, today men are so intimately associated in all parts of the world that they feel, as it were, as if they are members of one and the same household. *Therefore, the nations that enjoy a sufficiency and abundance of everything may not overlook the plight of other nations whose citizens experience such domestic problems that they are all but overcome by poverty and hunger, and are not able to enjoy basic human rights. . . .*

Mindful of our role of universal father, we think it opportune to stress here what we have stated in another connection: *"We all share responsibility for the fact that populations are undernourished. . . .*

As can be readily deduced, and as the Church has always seriously warned, *it is proper that the duty of helping the poor and unfortunate should especially stir Catholics, since they are members of the Mystical*

Body of Christ. "In this we have come to know the love of God," said
John the Apostle, "that He laid down His life for us; and we likewise
ought to lay down our life for the brethren. He who has the goods of
this world and sees his brother in need and closes his heart to him, how
does the love of God abide in him?" [emphasis added].[5]

While John instructs the rich nations to come to the aid of the poor, he also
warns the rich not to exploit the needs of the poor.

> *Moreover, economically developed countries should take particular*
> *care lest, in giving aid to poorer countries, they endeavor to turn the*
> *prevailing political situation to their own advantage, and seek to domi-*
> *nate them.*
>   Should perchance such attempts be made, this clearly would be but
> another form of colonialism, which, although disguised in name,
> merely reflects their earlier but outdated dominion, now abandoned by
> many countries. When international relations are thus obstructed, the
> orderly progress of all peoples is endangered.
>   *Genuine necessity, as well as justice, require that whenever countries*
> *give attention to the fostering of skills or commerce, they should aid the*
> *less developed nations without thought of domination*, so that these
> latter eventually will be in a position to progress economically and so-
> cially on their own initiative [emphasis added].[6]

In *Pacem in Terris* John XXIII provides us with a list of rights to which all
human beings are entitled by virtue of the dignity conferred upon them by
God. He begins by stating that:

> Every man has the right to life, to bodily integrity, and to the means
> which are necessary and suitable for the proper development of life.
> These means are primarily food, clothing, shelter, rest, medical care,
> and finally the necessary social services."[7]

All people, John argues, are entitled to respect, to the freedom to express
themselves, and "to be informed truthfully about public events."[8] All people
also have the right to education; and by virtue of our nature all people are
entitled to work, to just working conditions, and to a just wage. To insure
that all members of the human race receive the rights to which they are entitled, John states, we must join together and work to preserve our own rights
and those of others. In his words:

> Since men are social by nature, they are meant to live with others and to
> work for one another's welfare. Hence, a well-ordered human society
> requires that men recognize and observe their mutual rights and duties.

It also demands that each contribute generously to the establishment of a civic order in which rights and duties are progressively more sincerely and effectively acknowledged and fulfilled.[9]

Gaudium et Spes *(Pastoral Constitution on the Church in the Modern World)*

One of the most important documents of Vatican II that deals with the issue of social justice is *Gaudium et Spes* (1965). Some of the themes discussed above appear again in this document, but are given more specificity. This reflects to a large extent a growing awareness on the part of the church of the role that institutions, systems, and concrete historical situations play in mediating human dignity. *Gaudium et Spes* affirms the dignity of the human person and charges all Christians to respond to the needs of those whose dignity suffers because of poverty, hunger, and other forms of exploitation.

In our times a special obligation binds us to make ourselves the neighbor of absolutely every person, and of actively helping him when he comes across our path, whether he be an old person abandoned by all, a foreign laborer unjustly looked down upon, a refugee, a child born of an unlawful union and wrongly suffering for a sin he did not commit, or a hungry person who disturbs our conscience by recalling the voice of the Lord: "As long as you did it for one of these, the least of my brethren, you did it for me" (Mt. 25:40).[10]

It reaffirms the fact that socioeconomic systems are to serve the needs of all human beings, and that people should never be the servants of socioeconomic systems. Moreover, such systems are created and should be managed to meet the needs of all and not of the privileged few:

In the socio-economic realm, too, the dignity and total vocation of the human person must be honored and advanced along with the welfare of society as a whole. For man is the source, the center, and the purpose of all socio-economic life. . . .

The fundamental purpose of this productivity must not be the mere multiplication of products. It must not be profit or domination. Rather, it must be the service of man, and indeed of the whole man, viewed in terms of his material needs and the demands of his intellectual, moral, spiritual, and religious life. And when we say man, we mean every man whatsoever and every group of men, of whatever race and from whatever part of the world. Consequently, economic activity is to be carried out according to its own methods and laws but within the limits of morality, so that God's plan for mankind can be realized [emphasis added].[11]

With regard to private property, the council states that the rights of those who suffer because of a lack of the basic necessities of life are prior to the rights of the well-satisfied to private property:

> For the rest, the right to have a share of earthly goods sufficient for oneself and one's family belongs to everyone. The Fathers and Doctors of the Church held this view, teaching that men are obliged to come to the relief of the poor and to do so not merely out of their superfluous goods. If a person is in extreme necessity, he has the right to take from the riches of others what he himself needs. *Since there are so many people in this world afflicted with hunger, this sacred Council urges all, both individuals and governments, to remember the saying of the Fathers: "Feed the man dying of hunger, because if you have not fed him you have killed him"* [emphasis added].[12]

The Council Fathers contend that certain structural changes will be needed if the inequality among nations and the suffering of the poor are to be alleviated:

> If an economic order is to be created which is genuine and universal, *there must be an abolition of excessive desire for profit, nationalistic pretensions, the lust for political domination, militaristic thinking, and intrigues designed to spread and impose ideologies.*
>
> Proposals are made in favor of numerous economic and social systems. It is to be hoped that experts in such affairs will find common bases for a healthy world trade. This hope will be more readily realized if individuals put aside their personal prejudices and show that they are prepared to undertake sincere discussions [emphasis added].[13]
>
> *As for the advanced nations, they have a very heavy obligation to help the developing peoples in the discharge of the aforementioned responsibilities.* If this worldwide collaboration is to be established, certain psychological and material adjustments will be needed among the advanced nations and should be brought about.
>
> Thus these nations should carefully consider the welfare of weaker and poorer nations when negotiating with them. For such nations need for their own livelihood the income derived from the sale of domestic products.
>
> Let adequate organizations be established for fostering and harmonizing international trade, especially with respect to the less advanced countries, and for repairing the deficiencies caused by an excessive disproportion in the power possessed by various nations. Such regulatory activity, combined with technical, cultural, and financial help, ought to afford the needed assistance to nations striving for progress enabling them to achieve economic growth expeditiously [emphasis added].[14]

Populorum Progressio *(On the Development of Peoples)*

Of all the social encyclicals Pope Paul VI's *Populorum Progressio* (1967) bears most directly on the problem of poverty in the Third World and the moral responsibility of Christians in the First World to respond to that problem. More than any other pope, Paul VI linked the injustice of the present international economic order with a collapse in moral values. And he called on Christians everywhere to be true to the message of the gospel and the teaching of the church and to join together to build a more just and humane global community. Like Pius XII and the Fathers of the Vatican Council, Paul VI affirms that the right of the poor to meet their basic needs takes precedence over the right to own private property:

> "Fill the earth and subdue it": the Bible, from the first page on, teaches us that the whole of creation is for man, that it is his responsibility to develop it by intelligent effort and by means of his labour to perfect it, so to speak, for his use. If the world is made to furnish each individual with the means of livelihood and the instruments for his growth and progress, each man has therefore the right to find in the world what is necessary for himself. The recent Council reminded us of this: "God intended the earth and all that it contains for the use of every human being and people. Thus, as all men follow justice and unite in charity, created goods should abound for them on a reasonable basis". *All other rights whatsoever, including those of property and of free commerce, are to be subordinated to this principle.* They should not hinder but on the contrary favour its application. It is a grave and urgent social duty to redirect them to their primary finality [emphasis added].[15]

Paul goes on to say that in helping the poor and hungry we are not engaging in charity but giving them what rightfully belongs to them:

> To quote Saint Ambrose: "You are not making a gift of your possessions to the poor person. You are handing over to him what is his. For what has been given in common for the use of all, you have arrogated to yourself. The world is given to all, and not only to the rich." That is, *private property does not constitute for anyone an absolute and unconditioned right. No one is justified in keeping for his exclusive use what he does not need, when others lack necessities.* In a word, "according to the traditional doctrine as found in the Fathers of the Church and the great theologians, the right to property must never be exercised to the detriment of the common good" [emphasis added].[16]

Paul draws attention to the fact that the private pursuit of material goods can blind us to the human good; in no uncertain terms he condemns nations and individuals for whom the pursuit of private material gain has become an end in itself.

> Increased possession is not the ultimate goal of nations nor of individuals. All growth is ambivalent. It is essential if man is to develop as a man, but in a way it imprisons man if he considers it the supreme good, and it restricts his vision. Then we see hearts harden and minds close, and men no longer gather together in friendship but out of self-interest, which soon leads to oppositions and disunity. The exclusive pursuit of possessions thus becomes an obstacle to individual fulfillment and to man's true greatness. Both for nations and for individual men, avarice is the most evident form of moral underdevelopment. . . .[17]
>
> When so many people are hungry, when so many families suffer from destitution, when so many remain steeped in ignorance, when so many schools, hospitals and homes worthy of the name remain to be built, all public or private squandering of wealth, all expenditure prompted by motives of national or personal ostentation, every exhausting armaments race, becomes an intolerable scandal. We are conscious of Our duty to denounce it. Would that those in authority listened to Our words before it is too late![18]

The pope blames not only the activities of nations and individuals for the situation of the poor but also the systems that spawn such actions:

> But it is unfortunate that on these new conditions of society *a system has been constructed which considers profit as the key motive for economic progress, competition as the supreme law of economics, and private ownership of the means of production as an absolute right that has no limits and carries no corresponding social obligation.* This unchecked liberalism leads to dictatorship rightly denounced by Pius XI as producing "the international imperialism of money". *One cannot condemn such abuses too strongly by solemnly recalling once again that the economy is at the service of man.* But if it is true that a type of capitalism has been the source of excessive suffering, injustices and fratricidal conflicts whose effects still persist, it would also be wrong to attribute to industrialisation itself evils that belong to the woeful system which accompanied it [emphasis added].[19]

The encyclical tells the rich nations and individuals that they have a moral obligation to come to the aid of the poor:

> This duty is the concern especially of better-off nations. Their obligations stem from a brotherhood that is at once human and supernatural, and take on a three-fold aspect: *the duty of human solidarity—the aid that the rich nations must give to developing countries; the duty of*

> *social justice—the rectification of inequitable trade relations between powerful nations and weak nations; the duty of universal charity—the effort to bring about a world that is more human towards all men, where all will be able to give and receive, without one group making progress at the expense of the other.* The question is urgent, for on it depends the future of the civilisation of the world [emphasis added].[20]
>
> We must repeat once more that the superfluous wealth of rich countries should be placed at the service of poor nations. The rule which up to now held good for the benefit of those nearest to us, must today be applied to all the needy of this world.[21]

Our responsibility, however, should take the form not only of increased aid but of fundamental structural and systemic change. The pope questions the justice of the present systems of world trade and ultimately calls for a restructuring of world trade, stable prices for the exports of the Third World, and access for the Third World to the markets of the First World:

> In other words, the rule of free trade, taken by itself, is no longer able to govern international relations. Its advantages are certainly evident when the parties involved are not affected by any excessive inequalities of economic power: it is an incentive to progress and a reward for effort. That is why industrially developed countries see in it a law of justice. But the situation is no longer the same when economic conditions differ too widely from country to country: prices which are "freely" set in the market can produce unfair results. One must recognize that it is the fundamental principle of liberalism, as the rule for commercial exchange, which is questioned here.[22]
>
> The teaching of Leo XIII in *Rerum Novarum* is always valid: if the positions of the contracting parties are too unequal, the consent of the parties does not suffice to guarantee the justice of their contract, and the rule of free agreement remains subservient to the demands of the natural law. What was true of the just wage for the individual is also true of international contracts: an economy of exchange can no longer be based solely on the law of free competition, a law which, in its turn, too often creates an economic dictatorship. Freedom of trade is fair only if it is subject to the demands of social justice.[23]
>
> In trade between developed and under-developed economies, conditions are too disparate and the degrees of genuine freedom available too unequal. In order that international trade be human and moral, social justice requires that it restore to the participants a certain equality of opportunity.[24]

Finally Paul VI instructs those who are rich to carry out their obligation to the poor even at the cost of depriving themselves of luxuries and the lifestyle to which they have grown accustomed:

But neither all this nor the private and public funds that have been invested, nor the gifts and loans that have been made, can suffice. It is not just a matter of eliminating hunger, nor even of reducing poverty. The struggle against destitution, though urgent and necessary, is not enough. It is a question, rather, of building a world where every man, no matter what his race, religion or nationality, can live a fully human life, freed from servitude imposed on him by other men or by natural forces over which he has not sufficient control; a world where freedom is not an empty word and where the poor man Lazarus can sit down at the same table with the rich man. *This demands great generosity, much sacrifice and unceasing effort on the part of the rich man. Let each one examine his conscience, a conscience that conveys a new message for our times. Is he prepared to support out of his own pocket works and undertakings organised in favour of the most destitute? Is he ready to pay higher taxes so that the public authorities can intensify their efforts in favor of development? Is he ready to pay a higher price for imported goods so that the producer may be more justly rewarded? Or to leave his country, if necessary and if he is young, in order to assist in this development of the young nations?* [emphasis added].[25]

Statement of the Synod of Bishops

In 1971 the Second General Assembly of the Synod of Bishops issued a statement entitled *Justice in the World*. The bishops begin by acknowledging that all of us are a part of the same human family and share the same world. In their words we are "indissolubly linked with one another in the one destiny of the whole world, in the responsibility for which . . . all share."[26] Despite our common ties, a number of problems threaten the possibility of achieving real unity. One of the most pressing is the underdevelopment of the poor nations of the world. Yet the right to development is a fundamental right. The bishops affirm that "the right to development must be seen as a dynamic interpenetration of all those fundamental human rights upon which the aspirations of individuals and nations are based."[27] Pointing out that the right to development cannot be met until individual and systemic obstacles are overcome, they claim that the right to development demands:

. . . that the general condition of being marginal in society be overcome, so that *an end will be put to the systematic barriers and vicious circles which oppose the collective advance towards enjoyment of adequate remuneration of the factors of production, and which strengthen the situation of discrimination with regard to access to opportunities and collective services from which a great part of the people are now excluded.* If the developing nations and regions do not attain liberation through development, there is a real danger that the conditions of life created especially by colonial domination may evolve into a new form of colonialism in which the developing nations will be the victims of the interplay of international economic forces [emphasis added].[28]

It is precisely to the task of overcoming these obstacles—liberation—that Christians in both the Third and First Worlds are called. In the words of the bishops:

According to the Christian message, therefore, man's relationship to his neighbour is bound up with his relationship to God; his response to the love of God, saving us through Christ, is shown to be effective in his love and service of men. *Christian love of neighbour and justice cannot be separated.* For love implies an absolute demand for justice, namely a recognition of the dignity and rights of one's neighbour. . . . The mission of preaching the Gospel dictates at the present time that we should dedicate *ourselves to the liberation of man even in his present existence in this world.* For unless the Christian message of love and justice shows its effectiveness through action in the cause of justice in the world, it will only with difficulty gain credibility with the men of our times [emphasis added].[29]

Like Paul VI, the bishops recommend specific measures that the rich nations of the world must take if the Third World is ever to realize its God-given rights. These include a transfer of income from the rich to the poor, a restructuring of the terms of world trade, preferential treatment for the products of the Third World, and a greater voice for the Third World in international economic relations. These recommendations are worth quoting in detail:

Let the aims of the Second Development Decade be fostered. These include the transfer of a precise percentage of the annual income of the richer countries to the developing nations, fairer prices for raw materials, the opening of the markets of the richer nations and, in some fields, preferential treatment for exports of manufactured goods from the developing nations. These aims represent first guidelines for a graduated taxation of income as well as for an economic and social plan for the entire world. . . .

The concentration of power which consists in almost total domination of economics, research, investment, freight charges, sea transport and insurance should be progressively balanced by institutional arrangements for strengthening power and opportunities with regard to responsible decision by the developing nations and by full and equal participation in international organizations concerned with development. Their recent *de facto* exclusion from discussions on world trade and the monetary arrangements which vitally affect their destiny are an example of lack of power which is inadmissible in a just and responsible world order.[30]

The bishops not only recommend structural changes on the part of the rich nations but they call for a change in lifestyle of individuals in the First World as well:

> It is impossible to see what right the richer nations have to keep up their claim to increase their own material demands, if the consequence is either that others remain in misery or that the danger of destroying the very physical foundations of life on earth is precipitated. Those who are already rich are bound to accept a less material way of life, with less waste, in order to avoid the destruction of the heritage which they are obliged by absolute justice to share with all other members of the human race.[31]

As for the responsibility of the institutional church for the liberation of the Third World, the bishops maintain that the church must point out and denounce specific instances of injustice:

> The Church has received from Christ the mission of preaching the Gospel message, which contains a call to man to turn away from sin to the love of the Father, universal brotherhood and a consequent demand for justice in the world. This is the reason why the Church has the right, indeed the duty, to proclaim justice on the social, national and international level, and to denounce instances of injustice, when the fundamental rights of man and his very salvation demand it.[32]

Finally the bishops see work for justice as holy work and ultimately meaningful in terms of the kingdom:

> Hope in the coming kingdom is already beginning to take root in the hearts of men. The radical transformation of the world in the Paschal Mystery of the Lord gives full meaning to the efforts of men, and in particular of the young, to lessen injustice, violence and hatred and to advance all together in justice, freedom, brotherhood and love.[33]

John Paul II's Homily at Yankee Stadium

In his 1979 visit to the United States, Pope John Paul II delivered one of his most powerful pleas to Christians in the First World to accept responsibility for alleviating world poverty and hunger. He called on Christians to be mindful of the parable of the rich man and Lazarus and to translate it into contemporary terms, ". . . in terms of economy and politics, in terms of all human rights, in terms of relations between the 'first,' 'second' and 'third world.' "[34] It is not right for extreme poverty to exist alongside such great wealth in the world. In his words, "We cannot stand idly by, enjoying our own riches and freedom, if, in any place, the Lazarus of the 20th century stands at our door."[35] Nor is it right that the standard of living the rich enjoy be maintained by drawing the energy and resources that belong to all people.

The pope admonishes First World Christians not to shrink from the demands of justice. Charitable works must always respect the freedom and dignity of the recipients, but charity is no longer sufficient for Christians:

> Within the framework of your national institutions and in cooperation with all your compatriots, you will also want to seek out the structural reasons which foster or cause the different forms of poverty in the world and in your own country, so that you can apply the proper remedies. You will not allow yourselves to be intimidated or discouraged by oversimplified explanations, which are more ideological than scientific —explanations which try to account for a complex evil by some single cause. But neither will you recoil before the reforms—even profound ones—of attitudes and structures that may prove necessary in order to re-create over and over again conditions needed by the disadvantaged if they are to have a fresh chance in the hard struggle of life.[36]

Besides their responsibility to work for structural change, Christians are warned not to get caught up in the consumer society and urged to live a simple lifestyle:

> Christians will want to be in the vanguard in favoring ways of life that decisively break with a frenzy of consumerism, exhausting and joyless. . . . It is not a question of slowing down progress, for there is no human progress when everything conspires to give full reign to the instincts of self-interest, sex and power.[37]

In sum, it is by our action for justice that we proclaim the worth and dignity of all people made in the image and likeness of God. In John Paul's words:

> Jesus Christ makes us sharers in what He is. Through His Incarnation, the Son of God in a certain manner united Himself with every human being. In our inmost being He has recreated us; in our inmost being He has reconciled us with God, reconciled us with ourselves, reconciled us with our brothers and sisters: He is *our* peace. . . . We are bearers of the justice and peace of God.[38]

THE POSITION OF THE PROTESTANT CHURCHES

Let us now examine the views of the major Protestant denominations about the problem of poverty and hunger in the Third World. Perhaps the best sources of information are the statements issued by the World Council of

Churches and by regional conferences and assemblies held in the years between the five world assemblies of the World Council of Churches.

We should first of all note a difference in the authoritative nature of statements issued by the popes and bishops of the Catholic church and those of the World Council.

The papal encyclicals, the documents of the Second Vatican Council, and the statements of the Synod of Bishops are exercises in the teaching authority of the Catholic church. While not infallible statements, they nevertheless do have authority. This means that all Catholics are obliged to listen seriously to such teachings and to follow them.

On the other hand, statements issued by the World Council of Churches and by regional conferences and special assemblies have a more subtle kind of authority. Paul Bock, a specialist on the social teachings of the World Council of Churches, recalls that ever since the Reformation Protestants have rebelled against any form of hierarchical authority.[39] Thus statements that have come out of the general and special assemblies and regional conferences do not represent the official teachings of the Protestant churches and are not binding on individual member churches. The constitution of the World Council of Churches clearly states that the World Council of Churches has neither authority over its member churches nor power to speak for them.[40] Although the statements emanating from the World Council of Churches do not represent the official teaching of the Protestant churches, they are important policy pronouncements that are taken seriously by church members. The First General Assembly of the World Council of Churches in Amsterdam in 1948 made the following comment:

> With respect to public pronouncements, the Council regards it as an essential part of its responsibilities to address its own constituent members as occasion may arise, on matters which require united attention in the realm of thought or action. Further, important issues may arise which radically affect the Church and society. While it is certainly undesirable that the Council should issue such pronouncements often, and on many subjects, there will certainly be a clear obligation for the Council to speak out when vital issues concerning all churches and the whole world are at stake. But such statements will have no authority save that which they carry by their own truth and wisdom. They will not be binding on any church unless that Church has confirmed them, and made them its own. But the Council will only issue such statements in the light of God's revelation in Jesus Christ, the Lord, and the living Head of the Church; and in dependence on the power of the Holy Spirit, and in penitence and faith.[41]

Thus the World Council of Churches' statements do have authority but their authority, as Bock says, "rests largely in the authority of 'their own truth and wisdom.' "[42]

Since its founding in 1948 the World Council of Churches has convened five world assemblies: at Amsterdam in 1948; at Evanston in 1954; at New Delhi in 1961; at Uppsala in 1968; and at Nairobi in 1975. Between those world assemblies, a number of regional conferences and special assemblies were also held. Out of these conferences have come some significant statements on the problem of poverty and hunger in the Third World. We shall turn to such gatherings in an attempt to arrive at a better understanding of where some Protestant churches stand on the issues we have been discussing.

If we were to single out one concept that appears with some regularity in the statements about justice made by various assemblies and conferences, it would be the concept of a "responsible society." As conceived originally, a responsible society is one in which "individual freedom is guaranteed, distributive justice is practised and the state is responsible to and controlled by the electorate."[43] According to Bock, the concept of a responsible society has assumed a much broader connotation and has been divested of much of its western, democratic, and naive political tone through the efforts of Protestant churches in the Third World.

The Lucknow Conference of 1952

Between the Amsterdam Assembly of 1948 and the Evanston Assembly of 1954, two conferences were held in Asia which, Bock tells us, affected the direction of Protestant thinking on social justice. A report from the second conference at Lucknow, for example, deals with the problem of the standard of living in Asia. It attempts to address issues of balanced development, land reform, and the role of the churches in effecting change. The report specifically calls on the industrial nations to financially assist Asia as a matter of social justice; and it specifies that conditions should not be attached to the First World's aid.

The Evanston Assembly of 1954

At Evanston the problem of social justice was again taken up. But this time the discussion focused on justice on a global scale. The Evanston Assembly agreed on the need to set specific development goals in line with the recommendation of the Lucknow Conference. With regard to the specific responsibility of industrialized nations, the section on international affairs states:

The response of more developed countries through expanded international programs of technical assistance is one of the brightest pages of recent history; but the effort thus far has been small in comparison with the needs of the less developed countries and the resources of those more developed. A progressively sustained effort will for a long time be required and involves mutual responsibilities and benefits which challenge all who cooperate in such endeavors.

Many of the politically new nations are old nations with centuries of culture and civilization behind them. In this partnership of sharing they have their own distinctive contribution to make. But for the partnership to be fruitful there is required in nations "young" or "old" a readiness to learn from one another.[44]

The Arnoldshain Study Conference of 1955

At a study conference in Arnoldshain, Germany, representatives of the churches of Europe and North America discussed the issue of a responsible international society. They recommended that the churches of the industrialized world acknowledge the responsibility of people in the First World to accept higher taxes so that their governments could assist the Third World more effectively. They stressed the responsibility of First World Christians to support greater cooperation between their countries and the Third World.

Bock points out that when the Third World Assembly convened at New Delhi in 1961, eighteen of the twenty-three new members of the World Council of Churches were churches from the Third World. This gave not only the World Council of Churches but the conference itself a more global character. The international perspective was reflected in some of the major addresses of the assembly. Bock cites two in particular, one by Masao Takenaka of Japan and the other by Egbert de Vries of the Netherlands. Takenaka called on Christians to witness Christ in more ways than charity. He challenged them specifically to work for social justice. De Vries, on the other hand, stressed the need for churches to help people become more aware of the global context in which their lives were lived. Finally, the assembly urged Christians to work courageously for change:

The Christian is not afraid of change, for he knows how heavy are the burdens of poverty and privation carried today by the majority of mankind. He is ready to initiate changes and forward reforms that serve the ends of freedom and justice, that break the chains of poverty; and is willing to cooperate with all who share his concern for the welfare of mankind. He knows that the gifts of God can be perverted and directed to evil ends, but he knows also that this is God's world. In his time his purpose will prevail, and it will be manifest that he is indeed in control.

In the specific field of economic development, we welcome the vigorous effort to increase production and raise living standards. In much of the world the basic needs of man for food, clothing, shelter and health remain unmet or are constantly endangered. There are areas of particular frustration remaining static in the midst of surrounding progress. There are countries where economic progress has been slow or erratic, because they depend on the fluctuations of a market outside their control and—to remind us that man does not live by bread alone—

there are wealthy societies plagued by anxiety and frustration because the demands of people seem to be endless.[45]

The Uppsala Assembly of 1968

Between the New Delhi and Uppsala world assemblies, a number of important international and national conferences concerned with peace and justice took place. Among the more notable of them were the Study Conference on Church and Society in 1966, the SODEPAX Conference, a conference jointly sponsored by the World Council of Churches and the Pontifical Commission on Justice and Peace in 1968, and a special conference held in Zagorsk, U.S.S.R. Paul Bock makes the point that these conferences provided impetus for the choice of "World Economic and Social Development" and "Towards Justice and Peace in International Affairs" as two of the four sections of the Uppsala Assembly. The report of Section III, World Economic and Social Development, calls on Christians to recognize their moral responsibility not only to those who live within their national borders but also to those living in other countries. It calls on Christians to be in the forefront of the struggle against provincialism:

The great majority of men and also of Christians are aware of their responsibility for members of their own national societies who are in need. But few have discovered that we now live in a world in which people in need in all parts of the world are our neighbors for whom we bear responsibility. Christians who know from their Scriptures that all men are created by God in his image and that Christ died for all, should be in the forefront of the battle to overcome a provincial, narrow sense of solidarity and to create a sense of participation in a world-wide responsible society with justice for all.[46]

A report of the section on the Dynamics of Development states that justice can be attained only through fundamental, systemic, and institutional change in developing countries, developed countries, and the international economy. In its words:

At all three levels it is necessary to instill social and economic processes with a new dynamic of human solidarity and justice. In several developing nations ruling groups monopolize the produce of their economy and allow foreign resources to aid and abet them in such action. In the international economy, the amount received as aid is often neutralized by inequitable patterns of trade, excessive returns on private investment, and the burden of debt repayment.[47]

The priorities of the developed nations in particular must undergo a radical transformation. Uppsala urges the churches to assume a prophetic role by bringing the systems and institutions of society under critical scrutiny and by calling on all Christians to assume their responsibility to work for justice.

As a practical recommendation to the rich nations, the assembly urges them to contribute at least 1 percent of their GNP as aid to the Third World. The aid, however, is not to be a substitute for a fundamental restructuring of the First World's trade and investment relations with the Third World but an additional measure to insure economic justice. This point cannot be emphasized enough. Uppsala saw fundamental structural and systemic change as a necessary condition for justice in the world, and it placed the responsibility for attaining justice on the conscience of each and every Christian.

The Nairobi Assembly of 1975

The most recent assembly of the World Council of Churches was held at Nairobi. Reemphasizing that poverty is rooted in unjust systems and structures, it called for a critical examination of the political and economic goals, the structure of ownership and distribution of wealth, and the decision-making process on the national and international levels. Nairobi summoned the churches to challenge unjust structures; like Uppsala, it argued the need for fundamental structural and systemic change.

SUMMARY OF PART II

Let us review briefly the main points covered in Part II. First of all, we discussed the crisis in values that our society is traversing today. In the First World we have become obsessed to such an extent—both personally and nationally—with the pursuit of private material gain that we are unable to make the profound value choices needed to alleviate and eliminate global poverty and hunger. It was suggested that our religious tradition might help in the sorely needed transformation of our social values.

Next we took up the philosophical, rational arguments supporting the contention that all of us have a responsibility to act on behalf of the poor and hungry. By comparing the philosophical concepts of beneficence and benevolence with the Christian concept of agape or love, we concluded that the responsibility of Christians exceeds the responsibility based on reason alone.

Chapters 9, 10, and 11 sought to define the specific responsibility of Christians toward the poor and hungry. It was pointed out that unless Christians break out of their present narrow understanding of faith, they will continue to interpret their responsibility toward the Third World in terms of charity alone. By examining some insights of the political and liberation theologians, we concluded that faith is not just a private matter but something public and political in nature. After studying the methodology of liberation theologians, we learned the importance of beginning with the concrete problem of world hunger using the tools of the social sciences in our theological reflection, examining our findings in the light of faith and acting on the basis of our reflection.

Finally, in Chapters 12 and 13, we examined the problem of world hunger and our responsibility to overcome it in the light of the Judeo-Christian tradition and the teaching of the Christian churches. We concluded that the struggle to bring about a more just social order is the struggle for the kingdom of God.

We are now ready to take up the specific contribution that Christian education can bring to the task of alleviating or ending the problem of world hunger.

PART III

EDUCATING FOR JUSTICE

Chapter 13

THE ROLE OF RELIGION IN MAINTAINING THE STATUS QUO

When Christian educators discuss the role of the church and school in promoting social change, they frequently overlook two important facts. First of all, the school is only one of the agencies charged with education in our society. As we shall see, churches and synagogues, the family, the media, corporations, and government and other social agencies play a significant educational role—one that in some respects has more lasting effect than that of the school. Second, while it is true that churches and schools have the potential to effect social change, they also are subject to many of the concerns that dominate all our social institutions. For this reason religion and education often help maintain the existing social order.

EDUCATIONAL AGENCIES IN ADDITION TO THE SCHOOLS

Churches and Synagogues

The American educational historian Lawrence Cremin defines education as "the deliberate, systematic, and sustained effort to transmit, evoke, or acquire knowledge, attitudes, values, skills, or sensibilities, as well as any outcomes of that effort."[1] If we accept Cremin's definition, it becomes obvious that schools are not the only institutions in society engaged in education. There can be little doubt that churches and synagogues engage in deliberate, systematic, and sustained efforts to transmit knowledge of their traditions, to form attitudes, values, and sensibilities, and to develop correct patterns of behavior. The means by which churches and synagogues educate their congregations vary. The most obvious is, of course, the church or synagogue school. But for those who never attend the church or synagogue school, preaching, reading sacred texts, rites, rituals, symbols, and liturgical music serve as primary vehicles of religious education. Each of them is performed for the express purpose of developing and sustaining a sense of the sacred.

While it may be stretching our definition of education a bit to say that religious denominations also educate by their choice of architecture, the interior design of their houses of worship, the geographic location of their churches and synagogues, the naming of rooms for benefactors, etc., we can safely say that all these factors influence the congregation's perception of the denomination's values and priorities.

The Family

Another institution in society that unquestionably plays a significant educational role is the family. For the first eighteen or so years of life, it is usually the most consistent and influential source of education for children. Through the family's deliberate, systematic, and sustained efforts, children acquire the knowledge, attitudes, values, skills, and sensibilities that will enable them to deal intelligently and meaningfully with their environment. It is through the family that children first develop a view of themselves, others, and the world. The importance that the family plays in educating the child is gaining increasing recognition among educators. Today many religious educators maintain that if the religious education of children is to be effective, the parents will need to be reeducated or resocialized in the faith. The Protestant religious educator and author John H. Westerhoff III, for example, writes, ". . . adults will have to be a primary concern of our ministry on behalf of children; they are the agents of all religious socialization."[2]

The Media

Much of our knowledge of the worlds of politics, science, business, and the arts is acquired through newspapers, journals, magazines, films, television, and radio. While the media's role in transmitting knowledge is apparent, we often overlook the influence of the media on our values, attitudes, and sensibilities. Documentary films like *Harvest of Shame, Hunger in America,* and *Hearts and Minds* clearly have as their purpose not only the presentation of factual information but also the change of attitudes. By skillfully arranging actual film footage of the destruction of villages and hamlets in Vietnam, the activities of off-duty American soldiers in Saigon, and taped interviews with American soldiers during and after the war, the producer of *Hearts and Minds* painted a convincing portrait of the barbarity of war.

The media's selection of news events, the amount of time or space allotted to reporting events, the manner in which events are reported, and the frequency with which they are reported—all these factors affect the public's perception of such events. There is significant controversy as to whether the manner in which the media handle news events is a deliberate or unintentional attempt to shape attitudes, values, and sensibilities toward the events themselves. The fact remains, however, that the way in which events are reported influences the public's attitude toward the events.

Attitudes, values, and sensibilities are also shaped through entertainment programming. Again there is controversy as to whether producers intentionally set out to shape values. Producers of shows like "All in the Family" and "MASH" certainly do, but with others the intent is less clear. Thanks to the militant elderly, women, blacks, and other groups in our society, we have become more conscious of how entertainment programming can breed prejudice. As a result of the efforts of those groups, some producers have systematically attempted to reverse negative images previously shown on their programs.

Corporations

Business corporations spend billions of dollars to educate their employees, government officials, and the public at large. Besides providing on-the-job training, corporations like IBM and XEROX maintain schools where their employees are taught necessary technical skills as well as attitudes and behavior regarded as desirable. Corporations also spend time and money to educate public officials. For it is in the corporation's interest to see that those in public office are "properly informed" about corporate activities and that they acquire a correct attitude toward the corporation. Finally, the education that we, the public, receive from corporations is no less deliberate, systematic, or sustained than the education that we receive from schools, churches, the family, and the media. Moreover, the hold that a corporation has over us may last not just for twelve or eighteen years but for a lifetime.

Through advertising, corporations teach us to need, to choose, to use, and to waste their goods and services. Through advertising they shape not only our understanding of goods but also of what the "good life" is. It is precisely the vision of the "good life" favored by corporations that prevents us from choosing the human good over the accumulation of goods.

If we accept the fact that schools do not have a monopoly on educating the public, what are the implications for social change? It is important, I believe, to avoid the trap of placing the full burden and responsibility for social change on schools. Just as schools are only one of the educational forces in society today, they must be viewed as only one of the sources of social change. Churches and synagogues, the family, the media, corporations, and other institutions have as much if not more influence as schools in preventing and promoting social change. Teachers realize that the efforts of even the most critical and creative teachers can be neutralized by the educational activity of any of these institutions.

To locate the primary responsibility for change with the schools can be misleading. For it allows society to overlook or minimize the powerful influence that those other institutions have in shaping social attitudes and values. Thus the attitudes and values that other institutions promote escape critical examination and challenge. By locating the primary responsibility for change with schools, we also enable those other institutions to neglect their responsibility for creating a more humane social order. In short, if the revolution in values discussed in Part I is ever to occur, the values promoted by churches and synagogues, the family, the media, corporations, and other institutions must be challenged. Those same institutions must become agencies for humanization rather than dehumanization.

RELIGION AS A SUPPORT FOR THE STATUS QUO

In our enthusiasm to work for social change, we often overlook the fact that religion and education support the status quo as much as or more than they challenge it. The policies and structures of religious and educational institutions and the role that we play in these institutions may sanction and even reinforce the prevailing social order. Thus positive actions in one sector may be cancelled out or negated by institutional policies, structures, or our own actions in another sector. It is essential, therefore, for us to become conscious of how churches, schools, and we ourselves maintain the social order as we analyze our obligation to alleviate world hunger.

The American Faith in Religion

The most significant work on the relationship between religion and society has been done in the field of the sociology of religion. Max Weber, Talcott Parsons, Charles Y. Glock and Rodney Stark, Gerhard Lenski, Andrew M. Greeley, Will Herberg, and others have examined the extent to which religion influences the economic, political, and social lives of individuals and society at large.[3] We cannot here summarize the detailed findings of all those sociologists. Instead, let us review briefly the highlights of Will Herberg's well-respected work *Protestant, Catholic, Jew.*

Herberg observes that "what Americans believe in when they are religious is . . . religion itself."[4] Religion is a very important part of American life. Almost every American belongs to, or at least identifies with, one of the major western religious traditions: Protestantism, Catholicism, or Judaism. In our society there are few Hindus, Buddhists, or Muslims except for some recent immigrants. Perhaps even more noteworthy is the fact that there are few self-proclaimed atheists or agnostics. So closely do Americans identify religion with the American way of life that not to belong to or identify with one of the great western religions is tantamount to being unpatriotic or un-American.

On closer examination Herberg found that apart from theologians and a few theologically sophisticated believers, the specific content of a tradition—its doctrines and dogmas, for example—is not what matters most to Americans. What is of utmost importance is for "everyone to have some religion." In other words the faith of Americans is a faith in religion itself—in the intrinsic goodness of religion and the necessity of "having religion."

Religion as Security and Moral Justification

If the particular articles of faith do not matter very much to Americans, what then do we look for in religion? Herberg answers in one word—security. Religion is viewed as a source of comfort in time of stress and a source of social stability.

By identifying ourselves as Protestant, Catholic, or Jewish, we acquire social acceptance. The more we are involved in the life of a church or synagogue, and the higher we rise in its hierarchy, the more likely are our prospects for social acceptance. Religion also affords a sense of identity. It enables us to locate ourselves better in the larger society, and this feeling enhances our sense of social belonging. In other words religion is a means of social adjustment.

Finally, religion provides us with a sense of personal moral respectability. Identification with a religion enables us to view ourselves in essentially positive moral terms, regardless of our personal actions, values, or goals. A tendency thus develops to equate being a Protestant, a Catholic, or a Jew with being moral. In a society where everyone claims to be a Christian or a Jew, it becomes difficult to define what being Christian or Jewish in fact means.

Religion affords security and moral justification not only to us as individuals but also to society as a whole. Its importance to our nation is reflected in many ways: the mention of God on our coins and our national hymns; the pledge of allegiance; public oaths; the presence of chaplains in Congress and the armed forces; and other public acts. As every schoolchild learns, the Pilgrims, our founding fathers and mothers, and the leaders of our nation were all reportedly people of deep faith. Ours is a nation established on religious principles and dedicated to the pursuit of those principles. This close identification of our nation and its purposes with God has produced a form of religious self-righteousness. We tend to view the American way of life as divinely ordained. We firmly believe that it ought to be the way of life for everyone. Challenges to the American way of life, therefore, appear to be malicious at best and the work of the devil at worst. Coupled with devotion and zeal for the American way of life is an attitude that could almost be termed "reverence" for American foreign policy. So closely do we identify the cause of our nation with the cause of God that most of us reject any criticism of the foreign conduct of our government or of American corporations. We simply refuse to believe that our nation could use food for political or strategic purposes or that it is more interested in keeping the Third World dependent than supporting its self-reliance. Herberg has coined a phrase that captures very well the relationship between our religion and society. He calls this civic religion the "cult of culture." In his words:

> Civic religion is a religion which validates culture and society, without in any sense bringing them under judgment. It lends an ultimate sanction to culture and society by assuring them that they constitute an

unequivocal expression of "spiritual ideals" and "religious values." Religion becomes, in effect, the cult of culture and society, in which the "right" social order and the received cultural values are divinized by being identified with the divine purpose.[5]

In a society in which religion has become so intimately connected with maintaining our way of life, what happens to the prophetic dimension of the Hebraic-Christian tradition? Quite simply it becomes submerged or lost to consciousness. Neither churches nor individual Christians and Jews wish to lose the rewards that the American way of life provides, regardless of the cost at which they have been obtained. Anything, including a religious prophetic tradition, that appears likely to disturb that way of life is viewed as a threat. We cannot afford to listen to or to take seriously a religious tradition that would judge the worth of our system, goals, and values on the basis of whether we have fed the hungry, clothed the naked, or sheltered the homeless. In a society in which religion is so closely associated with well-being, comfort, and security, the prophetic tradition appears "repugnant" and terribly "unsociable."[6] The religion that we Americans settle for, therefore, is a religion:

> . . . without serious commitment, without real inner conviction, without genuine existential decision. What should reach down to the core of existence, shattering and renewing, merely skims the surface of life, and yet succeeds in generating the sincere feeling of being religious. *Religion thus becomes a kind of protection the self throws up against the radical demand of faith* [emphasis added].[7]

The result is that we become morally insensitive and indifferent to issues of social justice. We become preoccupied with meeting our own private material needs, all the while believing that we are a religious people. Because churches and synagogues refuse to subject themselves or their membership to the judgment of the prophetic element in their tradition, they increasingly lose the capacity to challenge the status quo.

SPECIFIC CONTRIBUTIONS OF THE CHURCHES

There are numerous ways in which churches specifically contribute to maintaining the status quo. One of the most obvious ways is by focusing primarily on the private realm. The gospel is preached in essentially private, individualistic, and personalistic terms. It is presented as the biography of a private individual who promises personal salvation. The way to salvation is through an intimate relationship with Jesus fostered by a life of prayer, the sacraments, and liturgical worship. While the congregation is instructed to "love our neighbor," this love is voluntary and has nothing to do with justice—especially with the establishment of just systems, structures, and relationships in our own society.

In their preaching churches seldom refer to the economic, political, and social events of the day unless those events have some direct bearing on matters of private or sexual morality or the church's privileged position in society. The decisions and policies of corporations, banks, the government, and the military are virtually excluded from ethical consideration and regarded as beyond the purview of religion. Consequently members of the congregation are spared an ethical examination of how structures and systems may be the instruments of injustice today and of how they themselves, by their participation in and endorsement of those systems and structures, may be accomplices in injustice.

Churches contribute to the status quo by adopting an apolitical or neutral stance with regard to political, economic, and social issues, institutions, and values. The reason usually offered is that the mission of the church is not of this world, therefore the church has no need to involve itself in matters of economics and politics. Churches also offer "unity" as a reason for their apolitical stand. The unity of the church, it is argued, must be preserved at all costs. But there is no such thing as true neutrality. Neutrality is tantamount to choosing—but choosing for what already exists. By pleading neutrality, churches are denying the historical and political character of their own existence. They are denying both the power and responsibility they have to contribute to a more just and humane social order. Like other social institutions, churches play a significant role in determining the quality of life in society by what they do and do not support.

The reasons for the churches' neutrality do not hold up under scrutiny. If the gospel is not calling us to work for peace, justice, and love in this world, then in what world are we to work for them? We must not fall into the trap of assuming that peace, justice, and love are merely interior attitudes. While they may indeed be interior attitudes, they also must be expressed in concrete action, systems, and structures. The mission of the churches is not just to change attitudes but also to call people to put an end to war, to establish just economic, political, and social structures, and to make the needs of all who are oppressed and exploited their own.

Juan Luis Segundo offers a good response to the argument that the churches must preserve unity:

> . . . the internal unity of a Christian church can be attained or maintained today only by minimizing and playing down the radical historical oppositions that divide its members. In other words, one must pass over in silence such matters as color, social class, political ideology, the national situation, and the place of the country in the international market. At the same time one must stress the values that are presumably shared by all the members of the Church in question. *In short, the Church must pay a high price for unity. It must say that the issues of suffering, violence, injustice, famine, and death are less critical and decisive than religious formulas and rites* [emphasis added].[8]

The question must be raised as to whether the churches use the "mission and unity" arguments as a way of maintaining their own secure position in society.

Churches also contribute to the status quo by an excessive preoccupation with their own internal affairs. While such concerns as papal authority, the correct interpretation of church teaching, and proper liturgical form are important, the amount of attention allotted to them gives the impression that these are the only concerns that matter. Ecclesiastical and pastoral reform must be placed in their proper perspective. As Hugo Assmann writes:

> In theological terms one can ask whether they [the churches of the affluent world] are actually remaining true to their own doctrine on the nature of the Church, which is to be an organ of service to mankind. The Church cannot find its *raison d'etre* in itself, in the internal workings of its structures, because its vocation is one of radical service to the world.[9]

Although the official teaching of the Christian churches on social justice is strong on certain issues, it is largely unknown among the local churches. One wonders if this is due to the fact that pastors may be generally uninformed on the subject or are unwilling to offend their parishioners with statements critical of the parishioners' own economic and political systems. Moreover, when the gospel is preached in local churches, it is often preached in vague abstract terms with little attempt to relate it to the specific situations of injustice today. Because of the level of abstraction, those who hear such preaching have no clear idea as to who the poor, hungry, homeless, and imprisoned are and what it means specifically to love our neighbors, to work for justice, and to establish peace today. Consequently to the majority of Christians the gospel appears to be nothing more than a beautiful story or ideal. Churches have only themselves to blame for generating what Will Herberg calls a religion "without serious commitment, without real inner conviction, without genuine existential decision."[10]

We have so far discusssed only a number of the most obvious ways in which churches reinforce the status quo in the United States. There are other more subtle methods, which perhaps should be mentioned briefly at this point. They include the close relationship that churches cultivate between themselves and the upper classes of our society; the presence of members of the clergy at civil functions and of civil leaders at religious functions; the existence of the military chaplaincy; the affluent lifestyle of many members of the clergy; and the investments held by many churches in corporations involved in arms production or the exploitation of workers here and abroad.

In the following chapter we shall subject the American educational establishment to the same kind of scrutiny that we have turned here onto the churches in order to see how our educational system also sanctions and reinforces the American way of life.

Chapter 14

THE ROLE OF EDUCATION IN MAINTAINING THE STATUS QUO

OUR EDUCATIONAL SYSTEM AS THE "GREAT EQUALIZER"

The strongest criticism of the way our educational system functions has come from a group of educational historians, sociologists, and political scientists who are often referred to as "the revisionists." Some well-known revisionists are Colin Greer, Raymond Callahan, Michael Katz, Joel Spring, Clarence J. Karier, Samuel Bowles, and Herbert Gintis. To this list we might add Richard H. deLone, who completed a study in 1979 for the Carnegie Council on Children that supports many findings of the revisionists.

The revisionists bring a critical perspective to the field of education at a time when many Christian educators may be unaware of important factors shaping much of the educational activity in our schools. Briefly put, the main criticism of the revisionists is that our educational system has from its beginning aimed to provide stability to the capitalist economic system.

It is commonly believed that the American educational system is the "great equalizer." That is, Americans believe that all individuals, regardless of their race, color, class, or creed are afforded the opportunity through education to succeed in this society. We base this assumption on the story of the European immigrants who came to this country around the turn of the century and who through education and hard work advanced economically and socially. If the immigrants of that period prospered, we argue, so too can minority groups today who have equal access to education. If they fail, they have only themselves to blame.

Colin Greer calls this belief "the great school legend." In an effort to determine the extent to which education actually did contribute to the immigrants' economic and social mobility, Greer studied the experience of European immigrants to the United States at the turn of the twentieth century. His findings are very different from the legend that you and I have been led to believe. In brief, Greer finds that the immigrants who succeeded in America did so in spite of rather than because of the schools. Schools at the turn of the century, much like schools today, reproduced and reinforced the class bias of the existing society.

Greer reports that a significant number of immigrant children failed in school or were forced to drop out of school, thus limiting their chances of socioeconomic success. For example, in 1898:

> No more than 60 percent of Chicago's public school pupils were recorded at "normal age" (grade level). The rest, to use the deceptive language of the school study, were either "overage" (one or two years behind), or "retarded" (three to five years behind). In Boston, Chicago, Detroit, Philadelphia, Pittsburgh, New York, and Minneapolis, failure rates were so high that in not one of these systems did the so-called normal group exceed 60 percent, while in several instances it fell even lower—to 49 percent in Pittsburgh, and to 35 percent in Minneapolis.[1]

The success of certain immigrant groups in our society, Greer maintains, can be attributed to a number of factors besides the schools. The most important factor was the cultural patterns of the ethnic group. The specific cultural patterns that the ethnic group brought with it from its homeland and the patterns that were formed as a result of having to survive in an alien environment determined to a large extent the degree to which the ethnic group would be assimilated and would succeed in its new culture. The cultural patterns shaped the immigrant group's self-image and prepared their children for the experience of the public school. The more closely the values, social habits, and personality traits of the immigrant groups resembled those of the host country, the more easily were they assimilated.

Another factor that significantly contributed to the upward mobility of certain ethnic groups was their economic status as an ethnic group. Immigrant groups that achieved economic and social mobility initially established themselves as members of a strong middle class. They then worked their way through various economic and social channels, including the schools, into the middle strata of the larger society. They came, for the most part, from non-peasant, nonlaboring backgrounds and possessed skills that were not only needed by society but would be of value in a rapidly changing society. Greer gives Jews and Greeks as examples of immigrant groups that achieved upward mobility in our society better than others. They prospered more than Italians or Irish, principally because they could draw on largely nonpeasant experience from their lands of origin. Moreover, they were familiar with urban culture, knew the value of education, and prepared their children for it.

Although schools may have helped immigrant children whose parents had the advantages mentioned above, they posed an obstacle to disadvantaged children. They provided a form of "negative credentialling,"[2] that is, they certified children of immigrants who did not possess the proper economic and social characteristics as intellectually inferior. This limited the access of such children to higher levels of schooling and ultimately to socioeconomic success. The various means by which schools certify children as intellectually inferior will be discussed in more detail later in this chapter.

THE SORTING FUNCTION OF SCHOOLS

Samuel Bowles and Herbert Gintis come to a similar conclusion regarding the function of schools in a capitalist society. In *Schooling in Capitalist America* they argue that schools neither increase nor decrease the inequality that exists in a capitalistic society. They simply reproduce it and legitimate it.[3] Using American census data and their own statistical studies, Bowles and Gintis examine the relationship between education and social mobility. They report that even though education has been more evenly distributed among the population, and even though the general level of schooling has increased since World War I, the degree of social mobility (the achievement of economic success independent of family background) has not measurably increased. Although higher levels of schooling can be correlated with economic success, Bowles and Gintis find that the level of schooling attained is as dependent on socioeconomic status today as it was thirty years ago. If education, therefore, does not facilitate social mobility as is commonly believed, what then is its function in society? Bowles and Gintis maintain that schools basically assign individuals to unequal positions in the hierarchical division of labor on the basis of their socioeconomic status. Moreover, they legitimate the existing inequality through the meritocratic principle.

The Influence of Business on Schools

Some of the mechanisms by which schools allocate individuals to positions within the hierarchical divison of labor are testing, tracking, vocational guidance, and vocational education. Those mechanisms are by-products of the industrial efficiency movement developed in the early part of this century. The industrial efficiency movement—commonly referred to as "scientific management"—was spearheaded by Frederick W. Taylor. Taylor believed that there was essentially a best way to perform every job, and set out to determine what that way was by observing the performance of the most efficient industrial workers. By timing and recording their movements, Taylor determined the most efficient method for performing each industrial task. He then standardized the movements and time for different phases of the production process.

Under Taylor's system, each employee would receive instructions from the plant's planning department daily, indicating what job was to be performed, how it was to be performed, and the amount of time in which it was to be performed.[4] By working closely with planning departments, Taylor enabled industry to extract the maximum amount of work from each employee. As might be expected, Taylor's scientific management captured the imagination of industry. Its influence soon spread to government and all kinds of public institutions, including schools.

In tracing the effects of scientific management on schools during the early part of the twentieth century, Raymond Callahan finds that the business industrial ideology crept into every aspect of education. The size of the school board, for example, was reduced, and its members were increasingly drawn from the business community. School administrators, to increase their schools' prestige and enhance their own reputation, began to operate schools like businesses. They applied cost analysis to class size, teaching load, the curriculum, texts, and every other aspect of education. Thus economics rather than educational considerations increasingly became the basis of school decisions. Callahan tells of a typical case in which cost analysis was applied to the curriculum. In deciding whether music or Greek should be taught in schools, one of the leaders of educational cost accounting named Franklin Spauling reasoned that since Greek cost more to teach, it was less valuable educationally.[5] In short, the scientific management movement pressured schools to become more responsive to the values and interests of the business community.

Schools also responded to the interests of the business community in another way by developing or implementing mechanisms for channeling young people into vocations that would supposedly match the student's abilities. Some of the mechanisms included tracking, vocational guidance, testing, and vocational education. Those reforms, as we will see, served the interests of the business community and the social elite more than the needs of the individual students.[6]

The Differentiated Curriculum

The rise of industrialism brought an influx of immigrants from eastern and southern Europe to the urban centers of the United States. Soon the leaders of society in big American cities were experiencing the need to socialize the immigrants "to behavior that [would] decrease crime, diminish expenditures on public welfare, promote safety on the streets, and contribute to industrial productivity."[7] This responsibility fell to the schools. An obvious solution was to extend the age of compulsory schooling, thus keeping children off the streets and under school influence for a longer period of time. But in doing so, the schools faced a dilemma. Since at that time high schools primarily prepared children of the upper classes for college, what was to be done with so many working class and immigrant children who would be attending public high schools for the first time in history? Rather than change the orientation and original purpose of the high school, educational reformers decided to introduce the differentiated curriculum.

The rationale behind the differentiated curriculum was that it would tailor the curriculum to meet the specific capabilities and needs of students. But as

it functioned in the early part of the twentieth century, it effectively chan-
neled working-class and immigrant children into business and vocational
training, while preserving the academic curriculum for children of the upper
classes.[8] Thus the differentiated curriculum served the purpose not only of
keeping lower-class children from dropping out of school but also of providing them with skills that would enable them to find jobs in the work force
appropriate to their social class. As Bowles and Gintis explain:

> . . . the expansion of public secondary education, and its transforma-
> tion from an upper class preserve to a mass institution was eminently
> consistent with democratic and egalitarian traditions. In the context of
> a rapidly developing corporate division of labor, however, such de-
> mands spelled not equality and democracy, but stratification and bu-
> reaucracy.[9]

Vocational Guidance

The stratification and smooth integration of young people into the labor
force was facilitated by another educational reform, the vocational guidance
movement. Leaders of this movement believed that the adolescent years were
the most productive for shaping vocational goals and proper attitudes. Using
a battery of psychological and intelligence tests administered in junior high
school, vocational guidance counselors attempted to differentiate and sort
students according to ability groupings and future occupational positions as
early as possible. By the seventh and eighth grades, therefore, students were
matched to their future occupations and courses of study. By the time they
reached the ninth grade, they had already made their vocational choice and
were ready to be placed in a track within their field.[10] Leaders of the vocational guidance movement firmly believed that vocational guidance, especially in junior high school, not only reduced inefficiency but supplied labor
tailored to the needs of students and the corporate sector.[11] The fact that the
student was often referred to as the "raw material for the industrial machine"[12] in the early days of the vocational guidance movement tells us something about the close relationship between the vocational guidance movement and business and industry.

Educational Testing

If the vocational guidance movement facilitated the early stratification of
students and their smooth integration into the hierarchical division of labor,
the educational testing movement legitimated this whole procedure. Educational testing lent an aura of scientific objectivity to educational stratification. Frank Freeman, like other proponents of educational testing, believed
that it would be undemocratic to track students on the basis of wealth or
birth. If, however, students were tracked on the basis of their inherent abili-

ties, then tracking was not only justified but necessary for the good of society.[13] The standard used for measuring a student's "inherent" ability was taken from the early educational testers' observation of society.[14] Intelligence tests were based on class differences with the expectation that the different classes would perform differently on the tests. Testers like Binet, Terman, Thorndike, Goddard, and Yerkes believed that members of the upper classes had superior intellectual, physical, and moral abilities. And because the prejudices of the testers were confirmed by their tests, they believed that their tests were valid instruments for sorting individuals. The following statements by Binet and Simon reflect the class bias of the early educational testers:

> An individual is normal when he is able to conduct himself in life without need of the guardianship of another, and is able to perform work sufficiently remunerative, to supply his personal needs, and finally when his intelligence does not exclude him from the social rank of his parents. . . .[15]
>
> Our personal investigations as well as those of many others, have demonstrated that children of the poorer class are shorter, weigh less, have smaller heads and slighter muscular force, than a child of the upper class; they less often reach the high school; they are more often behind in their studies. Here is a collection of inferiorities which are slight, because they are only appreciated when large numbers are considered, but they are undeniable. Some probably are acquired and result from unavoidable and accessory circumstances; others are congenital.[16]

In short, intelligence tests reflected the class bias of the testers and society at large.

The widespread acceptance of intelligence testing in schools is reflected by the following statistics. Between 1921 and 1936 over four thousand articles on intelligence testing were published and more than four thousand intelligence tests were in circulation; 75 percent of the 150 city school systems polled in 1930 used intelligence tests to track students.[17] As mentioned above, vocational guidance counselors relied heavily on intelligence tests in planning student's future in school and the job market. The fact that higher test scores were correlated with occupations in the upper levels of the hierarchical division of labor and lower test scores with lower levels in the division of labor is reflected in the following statement by Lewis Terman:

> At every step in the child's progress the school should take account of his vocational possibilities. Preliminary investigations indicate that an IQ below 70 rarely permits anything better than unskilled labor; that the range from 70 to 80 is pre-eminently that of semi-skilled labor, from 80 to 100 that of the skilled or ordinary clerical labor, from 100 to 110 or 115 that of the semi-professional pursuits; and that above all these are the grades of intelligence which permit one to enter the professions or

the largei fields of business. . . . This information will be a great value in planning the education of a particular child and also in planning the differentiated curriculum here recommended.[18]

As we will see, the general use and acceptance of intelligence tests as valid measures of intelligence in the past as well as in the present has the effect of shifting attention from the economic system to the individual to account for inequality in society. We assume that people who are wealthy are intelligent and have worked for their wealth, and people who are poor are either unintelligent or lazy and thus deserve their condition.[19] Bowles and Gintis set out to measure the relationship between merit and economic success through a series of statistical studies. They have discovered that "IQ is not an important criterion for economic success"[20] and that "economic success tends to run in the family. . . almost completely independently from any inheritance of IQ, whether it be genetic or environmental."[21] With respect to an association between economic success and the achievement of cognitive or technical skills rewarded and certified by schools, Bowles and Gintis report:

> . . . mental-skill demands of work are sufficiently limited, the skills produced by our educational system sufficiently varied, and the possibilities for acquiring additional skills on the job sufficiently great so that skill differences among individuals who are acceptable for a given job on the basis of other criteria including race, sex, personality, and credentials are of little economic import. At most levels in the occupational hierarchy mental skills are productive, but are not scarce, and hence do not bear a direct monetary return.[22]

In short, Bowles and Gintis find that neither the skills acquired and certified by schools nor the IQ test scores used to assign individuals to vocational or academic course streams or ability tracks are important determinants of economic success. Economic success is as dependent on social class today as it was before the institution of the various educational sorting mechanisms. Bowles and Gintis go so far as to say that the meritocratic orientation of school functions as a "facade that facilitates the stratification of the labor force."[23]

Effects of the Educational Sorting Mechanisms

Besides assigning individuals to different levels of schooling, the educational sorting mechanisms also help shape their personality traits. Personality traits, according to Bowles and Gintis, are among the significant factors that determine the level at which people enter the labor force. And as is well known, access to the upper levels in the work force is restricted by the level at which people enter.

Bowles and Gintis argue that there is a correspondence between the social relations of education and the social relations of production. At least three personality traits are necessary for production: respect for rules, dependability, and internalization of the values and norms of the operation. Certain traits are necessary and emphasized for certain levels of production. Employees at the lower levels of production usually exhibit a respect for rules and the ability to follow orders. Employees at the middle level exhibit diligence and the ability to carry out orders. And employees at the higher levels have usually internalized the norms and values of the operation and can act on their own initiative.

Bowles and Gintis maintain that different levels of schooling as well as different schools prepare individuals for the level at which they will enter the labor force by shaping their personal attitudes and expectations. The lower levels of schooling like the junior high school and the high school, for instance, generally foster rule-following behavior. The middle level of schooling, or the community or teacher college, encourage more independence and rely less on supervision. The higher levels (the four-year colleges and elite institutions) generally stress the internalization of norms.[24] The same observation can be made of the various tracks within schools. The vocational and business tracks, for example, emphasize rule following, while the academic tracks encourage more intiative and self-direction and motivational control.

According to Bowles and Gintis, the same generalization is true of schools catering to students from wealthier versus poorer families. Schools enrolling lower-income students generally emphasize followership and behavioral control, while schools enrolling upper-class students generally foster leadership skills and motivational control.[25] Thus schools through the use of educational sorting mechanisms can effectively lock individuals into their social classes by limiting their access to higher levels of schooling and by shaping their personal attitudes and expectations.

Finally, students learn to accept the hierarchical division of labor in schools through rather subtle ways—through observing and experiencing the relationships that exist among administrators, faculty, and students, for example. They also learn to accept the alienation that they will experience in the work force through experiencing alienation in the classroom. They have no control over who teaches them, what is taught, or how it is taught. Moreover, the schools foster a spirit of working for personal external rewards rather than a spirit of working for the good of the community.

Let us summarize the educational revisionists' argument thus far. The educational system in our society supports the status quo by channeling students into vocations appropriate to their social class, thereby providing a stratified labor force for the smooth functioning of the capitalist system.

THE LEGITIMATING FUNCTION OF THE SCHOOLS

Educational Reform as a Substitute for Social Reform

The educational system, according to the revisionists, supports the status quo in yet another way—by legitimating inequality in our society and obscuring its roots. As mentioned above, society has traditionally looked to schools to solve its social problems. This was true not only at the turn of the century when the immigrant population threatened the stability of the urban centers but it is also still true today. Americans continue to look to the schools to solve the monumental problems of poverty, unemployment, racism, and sexism in our society today. The tendency to regard education as a cure for social problems, Richard deLone has pointed out, is based on the assumption that poverty, unemployment, and other social ills are due to individual failures.[26] Americans, generally speaking, believe that the poor in our society have only themselves to blame. Their poverty is attributed to personal laziness or a lack of intelligence or talent. It is commonly assumed that in our country all of us can succeed, provided we take advantage of the opportunities society offers and are willing to work for a living.

Because poverty is so closely associated with individual failure, Americans tend to believe that the most effective way to combat poverty is by improving individuals. And what better way is there to improve individuals than through education? Since the children of the poor are the hope of the future, social reform easily becomes translated into educational reform. Michael Katz captures this sentiment well when he writes:

> There is a surface logic, which remains immensely appealing: Equipping children with appropriate skills and attitudes can cause the problems of unemployment and poverty to disappear. *The illnesses of society become diagnosed as simply a lack of education, and the prescription for reform becomes more education. The prescription, for one thing, unleashes a flurry of seemingly purposeful activity and, for another, requires no tampering with basic social structural or economic characteristics, only with the attitudes of poor people,* and that has caused hardly a quiver. The problem (and the determination with which people have refused to admit it is powerful testimony to the usefulness of the idea) is that this approach to social reform simply has not worked. In fact, insofar as *it has been a smoke screen, obscuring the nature of social problems, educational reform has hindered broader reform* [emphasis added].[27]

When the children of the poor fail to break out of the cycle of poverty, our assumption regarding the inferiority of the poor is confirmed.

The Role of Schools in Masking the True Causes of Social Ills

The problem with educational reform is twofold. It not only has failed to reduce significantly poverty and unemployment but it has also helped obscure the root causes of inequality in our society. The school obscures the sources of inequality essentially by perpetuating the myth that economic success in our society is due primarily to merit. Whether or not this is a deliberate attempt on the part of the school, children rather early in their educational career learn to associate wealth and power with intelligence. This association of wealth with intelligence has led not only children but also society at large to seek no further than the individual for the source of poverty and inequality in our society. By focusing on the individual, the systemic and structural roots of the problems go unnoticed. As the deLone study so aptly puts it:

> Implicit in attempts to solve inequality by helping individuals is the belief that social inequalities are caused by individual differences. This is a more sophisticated version of the notion that we are all masters of our fates and it is a natural companion of market economic theory. What this view, in both its cruder and its more sophisticated versions, fails to consider sufficiently is that causality also runs the other way, that social structure influences development. Accordingly, reformers' efforts to change social structure and its dynamics through changing individuals are often attempts to battle against the tides.[28]

As our analysis in Part I revealed, poverty and inequality on the international level are rooted in systems controlled and structured by the rich to their own advantage. The same argument can be made for the causes of domestic poverty. Individual differences alone cannot account for the vast amount of poverty and inequality in our society. If we are to solve the problems that plague society, we must look beyond the individual to the mechanisms that distribute wealth and privilege. Fundamental social change, in other words, requires us to strive to change the basis of producing and distributing wealth and power. We are only deluding ourselves if we persist in the belief that poverty can be eradicated simply by changing individuals without changing the economic system that produces such poor individuals. As Kenneth Keniston writes:

> . . . in the end, such reforms have failed in their lofty goals because they were not accompanied by more direct and structural change. Without structural change, education and efforts to equalize opportunity can at best only change the cast of characters who occupy preexisting numbers of position on the top and on the bottom.[29]

If the analysis of the revisionists is correct, one of the most damaging effects of our educational meritocratic system is its legitimation of positions of privilege. We are conditioned by our educational system to accept as normal and reasonable the positions of dominance and subordination that exist not only in our society but in the world as well. Because we have been socialized to attribute poverty and inequality to individual failure, we tend to assume that poor nations have only themselves to blame for their own condition. Thus we fail to look beyond the individual nations to the systems linking nations to other nations. The fact that the economic and political systems that keep one nation rich may be responsible for keeping another one poor, or the fact that our own nation exploits the Third World through its control of international systems escapes our examination.

Blaming the poor for their own poverty is an effective way of protecting our own positions of privilege. As Michael Katz points out, it "requires no tampering with basic social structural or economic characteristics, only with the attitudes of poor people."[30] Blaming the poor is also an effective way of escaping responsibility for rectifying the situation. Because actions to eliminate poverty or hunger in our own country or in the Third World are based on a faulty analysis of the roots of poverty and hunger, they assume the quality of charity rather than justice. Consequently, they merely tamper with the symptoms and leave intact the systemic causes of the problem. Thus actions on behalf of the poor that spring from charity instead of justice leave undisturbed our exploitative systems, our standard of living, and our consciences.

Once we understand that religion and education play an important role in supporting the capitalistic system, we shall realize that, in fact, they are supporting the very system that keeps the Third World in a condition of dependency and hunger. If our churches and schools are to become humanizing agencies, those who assume positions of leadership within them must encourage a critical evaluation of all the forces that shape those institutions.

Christian educators need to become aware of the contradictory interests embodied in religious and educational structures, theories, and practices. They need to examine the historical roots of the contradictions within their own institutions—how those contradictions evolved, who keeps them going, and why they are kept going. They should ask themselves who dominates the religious and educational institutions of which they are a part. What are the political and economic forces that structure those institutions?

One of the most serious errors we can make as Christian educators is to assume that the lofty ideals of our institutions are always practiced within the institutions themselves. Often idealistic language can mask complicity. If we examine our religious and social institutions within the context of the larger society, we shall discover that our churches and schools, like our other institutions, are deeply structured by the values and goals of a capitalist society. Instead of leading society, they have served it—often unwittingly. For this reason as Christian educators we must seek to change the relationship between our institutions and the larger society. Otherwise the efforts we mount to improve the conditions of the poor may be negated by our own institutions.

Finally, we must see that our efforts to change the relationship of churches and schools to the larger society fit into a larger context. Our efforts are a necessary part of the struggle to bring about a more humane social order. We must strive to liberate our institutions from serving the ideals, values, and goals of the capitalist system. This struggle, if we recall the words of the liberation theologians, is nothing less than the struggle for the kingdom of God.

Chapter 15

EDUCATING FOR CRITICAL CONSCIOUSNESS AND ACTION

What specific contribution can we make as Christian educators to alleviating hunger and poverty in the world? We must realize, first of all, the contradictions in our own economic system that produce poverty and hunger in the Third World, and we must have the moral courage to take action to change the systems and values of our society that cause the exploitation of people in the Third World.

THE HUMANIZING PURPOSE OF EDUCATION

What form of action should we take as Christian educators? Sociologist, Sister Marie Augusta Neal, has recommended a form of teaching that she called "disturbing the peace." She describes it in these words:

> . . . for religious educators to teach the skills needed for calling to account the functionaries of the government or of the economy for their exploitation of the people, and for providing reflective space for the people on every occasion to decide what to do in order to right this wrong, is to have such teaching defined as disturbing the peace.[1]

The educational methodology that in my estimate offers the most promise for developing the critical skills needed in our society has been described in the work of the Brazilian educator Paulo Freire.

For Freire the purpose of the educational process is to humanize, that is, to make individuals more humane and to bring about a more humane society. But in order to do so, the educational process must help us as individuals to become aware of the obstacles to humanization existing in our society. In other words, the educational process must enable us to perceive critically the way we exist in the world. It must enable us to examine the forces that restrict our humanization. And finally, it must help us realize the necessity and possibility of overcoming those forces.

"Banking Education"

A great deal of educational activity, Freire points out, impedes the development of critical consciousness and thus humanization. In fact, he argues that much education is structured to adjust individuals to the status quo rather than to help them critically evaluate it and transform it. Freire terms the type of education that dulls the consciousness of individuals and impedes humanization "banking education." The teacher deposits information in students, who merely receive it. In Freire's words, "the more completely [the teacher] fills the receptacles, the better teacher he is. The more meekly the receptacles permit themselves to be filled, the better students they are."[2] Banking education engenders passivity in students. It neither challenges them to examine the problematic nature of their social reality nor does it encourage them to assume responsibility for their social existence.

"Problem-Posing Education"

For the educational process to be a humanizing act, Freire holds that the banking method must give way to "problem-posing education." This method of education differs from banking education in essentially three respects. The relationship of domination and subordination between teacher and students is replaced by a relationship of cooperation and mutual respect. The role of teachers is changed from that of transmitting information to problematizing social existence. And the educational process becomes a dialogue in which teachers and students together analyze their social situation for the purpose of transforming it.

In problem-posing education the teacher is no longer the only one who teaches and the students are no longer only those who are taught. The teacher is no longer expected to be the sole source of information, while students function merely as recipients of that information. Teachers and students both teach and learn. Both recognize that knowledge and insight are not the special privilege or preserve of a certain class or educated elite. Each person brings a unique and valuable perspective to the problem at hand. Thus the relationship of dominance and subordinance that exists between teachers and students in banking education gives way to a relationship of cooperation, mutual trust, and respect. In problem-posing education teachers become both teachers and students, and students become both students and teachers. In short, both assume responsibility for the educational task.

The Role of the Teacher

The role of the teacher as well as the educational process itself are radically changed in problem-posing education. Instead of transmitting information about the world, the teacher poses the world as a problem. The teacher becomes essentially a "problematizer," someone who presents to students their own social reality as a problem that challenges their common humanity and demands a response. Through the problem-posing process students develop the capacity to confront their social existence as they gain a critical perspective on their society and the world at large.

Through dialogue the teacher and students critically analyze and evaluate their social reality. They examine the roots of the problems of their society, the interests that give rise to those problems, and the interests served by perpetuating those problems. Through dialogue the teacher and the students come to see more clearly the challenge such problems pose to their humanity and their obligation to change them.

The subject matter in problem-posing education, therefore, is neither contrived nor irrelevant. It is taken directly from the teacher's and the students' experience of the world. Moreover, in problem-posing education students come to perceive themselves as subjects rather than objects of history. Their concrete historical situation appears changeable rather than static or given. Freire points out the fundamental difference between banking and problem-posing education when he writes:

> Whereas banking education anesthetizes and inhibits creative power, problem-posing education involves a constant unveiling of reality. The former attempts to maintain the *submersion* of consciousness; the latter strives for the *emergence* of consciousness and *critical intervention* in reality.[3]

Thus by posing the contradictions that exist within the social order, the educational process can be a force for bringing about the emergence of critical consciousness that will transform the status quo on behalf of humanity.

Educating beyond Critical Consciousness

In problem-posing education the test of the teacher's effectiveness is the change that is brought about in the students' consciousness—an increased ability to think critically about their own social existence. But Ronald Marstin argues that the development of critical consciousness is not enough. In his words:

> It is well to remember that an extensive and well-funded industry—the knowledge industry—exists in large part to provide the necessary skills for dealing intellectually with the world's pain. The main problem is not that our colleges, classrooms, libraries, and study circles fail to acknowledge the justice issues. In liberal circles at any rate, our course lists and bookshelves are filled with discussion of these themes. But that is precisely the problem: while the situation cries out for action we continue the endless round of discussion, all the time convinced that in our wordy concern we are really addressing the issues. We are not. We are

avoiding them. Our failure to take the kind of action that might change an oppressive situation results less from any failure to consider the oppression or to be concerned about it than from our uncanny ability to keep channeling our outrage into a flow of words.[4]

While the development of critical consciousness is an essential element in educating for justice, it must never be taken for its final end. The goal of educating for justice is nothing less than changing the situation of injustice. Change, as we know, cannot come about by merely analyzing a situation or devising strategies, although both are important and necessary. Nothing short of action will do. Thus the responsibility of religious educators is really twofold: to develop critical consciousness and to engage in action for justice.

Since injustice is mediated not only through individuals but through systems and structures, action for justice must be expressed in action oriented toward transforming the economic, political, and social structures of society. The task of religious educators cannot be interpreted as anything less than that of working with students to change those structures. In sum, Marstin raises the right question for religious educators when he asks, ". . . should the maturity of faith be gauged by our ideas or our action, by the changes that come about in our minds or the changes we bring about in our society?"[5] The only gauge religious educators have for measuring the effectiveness of their efforts to educate for justice is the effectiveness of their own actions and the actions of their students in changing the political, economic, and social institutions of society.[6]

THE SOCIAL RECONSTRUCTIONISTS

The idea that the primary purpose of education is to develop critical consciousness and to stimulate action that will change unjust systems and structures is not as foreign to the American educational tradition as most people might believe. That very position was espoused by a group of prominent educators associated with Columbia University Teachers College. The Social Reconstructionists, as they are sometimes called, met regularly between 1927 and 1939 to discuss informally the public purpose of economic, political, and social institutions. Members of the group included William H. Kilpatrick, Edmund De S. Brunner, John Childs, George Counts, John Dewey, Harry Overstreet, and Harold Rugg. All were joined by a common belief that "education has an important, even strategic, role to play in the reconstruction of American society."[7]

The Social Reconstructionists attributed the inequality and poverty of the 1930s to laissez-faire capitalism and to a lack of critical consciousness in society. Since George Counts and Harold Rugg acted as spokesmen for the group, we can best understand through their works the position of the movement as a whole.

The Social Reconstructionists maintained that one of the most important responsibilities of educators was to enable students to examine and criticize the social order of which they were an integral part. They believed that the crucial first step in any critical analysis of society was to accurately describe its systems and forces. Rugg, in particular, argued that all the systems and forces operating in society must be exposed for public scrutiny despite the controversy inherent in such a procedure:

> The very foundation of education must be the study of the actual problems and controversial issues of our people. There is no other way by which the democratic principle of consent can be implemented. Consent based upon knowledge of only one aspect or side of a problem, upon the avoidance of controversy, is a travesty to both knowledge and democracy. To keep issues out of the schools is to keep thought out of it; it is to keep life out of it.[8]

Some of the aspects of our social order that in Rugg's judgment warranted examination were:

—Private profit as the chief motivating force in the maintenance of our economic order. . . .
—The continued inequality in the distribution of the social income, accompanied by the growing acceptance of the social nature of wealth. . . .
—The tendency toward greater concentration and integration in the organization and control of industries, business, wealth, income, credit, the press, and government. . . .
—The tendency for dominant economic classes to control local, State, and national government. . . .
—The rise and spread of economic imperialism—that is, the increasing export of capital by the larger industrial nations, the consequent development and control of resources of undeveloped countries, and the consequent danger of war. . . .
—The lag of the knowledge of human motives and conduct behind the accumulation of knowledge of mechanical power. . . .
—The struggle between the acquisitive and conformist traits on the one hand and the creative, expressive traits on the other; the tendency to enthrone mercenary goals as the chief objectives of life. . . .
—The tendency toward wasteful and ostentatious consumption by persons of wealth and the prevalence of imitation by the less wealthy classes.[9]

As we can see, the same issues are still very much with us today and are in no less need of critical examination.

The Social Reconstructionists were struck by the paradoxes and contradictions, particularly poverty and inequality, in a society that professed the principles of equality, justice, freedom, and opportunity for all people. Blaming the capitalist system for those ills, they maintained that the principles of laissez-faire capitalism and rugged individualism were no longer appropriate in the United States.

Counts describes the principle of laissez-faire capitalism as one that:

> . . . assumes that every man is supremely devoted to his own pecuniary interest, that he knows best what that interest is, that he himself can guard and advance that interest most effectively, and that, since the whole is equal to the sum of all its parts, if he will but mind his own business and dutifully think only of what is good for himself, then the greatest social good will be achieved.[10]

The Social Reconstructionists concluded that laissez-faire capitalism was detrimental to a society that was becoming increasingly cooperative and collective in behavior. In their judgment the technological revolution had brought about an integration of society never before experienced in history. The advances in industry, transportation, and communication made cooperation and interdependence within and beyond the nation not only possible but necessary. People were linked to each other through mass production, distribution, sales, consumption, communications, transportation, and finances. Whether or not people recognized it, they were dependent on each other as never before and could not reverse the trend. Since the philosophy and practice of laissez-faire capitalism ignored that fact, it jeopardized the well-being of the entire society.

The worth of an economic system, according to the Social Reconstructionists, should be judged on the basis not only of how well it produced goods and services but also of how well it distributed those goods and services. Distribution was as important as production:

> The natural endowment of the nation is exploited without thought of the future; a high-powered productive mechanism is harnessed to money-making rather than to supplying the population with needed goods and services; human labor is viewed as a commodity to be bought and sold in the market place; government is often converted into a dispenser of special favors and privileges to those who have; the speedy dissipation of a severely limited resource is regarded as an inalienable right of business enterprise; . . . extravagant consumption is converted into a resounding civil virtue; a philosophy of deliberate waste and improvidence is proclaimed as the highest economic wisdom . . . credits are granted to distant countries to enable them to absorb both commodity and capital surplus; the struggle for foreign markets leads to bitter competition and ultimately to war. . . the entire country rejoices at the news that the total wheat crop will be the smallest in a generation. . . .[11]

The Social Reconstructionists stated that the day of individualism was gone forever, and that the choice could no longer be between individualism and collectivism but between "two forms of collectivism: the one essentially democratic, the other feudal in spirit; the one devoted to the interests of the people, the other to the interests of a privileged class."[12]

In the critical analysis of the Social Reconstructionists, the lack of a public critical awareness was another source of the nation's problems at that time. Counts's description of the lack of social concern in the country nearly fifty years ago seems no less accurate of our society today:

> We are able to contemplate the universe and find that all is vanity. Nothing really stirs us, unless it be that the bath water is cold, the toast burnt, or the elevator not running; or that perchance we miss the first section of a revolving door. . . . We are moved by no great faiths; we are touched by no great passions. We can view a world order rushing rapidly towards collapse with no more concern than the outcome of a horse race; we can see injustice, crime and misery in their most terrible forms all about us and, if we are not directly affected, register the emotions of a scientist studying white rats in a laboratory.[13]

The Social Reconstructionists felt that this lack of critical awareness and concern was inextricably linked to the spirit of capitalism. In fact, they argued that the values generated by the economic system made it virtually impossible for people to think collectively or to act out of a motive other than profit.[14]

The Social Reconstructionists pointed out that the business community deliberately distracted society from contemplating its own ills and discovering the source of those ills because it was in the interest of business to do so.[15] The problems of society, they judged correctly, would be met only if those problems happened to correspond with the interests of private and corporate capital. They concluded that the economic system would have to be radically transformed in order to serve the human interest:

> With its deification of the principle of selfishness, its exaltation of the profit motive, its reliance upon the forces of competition, and its placing of property above human rights, it will either *have to be displaced altogether or changed so radically in form and spirit that its identity will be completely lost* [emphasis added].[16]

According to the Social Reconstructionists, our educational institutions could take the lead in the transformation of the economic order. The purpose of such institutions was not only to transmit civilization but also to rebuild it. In order to carry out this task, the schools would need a vision—a great and noble concept of life and civilization that would challenge people to build a new social order.[17] Members of the group believed that the principles of democracy, freedom, justice, equality as well as faith in the intrinsic worth and dignity of all people could provide such a vision. Counts describes that vision in these terms:

A Society fashioned in harmony with the American democratic tradition would combat all forces tending to produce social distinctions and classes; repress every form of privilege and economic parasitism; manifest a tender regard for the weak, the ignorant, and the unfortunate; place the heavier and more onerous social burdens on the backs of the strong; . . . strive for genuine equality of opportunity among all races, sects, and occupations; . . . and finally be prepared as a last resort, in either the defense or the realization of this purpose, to follow the method of revolution.[18]

Once educational institutions affirm the principles of the American democratic tradition, the task of educators would be to encourage students to critically evaluate the social order in terms of those principles. Students should be encouraged to examine the purposes and interests of the institutions of society. The Social Reconstructionists believed that where suffering and exploitation are concerned education cannot afford to adopt a position of neutrality. To do so, they said, was to deny its very purpose for existing.

Besides exposing the hypocrisies of our political, economic, and social institutions, educators are responsibile for inculcating a sense of social responsibility in students. Students must become conscious of the fact that with knowledge comes an obligation to use it for the public good. Instead of cultivating a sense of competition and narrow individualism, educators should instill a sense of service to the larger community.

Finally, the Social Reconstructionists believed that educators should encourage the study of the creative reconstruction of society based on the finest ideals of our democratic heritage and the changing character of our social existence. A program for the future must include the following:

(1) To increase production; (2) to secure an equitable distribution of goods and services to the masses of the people; (3) to foster wise and temperate consumption of these benefits; (4) to conserve those basic natural resources on which the economic life depends; (5) to organize industry so that it will quicken rather than destroy the intellectual and moral life; and, finally, (6) to inject into industry a new spirit which will call forth the will to serve in place of the will to exploit.[19]

The words of George Counts capture the challenge before educators: "To refuse to face the task of creating a vision of a future America immeasurably more just and noble and beautiful than the America of today is to evade the most crucial, difficult, and important educational task."[20]

STATEMENT OF THE SYNOD OF CATHOLIC BISHOPS

The foregoing discussion of the views of the Social Reconstructionists has focused on the role of schools in educating for justice. This does not mean, however, that other institutions in our society have no responsibility in this area, and that schools must shoulder the entire burden. Meeting in 1971, the Synod of Catholic Bishops issued *Justice in the World*, a formal statement of the church's task in educating for justice. (We have already noted this document in Chapter 12.) The bishops spoke of the need to develop in Christians both a critical consciousness and willingness to take action for justice. They condemn a tendency toward narrow individualism in today's society:

> The method of education very frequently still in use today encourages narrow individualism. Part of the human family lives immersed in a mentality which exalts possessions. The school and the communications media, which are often obstructed by the established order, allow the formation only of the man desired by that order, that is to say, man in its image, not a new man but a copy of man as he is.[21]

The purpose of education, the bishops maintain, is to humanize both individuals and society at large. This can only be accomplished through awakening critical consciousness and participating in constructing a just social order. They write:

> But education demands a renewal of heart, a renewal based on the recognition of sin in its individual and social manifestations. It will also inculcate a truly and entirely human way of life in justice, love and simplicity. It will likewise awaken a critical sense, which will lead us to reflect on the society in which we live and on its values; it will make men ready to renounce these values when they cease to promote justice for all men. In the developing countries, the principal aim of this education for justice consists in an attempt to awaken consciences to a knowledge of the concrete situation and in a call to secure a total improvement; by these means the transformation of the world has already begun.
>
> Since this education makes men decidedly more human, it will help them to be no longer the object of manipulation by communications media or political forces. It will instead enable them to take in hand their own destinies and bring about communities which are truly human.[22]

Finally, education for justice is an ongoing process. It cannot be confined to the years spent in formal education. Its most important lessons are, moreover, learned and learned best in actions for justice:

> Accordingly, this education is deservedly called a continuing education, for it concerns every person and every age. It is also a practical education: it comes through action, participation and vital contact with the reality of injustice.
>
> Education for justice is imparted first in the family. We are well aware that not only Church institutions but also other schools, trade unions, and political parties are collaborating in this.[23]

Chapter 16

THEORY AND PRACTICE OF EDUCATING FOR JUSTICE

EDUCATIONAL PRESUPPOSITIONS

This brings us to our final task—illustrating how religious educators might educate for justice on the problems of underdevelopment and world hunger. The following ideas reflect primarily my own experiences in teaching courses to college students about the religious and ethical dimensions of these problems. They are presented here not as a model for all religious educational situations but as a stimulus to you to develop the creative approach appropriate for your particular situation.

My educational methodology and goals have been influenced by Paulo Freire, whose approach was described in the preceding chapter. My educational goals are to humanize students, that is, to help them become sensitive and responsive to the needs and suffering of others, to become critically aware of the roots of human suffering, and to work to change the political, economic, and social causes of human suffering. These goals cannot be met, however, until students recognize and confront the obstacles to humanization in their own lives and in the larger society. My role as teacher, therefore, is to problematize—to make a problem out of what was never perceived to be a problem before—to take the taken-for-granted, the normal, the acceptable and present it as if it could not be taken-for-granted and as if it were abnormal or unacceptable. Teachers, I believe, should not only initiate the problematizing process but should also serve as facilitators for the critical analysis needed to uncover the roots of the problem and to determine the steps that must be taken to resolve it. Finally, since the educational process cannot stop with the critical reflection, teachers and students together must become actively involved in changing the systems and structures that produce the problem.

POSING THE PROBLEM OF WORLD HUNGER

I begin my course on the ethical dimensions of world hunger by presenting world hunger as one of the most pressing moral problems of our day. Al-

153

though this may appear to be a rather easy task, I have not found it so. In the United States we have become so used to hearing about the problem of hunger, that its human face—the daily suffering of millions of human beings—is lost to our consciousness. The pain of people in the Third World over the suffering and death of their loved ones somehow appears less real and less pressing than our own personal problems and struggles. Even among nineteen- and twenty-year-old students there are few who express the belief that "this should not be!" It has become a normal and acceptable fact of life that 450 million people are suffering from hunger.

Our Own Insensitivity

To deal effectively with the problem, therefore, I begin by posing our own insensitivity to the suffering of others as an obstacle to becoming truly educated. Our insensitivity prevents us from realizing our potential as human beings.

Denis Goulet's discussion of the goals and principles of development in *The Cruel Choice* is especially helpful in this regard.[1] Goulet forces us to confront the meaning of the term "development," the relationship between goods and the "good life," the nature and degree of freedom achieved in so-called developed societies, and the responsibility of the rich to abolish poverty.

Since most of my students are Roman Catholic, the social encyclicals and in particular much of *Populorum Progressio* also have been helpful in this discussion. The teaching of the Catholic church about the dignity of human beings, the role of government and institutions, and the rights and duties of property owners has been an eye-opener for many students. Only after students confront the problematic nature of their own insensitivity can they begin to consider seriously world hunger not only as a problem of the Third World but also as one directly affecting themselves.

Evaluating Theories of World Hunger

To approach world hunger critically, I find it necessary to lead students through an examination and evaluation of the various explanations reported in Chapter 1, beginning with the Paddocks and ending with Susan George. For the biological/ecological section, I have had the assistance of a colleague who is a biologist and an ecologist. Together with the students we examine what constitutes an adequate diet, the effects of an inadequate diet, the meaning of malnutrition and undernutrition, and the repercussions of our own eating habits on people in the Third World. We also study the pressures that population and affluence place on the ecosphere—pressures that have resulted in the devastation of land, water pollution, shortages of fuel and fertilizer, and overfishing. In examining overpopulation and overconsumption, we inquire into their economic, political, and cultural causes and consider how the causes can be controlled.

The Meaning of Underdevelopment

After examining the theories of the Paddocks, Brown, and Borgstrom (see Chapter 1), we understand why overpopulation and overconsumption do not adequately account for the concentration of hunger in the Third World. This leads us to consider why the Third World is poor and what the relationship is between its poverty and its hunger. Since we have already discussed the term "development," we turn at this point to an examination of the term "underdevelopment."

Recalling first of all that language often masks or hides the reality of a situation, we consider some of the Third World's criticism of the label "underdeveloped." We ask whether it captures the Third World's experience of its own situation. Are the nations of the Third World simply not yet developed? Are they at a lower stage in the development process? Or have they in fact been kept in a state of "underdevelopment," that is, a state of dependency? Is it true, as some critics argue, that the term serves to hide the history of the exploitation of the Third World, that is, the assymetrical power relationship between the First World and the Third World, as well as the economic, political, and cultural vulnerability of the Third World?

Criticism of the term "underdeveloped" provides an opening to discuss the causes of the Third World's so-called underdevelopment as seen through the eyes of people in the Third World. Students, it must be pointed out, tend to label any criticism of the policies of their own government or corporations as communistic and to dismiss them as factually untrue. But they gradually become more open once they understand the reason for conducting the analysis from the perspective of the oppressed, and once they are given adequate documentation of specific criticisms of the First World.

I explain to the students that if someone is injured, you don't ask the persons who have inflicted an injury how it feels, nor do we expect them to be able to report on the extent of the injury. Moreover, we cannot trust the persons who are responsible for the injury to admit that they inflicted it or how they did the inflicting. It makes sense to ask the victim first. Applying this line of reasoning to the Third World, Robert McAfee Brown reports:

> . . . the way the poor view the world is closer to the reality of the world than the way the rich view it. Their "epistemology," i.e., their way of knowing, is accurate to a degree that is impossible for those who see the world only from the vantage point of privileges they want to retain.[2]

In documenting the Third World's criticism of the First World, I have found AID reports, congressional testimony, Senate reports, and the like especially helpful in confirming that self-interest has been a dominant motive in our nation's dealings with the Third World.

World Trade, Aid, and Investment

Next we use documents that emerged out of the Sixth and Seventh Special Sessions of the General Assembly of the United Nations calling for the establishment of a new international economic order (NIEO) as our point of reference. We then proceed to examine critically the systems of world trade, aid, and investment. In time the control that the First World exercises over those systems and the interests that they serve become apparent. Only after students understand how the international economic order is structured to the advantage of the First World and to the disadvantage of the Third World can they begin to examine food aid, trade in food, and the practices of the multinationals involved in food production. Then they are able to see how the problem of hunger is related to the larger problem of development. Hunger thus becomes not a problem in itself but a symptom of the systematic subjugation of the Third World by the First World.

At this point I challenge students to consider whether the NIEO reforms called for by the United Nations are themselves only palliative incremental measures. Do they merely tamper with the symptoms and leave the roots of the problem undisturbed? Is it possible to change fundamentally the inequitable relationship between the First and Third Worlds without radically restructuring the economic system that produced that relationship and continues to make it necessary? On the other hand, if we adopt the more radical position, must we abandon the NIEO reforms? Or is it possible to view those reforms as steps in the longer process of radically transforming the market system? In other words is it possible to approach the NIEO reforms in such a way that they become not palliative but creative incremental changes— changes that spur us on to work for deeper and long-lasting change?

My experience is that people must first realize that hunger is not simply the result of bad weather or overpopulation but of systems that make our overconsumption possible. Once they have grasped this fact, they can begin to make a connection between their own lives and the hunger of the people in the Third World. It becomes clear that hunger will not be alleviated by merely initiating population control measures in the Third World; it requires a fundamental change in the economic, political, and social systems and personal lifestyles of the First World. This awareness is usually accompanied by a change in the attitudes of students toward charity. While they see the positive effects of aid in terms of meeting immediate needs, they also recognize the fact that aid offers no panacea. If the terms of aid are not radically changed and linked with more fundamental structural change, aid may itself contribute more to the problem than to its solution.

The Moral Responsibility of Christians

Our analysis of world hunger and its relationship to our own systems and lifestyles provides an opportunity to consider the moral responsibility of

Christians in the First World. The social encyclicals provide a clear directive to Christians to work for personal and systemic change. Students frequently express surprise at the strong position of the Catholic church in these matters. They are puzzled because they have not previously been introduced to the social teaching of the church; they ask whether Christians can be expected to work for justice if the church with which most of them are familiar does not appear to be doing so.

We try to give the students a better understanding of what the church is doing in some parts of the world on behalf of justice. We also try to give them a stronger theological foundation for their own ethical reflection and action. Then we look at the church in Latin America and at the work of some Latin American liberation theologians. From time to time Maryknoll missioners returning from the Third World share their experiences and reflections on the church in both the Third World and the First World with the class. The activity of the church on behalf of the poor and oppressed in some parts of the world is an eye-opener. It provides a basis for a discussion of how the North American church might become more involved in and take a stronger position of leadership with regard to global poverty and hunger.

ACTION FOR JUSTICE

Student Projects

My course does not consist simply of readings and discussions. One aspect of the course that has been perhaps most meaningful for many students is the emphasis on student projects. The value of the projects is based on the old adage: "I hear and I forget; I see and I remember; I do and I understand." Student projects fulfill the following purposes:

1. They help students see that what we are studying is not just another "academic" problem. The lives of millions of people in the Third World depend to a large extent on how we in the First World perceive the hungry and relate to their sufferings. The way that we think and act as individuals and as a society can determine whether or not the poor can manage to live full, productive lives.

2. They help students both identify the hungry in our own society and develop a feeling of identity with them.

3. They can help students relate their major field of study and their future occupation to the problem of hunger.

4. Finally, they put students in touch with people and organizations in our society that are striving to combat world poverty and hunger. In this way students can see firsthand the channels available to us to work for global change.

Before describing some student projects and their outcomes, I need to explain that the projects are worked on throughout the semester by students as individuals or as members of a group. After they become involved in their projects and begin to relate their own experiences in the projects to the problems we are confronting in class, a change can be seen in the teacher/student relationship. In my opinion the students come very close to what Freire would call student/teachers. They actually begin to take possession of the teaching/learning act. Although I remain the teacher, I am no longer perceived as the sole source of information. The students themselves become experts and problem posers. It is exciting for me as a teacher to witness the change as students begin to take over their own educational process. What follows is a brief description of some of my students' projects.

Understanding undernutrition and powerlessness. A group of biology students chose a project in which they could study the effects of malnutrition and undernutrition. Under the supervision of the biologist mentioned previously, the students fed one group of mice an adequate diet and another group an inadequate diet. As the semester went by, the students kept close tabs on the mice, charting the physical development of both groups. It was noticed that the undernourished mice began to deteriorate physically and in time became so listless that they did not even have enough energy to respond when food was offered to them. Besides learning about the physical effects of undernutrition and malnutrition, the students made an unexpected discovery. They told the class how they had discovered the meaning of power as well as the power that comes through control of food. They spoke of the ease with which the powerful can make decisions affecting the lives of the powerless and how, given the absence of personal or societal moral restraints, the power of the powerful is limitless. They also gained a new appreciation of the word "dependency" and learned something about the advantage of controlling resources and keeping others dependent.

Understanding systemic injustice. Another group of students volunteered for the Meals-on-Wheels program for the semester. They delivered frozen meals prepared by area volunteers to elderly and housebound people living in the vicinity. The students received valuable personal contacts with individuals in need of food. They discovered that the elderly in our society are often hungry and dependent. They were disturbed that a so-called developed society could cast off those who were no longer economically productive, and that the reward for a lifetime of labor might be poverty and dependency. They wondered what might happen to their parents and themselves in old age. This experience led them to discuss with parents and grandparents the justice of our Social Security system, forced retirement, the tax system, and care for the elderly. The meaning of systemic injustice became a reality and not just an idea to students who saw firsthand that the hungry they encountered were hungry not through personal failure but through a failure of systems. Experience with the Meals-on-Wheels program led some students to research the treatment of the elderly in societies that we consider less "advanced" than our own. The students also learned what it means to be responsible for feeding the hungry. For example, if the Meals-on-Wheels program was suspended for a holiday or if a volunteer did not show up, the people who depended on the program would simply not eat.

Understanding bias in the news. A journalism major studied the coverage of hunger in several newspapers. Becoming adept at judging the quality of the reporting on hunger, she found that the political, more controversial aspect of the issue was rarely treated. Moreover, she began to see that so-called unbiased reporting was never really unbiased. All stories were written from a particular perspective. In the case of news reports on hunger, she found that they rarely challenged the United States government's perspective. As part of her project she wrote a column on hunger for the school newspaper and did a fine job of keeping the campus informed of issues related to global poverty and hunger.

Getting the facts on the infant-formula controversy. A nurse in the course, who was pregnant at the time, was interested in the infant-formula problem in the Third World. At first she was skeptical that companies producing the infant formula would play on the ignorance of the poor, as had been reported. From the Interfaith Center on Corporate Responsibility she received as much information on the issue as possible. Then she personally got in contact with representatives of the companies involved to discuss her findings with them. She found the companies reluctant even to discuss the matter; some were openly antagonistic. Finally she decided to urge radio and television stations to increase their coverage of the bottle-baby issue. As a result of her work, a local TV station offered to do a half-hour talk show on the topic.

Learning about food-reform lobbies. One student wanted to find out more about how lobbies for food work. In Washington she conferred with a lobbyist from Bread for the World, a Christian citizens' lobby concerned about hunger. Together they attended a meeting of representatives of various organizations concerned with the domestic hunger problem. The student got a firsthand glimpse of the amount and type of lobbying that goes on between the government and various social service groups. For the first time, she told the class, she saw the power that the powerless have when they organize and bargain together. From her discussions with the lobbyist and representatives of other organizations she learned about the tactics the powerful use to defuse challenges to their power, for example, the delay tactic, the divide-and-rule tactic, and the cooptation tactic. This young women received not only a new understanding of the amount of lobbying that goes on in Washington but also an appreciation for the dedication of the Bread for the World lobbyists. She told the class that as a result of her visit she saw for the first time the possibility of working for change as a viable career option.

Food and clothing drives. Food and clothing drives for the poor are common on campus. As their project, some students tried to make our food drive different. They set out to educate the donors about the complexity of the issues and the need for other, more long-term actions. The students who ran the Thanksgiving food drive found that people would much rather deal with hunger on the level of charity. They did not want to hear about the causes of hunger and preferred merely to give cans of food rather than take another option such as writing to their congressional representative. The students also learned—much to their surprise—that their fellow students were as apathetic and insensitive, if not more so, as they believed the older generation to be.

Organizing the poor to help themselves. One student volunteered his time one day a week with a group called the Eastern Service Workers. The Eastern Service Workers assist the poor in the inner city to acquire the skills that are needed to organize themselves and effectively deal with unscrupulous landlords, employers, the power company, the welfare bureaucracy, etc. The effectiveness of the Eastern Service Workers' approach became apparent when the student found out that even the state welfare department would send people whom they could not help because of red tape to their organization. The student has continued to volunteer even after our course concluded because he found that organizational skills were one of the most effective ways of helping the poor to help themselves. He grew to respect the poor that he worked with and found in them the courage and strength he had found lacking in many of his own acquaintances.

Conferring with organizations in favor of structural change. Some students have opted to visit organizations like the Interfaith Center on Corporate Responsibility, the Interreligious Taskforce on U.S. Food Policy, the Campaign for Human Development, Catholic Relief, Church World Service, the Quixote Center, Network, and others. People at those organizations have been extremely helpful and generous of their time. Without the enthusiastic support of such representatives, the student projects could not have been as successful as they have been.

One student usually makes arrangements for a group of four or five students to spend a day visiting the organization. Information is obtained about the organization and its projects so that the group can become familiar with the organization before its visit. The students aim to obtain first-hand information about the purposes of the organization; projects in which it is involved; its function, funding, successes, and failures; obstacles to the achievement of its purposes; and specific contributions that individuals and churches are making to the work of the organization. The students generally meet as a group with a representative of the organization who explains its operation and answers questions. Then, depending on the students' individual research interests, each student confers with an expert within the organization who is working in the area of the student's interest. Students on a visit to the Interfaith Center on Corporate Responsibility (ICCR), for example, met first as a group with Tim Smith, director of the ICCR. Afterward one student conferred with the resource person for the infant-formula project; another, with the expert on bank loans to South Africa; a third, with the expert on church holdings of securities issued by corporations producing military products; and a fourth, with the expert on agribusinesses in the Third World.

After their visit the students carried on a fair amount of independent research in their areas of special interest. Using materials obtained about the organization and their own areas of special interest as well as the results of their own critical reflections, they drew up a report of their findings and shared it with the class.

The results have been impressive. A real change in critical awareness has taken place among students involved in the projects. Some of them have become seriously committed to working for justice, as the following examples illustrate.

Examples of Actions for Justice

When the news media were carrying distressing stories about the threat of starvation to the people of Cambodia, a group of students decided to find out why the Cambodians were suffering and what was being done to help them. They spent a day at the Catholic Relief office, studying the crisis and the response of various relief organizations to it. They paid attention to TV and radio special reports on that topic and read practically all the articles published at the time by newspapers, magazines, and journals. Yet they were not satisfied with what they had learned from the media. Wanting to study the roots of the crisis, they went back over the history of the Vietnam War and the United States' involvement in it. Since many of them had been youngsters at the time of the war, they were not well informed about it. Soon they discovered that starvation in Cambodia was due not only to an inadequate harvest, the obstinacy of the Kampuchean government, and fighting between the Pol Pot and Samrin forces, but also to our military involvement in Southeast Asia. They learned about the economic, political, and cultural vulnerability of an underdeveloped country like Cambodia and how its people were paying a price for the superpowers' ideological and military warfare. Food aid to the Cambodians, as they could see, was only a temporary solution. More deep-rooted structural and systemic change would be needed. The command that the students acquired of the Cambodian crisis enabled them to discuss it not only with the class but also with their friends and families. They remarked frequently about how uninformed and unenlightened the American public is on such a crisis. As a result of the project, one of the students, a nurse, has volunteered to spend a summer in a refugee camp in Thailand.

One of the students who visited the ICCR became interested in the infant-formula problem in the Third World. As part of her project, she decided to make people at the university more aware of the problem and managed to have Nestlé products removed from campus vending machines and the campus food service.

As a result of their projects, four students decided to acquire direct, personal experience of problems of the poor. They felt personally committed to working for justice. Two of them worked as summer volunteers with the Holy Child Sisters in Mexico, helping people who were living on a refuse dump and deriving their livelihood from it. Another student spent her spring break as a volunteer in Appalachia with a group organized by our Campus Ministry. A third student is now a Peace Corps volunteer.

In addition to individual projects, the class engaged in several common projects. One was a trip to Rodale Organic Farm at Emmaus, Pennsylvania. There the class learned about various forms of experimental farming that restore nutrients to the land and avoid the use of expensive and often destructive or harmful pesticides and fertilizers. They also learned about various forms of experimental technology that are less energy- and capital-intensive, which could be adapted for use in the Third World. Rodale is trying to reclaim types of food like amaranth that are vanishing so that the global food supply can be protected in case disasters render more recent hybrids useless. Some of these alternative foods are rich in protein, require little fertilizer, and are viable under a number of conditions. The class also received a vegetarian meal prepared at Rodale's Fitness House—their test kitchen and dining room for their employees. Here too they saw a number of people who have found a way to combine an interest in world problems with a career.

We have also taken a trip to the United Nations to confer with a representative of the UN Development Program. He reinforced many of the ideas we were examining in class. His anecdotes and examples made many of the theories we were studying more concrete.

Each student, I should mention, also keeps a clipping file of newspaper and magazine articles that relate to course issues. Through these files the students keep abreast of the latest developments and learn to read between the lines of the media coverage. They also get a sense that what we are studying together is no mere abstract "academic" concern but a very real problem that we have the potential to change. An exciting dimension of the clipping file is that students often come across the names of individuals with whom they have confered while working on their projects. One student, for example, who was interested in the concept of the simple life, met Bishop Gumbleton at a local meeting of the Catholic Peace Fellowship. During that same semester she read about the bishop in the *New York Times* and saw him on TV during his visit with the American hostages in Iran at Christmas. This direct contact with people who are making the news enables students to see that people struggling for justice are not eccentric; they are persons very much like themselves who have chosen to take a stand.

The clipping files have the added benefit of involving the students' families and neighbors, so that these people too are on the lookout for articles of interest. This frequently results in worthwhile discussions about what the students are learning.

Guest speakers provide another dimension of value. A representative from the Action Center in Washington, D.C., discussed what other college students are doing about hunger on campuses throughout the country. Our speakers have included a local U.S. congressman, a representative of an agribusiness firm, a director of a diocesan feeding project, a lawyer who gave up corporate law practice to take tax-resistance cases, and a Sister who represents her religious community with the ICCR. These speakers give students an opportunity to meet and discuss issues of significance with people who are directly working on food and poverty issues.

An increased sensitivity to food and nutrition is always a by-product of the course. The students begin to observe the waste in the college cafeteria and the nutritional quality of the food they eat. One semester some students prepared a different nutritional food to be shared with the class each week so that they could expand their taste to coincide with their new knowledge of nutrition.

Results of Student Projects

The projects have proven to be pedagogically invaluable for a number of reasons. First of all, they counter our common tendency to approach global poverty and hunger as theoretical, abstract, and academic problems. Through their projects some students encounter for the first time people who are hungry and hear about their situation. Other students get to know the people and to identify the faces behind organizations working to alleviate hunger. Still other students encounter people who are opposed to action on behalf of the hungry. Thus hunger becomes for students what it essentially is—a human problem. The immediacy of the problem is reinforced through reading and clipping articles from newspapers, magazines, and journals and by listening to radio shows and watching TV news reports and news specials.

Throughout the course I stress the fact that the students are the corporate executives, government officials, social workers, voters, and investors of tomorrow. What they learn and think about world hunger today may affect the lives of more than 450 million people tomorrow. Since this will probably be the only time in the students' lives that they will have the time and opportunity to examine the problem of hunger in depth, it is essential for them to find out as much as they can about the roots of the problem and the changes needed to put an end to the suffering of so many.

Not only does the project highlight the concreteness and immediacy of the problem but it also frees students from narrowly identifying education with schooling. The poor themselves, people in various organizations, the students' families, their friends, the church, and the media all become sources of education as students draw them into dialogue.

The critical questioning that emerges in conversation with their contacts and the information that students acquire both from their contacts and the media enable them to put the educational experience acquired in school in perspective. The students' discovery of educational sources and experiences beyond the school and their ability to identify those sources and experiences as educational make the possibility of a broad and long-lasting education outside of the school a reality.

The projects also afford other agencies that educate in our society an opportunity to assume a more overt educational role. Students who worked in the Meals-on-Wheels project, for example, received an outstanding course on aging in American society from the old men and women to whom they brought meals. Tim Smith, director of the ICCR, made six aspiring corporate executives aware of the fact that religious institutions are a force to be reckoned with. The student who interviewed Bishop Gumbleton learned the significance of a simple lifestyle for members of the clergy so well that she made an appointment with her pastor the following week to discuss the matter further with him. The students' families also became more overtly involved in the educational process. Not only were they on the alert for magazine and newspaper clippings and radio and TV specials but in many cases they acted also as sounding boards for the new ideas that the students were coming upon.

The projects gave the students themselves an opportunity to become student/teachers in conversations with their contacts, families, and friends. In sharing experiences and findings with the class, they became both experts and co-investigators in areas they had researched. It was exciting to watch the students' respect for one another's intellectual and critical ability develop during the course of the semester.

Beyond the immediate benefits just mentioned, the projects provided for many students an invaluable link between their chosen occupation and a possible solution to the problem of hunger. It became quite clear to many that unless they acted differently from their predecessors in business, law, politics, and other occupations, hunger and poverty would continue to plague our global society. Without a revolutionary change in values and actions, nothing will change.

Finally, for some students the projects provided contact with an organization that was not just talking about hunger but actually doing something concrete to alleviate it. On their visit to the organization, students met individuals who had chosen to take a stand and learned of a vast network of people concerned about the problems we were studying. A number of students remarked that the people they met appeared to be as normal as persons next door—not extremists or fanatics but middle-class Americans who had decided to work for what they believed in. The students were impressed with the soundness of their logic and the frankness of their speech. These personal contacts, I believe, made a lasting impression.

Although the students may not remember the content of our readings or class discussions, their projects will probably stay with them as a reminder of the fact that it is possible to work for change in our society and the world. After leaving school, they will not have to look very far for support of their own efforts on behalf of justice.

As with all educational endeavors, it is difficult to predict the long-term effect of our efforts on the lives of students. This is especially true if we measure success not on the basis of test scores or financial and professional achievements but on change in consciousness and on actions for justice.

The evaluations of my students at the end of our course have given me hope, however. Let me share just a few of their comments with you:

> The course urged me to become more aware of the present world situation. . . . I now feel interested and involved. I can carry on a knowledgeable conversation about world affairs and can contribute educated opinions. . . .

> The most valuable aspect of this course for me was how it made me open up and question my own beliefs and thoughts as a Christian. Our class discussions forced me to take a stand. . . .

> The most valuable aspect of the course was the opportunity it gave the students to reevaluate their lives, the world, and the part they play in the world. . . .

> At times the course seemed very trying and unsettling. It raised questions about my beliefs, values, and responsibilities. . . .

> The course made me critical of situations that usually would not stir much interest. It taught me to fight, not just to sit back. . . .

> I feel that I have grown so much in my ideas and thoughts. What was good was that I really began to apply what I had learned to my life and it helped me to deal with things. . . .

SUMMARY OF PART III

In Chapter 13 we discussed the role of the following agencies in supporting the status quo in our society: churches and synagogues, the family, the media, corporations, the government, and social agencies. Using the findings of sociologist Will Herberg, we discovered the extent to which Americans tend to identify adherence to a religion with belief in the American way of life. As a result, the prophetic dimension of the Hebraic-Christian tradition has become submerged or lost to our consciousness.

Next we examined critically the role of education in the United States. We saw how the schools have served as a sorting device to channel children of the upper and middle classes toward higher education and positions at the top of the social pyramid, while they at the same time direct lower-class children toward positions at the bottom of the social pyramid. It was proposed that the schools often mask the true causes of social ills.

In Chapter 15 the methodology of Brazilian educator Paulo Freire served as the basis for a consideration of the humanizing purpose of education. We studied the theories of education advocated by the Social Reconstructionist school and by the Synod of Catholic Bishops.

Finally we tried to illustrate ways of educating students to a greater sensitivity toward world hunger. On the basis of my own course, we learned about the use of such traditional methods as discussions and readings to achieve this purpose. Then we took up the method of student projects that seek to involve students in action for justice.

In conclusion, we cannot expect that educating for justice will solve the problem of world hunger. It is, however, a necessary and integral part of the process. It is needed in order to transform radically systems and values that produce today suffering for most members of the human race. The task that confronts Christian educators is neither easy nor popular. We can expect resistance from school administrators, church officials, our students, their families, and others. For what we are challenging is nothing less than the system and the values that have made the American way of life possible. The question that we need to keep raising for ourselves and others is "Has the American way of life become more sacred to us than life itself?"

I usually conclude my course by sharing one of my favorite parables by Daniel Berrigan with my students. So it is fitting to conclude this book in the same manner.

MY SON JOHN—A PARABLE BY DANIEL BERRIGAN

There was once a child who used to play only in the front yard, where everyone was like himself. One day, however, after a passage at arms with a younger brother, he was sent for punishment into the back yard.

Back yard? He hadn't known there was one. A sea change, a revelation! Tanners, shoemakers, alleys, gutters, children, wash women, markets, flower carts, beggars. There was not much time for tears. The child sat on the back stoop half frightened, totally fascinated.

After a while he was in the thick of it, playing with the others; after a few hours he too was dirty and joyful. It was as though a sprite, benign and mischievous, had led him blindfolded into a place of delights, and then whisked the darkness away.

His exile ended, as such things will. He was called back indoors, and on into the front yard. He went in with a new look on his face. He knew something for the first time. It had come to him with the delicacy and unpredictability of lightning, with the logic of nature, of water and sun, of the opening of a door. He knew now, that a front yard existed because a back yard existed. He knew alternatives; in the name of punishment, a dangerous gift was in his hands. Front will have back, rich will have poor, master will have slave, pride will have fall, blood will have blood.

He could also do sums in a new way. I mean, he would cry aloud in later years, I know why our ladder has fifty rungs. I know how we got up and stay up. I know whose filth and sweat make us smell like roses. I mean bodies, cordwood, something to walk on, human lives, good stupid rungs of wood locked in place, steady in the middle, tight in the socket, dumb, petrified. Count them, climb them, walk on them!

The boy went back indoors and got washed and admonished and kissed and came out the front door. Does he now smell like roses, look like his mother, talk like his father? Is he fervent for one kind of justice, which is to say, for his kind of injustice? Is he clean as a cravat, a good business head, ready for law or medicine or army—or chancery?

What had he lost; what had he gained? Was he tamed, housebroken, the rich kid unsullied by the barnyard, a good metallurgic triumph, papa's pride, mama's sacramental, the lion who lies down on command, the ambulatory hearthside rug?

No. The story has a happy ending. State didn't win. Neither did church. Nor papa nor mama nor dominations nor powers, nor fat ease nor lean revenge, nor height nor breadth nor depth. Our story has a happy ending. Which is to say:

The boy stood above the dirty water that had collected in a broken street. And he did a very simple thing. He took off his clothes. All the little boys and girls had done the same thing. They stood there together in the silence of an epiphany. The boy took off his clothes, and he saw himself. And he saw the world.

I see, he said, a boy looking back at me, a boy who is like myself; two hands, two arms, two eyes, a hairy head, a thingummy between two legs. I can scoop up dirty water and throw it. I can wade in. I can wade deeper. I can get in over my head. I can pee gently. Why, the whole world is like myself, looking back, smiling, frowning, mugging, pushing, joining hands, dancing. And getting hungry, and staying hungry. And sweating (he went on—because he stood there for years—the thing really had no end) and suffering, sinning, rejoicing, marrying, child bearing. And dying. And so on and so on.

The boy came back to the front lawn, to the tranquil house, to the poodles and terriers and doormen. But he was never again the same. How could he be? The question in his eyes was the measure of his awakening. It was himself; he was a question to himself. To ask the question at all was dangerous, as dangerous as it was to be alive. To listen to answers, to be grateful for help, to seek light in his perplexity—all this he did, and more. But the more was all the difference. For every answer fed the question. The fire could never be put out, never again.

How to be man, how to be himself, how to be messenger, how not to forget the message, how to bring the good news or the bad news from the back yard into the front yard? Ah, he had broken through.

Men, beware a man.[3]

It is my hope that what I have written here will help others to bring the good news or the bad news from the back yard into the front yard.

NOTES

CHAPTER 1
CAUSES OF THE PROBLEM

1. U.S. Department of Agriculture, Economic Research Service, *The World Food Situation and Prospects to 1985,* Foreign Agricultural Economic Report No. 98 (Washington, D.C.: Government Printing Office, 1974), p. 21.

2. Ibid., p. 60.

3. Ibid., pp. 21–22.

4. Ibid., p. 22.

5. Lester R. Brown, *The Twenty-Ninth Day: Accommodating Human Needs and Numbers to the Earth's Resources* (New York: W.W. Norton, 1978), p. 19.

6. Ibid., p. 19.

7. Ibid.

8. Ibid., pp. 19–20.

9. Ibid., p. 21.

10. U.S. Department of Agriculture, p. 3.

11. Ibid.

12. Ibid., p. 10.

13. Lester R. Brown, *By Bread Alone* (New York: Praeger Publishers, 1974), pp. 4–5.

14. William Paddock and Paul Paddock, *Famine 1975! America's Decision: Who Will Survive?* (Boston: Little, Brown, 1967), p. 46.

15. Ibid., p. 229.

16. Ibid., p. 209.

17. Although the morality of the application of triage to the Third World cannot be examined here, I refer you to an excellent study: George R. Lucas, Jr., and Thomas W. Ogletree, eds., *Lifeboat Ethics: The Moral Dilemmas of World Hunger* (New York: Harper & Row, 1976).

18. It should be noted that *Famine 1975!* was reissued in 1976 under the title *Time of Famines: America and the World Food Crisis.* Despite the appearance of new research on the complexity of the hunger issue, the authors' analysis of the problem and their response to it remain the same in the new book.

19. Brown, *By Bread Alone,* p. 6.

20. Ibid., p. 43.

21. Ibid., p. 184.

22. Ibid., p. 12.

23. Georg Borgstrom, *The Food and People Dilemma,* The Man-Environment System Series (North Scituate, Mass.: Duxbury Press, a Division of Wadsworth Publishing Co., 1973), p. 2.

24. Ibid., p. 38.

25. Ibid., p. 64.

26. Ibid., p. 57.

27. Ibid., p. 108.

28. Frances Moore Lappé and Joseph Collins, *Food First: Beyond the Myth of Scarcity* (Boston: Houghton Mifflin, 1977), p. 15.

29. Ibid., p. 200.

30. Ibid., p. 381.

31. Ibid., p. 373.

32. Ibid., p. 374.

33. Ibid., p. 408.

34. Ibid., pp. 407–8.

35. Susan George, *How the Other Half Dies: The Real Reasons for World Hunger* (Montclair, N.J.: Allanheld, Osmun, 1977), pp. 14–15.

36. Ibid., p. 98.

37. Ibid., p. 19.

38. Ibid., p. 18.

39. Ibid., p. xviii.

40. Ibid., p. 237.

41. Lappé and Collins, p. 8.

42. Denis Goulet, *The Cruel Choice: A New Concept in the Theory of Development* (New York: Atheneum Publications, 1971), pp. 282–3.

43. The discussion of the relationship of the rich and poor nations in ethical terms has been generated in part for me by the work of Denis Goulet. See especially on this point his book, *The Cruel Choice: A New Concept in the Theory of Development* (New York: Atheneum Publications, 1971), p. 53.

CHAPTER 2
ROOTS OF THE THIRD WORLD'S POVERTY

1. Theotonio Dos Santos, "The Structure of Dependence," in *The Political Economy of Development and Underdevelopment,* ed. Charles K. Wilber (New York: Random House, 1973), pp. 110–11.

2. James O'Connor, "The Meaning of Economic Imperialism," in *Readings in U.S. Imperialism,* ed. K. T. Fann and Donald C. Hodges (Boston: Porter Sargent, 1971), pp. 25–26.

3. Michael Harrington, *The Vast Majority: A Journey to the World's Poor* (New York: Simon & Schuster, 1977), p. 126.

4. Michael Barratt Brown, *The Economics of Imperialism* (Baltimore: Penguin, 1974), p. 256.

5. For this discussion of Marx I am grateful to Nancy Bancroft for conversations with her on Marx and for sharing the first chapter of her dissertation with me.

6. Karl Marx, *Grundrisse der Kritik der politschen Okonomie* (Berlin: Dietz Verlag, 1953), pp. 311–13, 19, as translated in Harrington, *The Vast Majority,* p. 118.

7. Paul M. Sweezy, *The Present as History* (New York: Monthly Review Press, 1953), pp. 205–10.

8. Ibid., p. 206.

9. Michael Harrington, *The Twilight of Capitalism* (New York: Simon & Schuster, 1975), p. 307.

10. Jack A. Nelson, *Hunger for Justice: The Politics of Food and Faith* (Maryknoll, N.Y.: Orbis Books, 1980).

CHAPTER 3
THE STRUCTURE OF WORLD TRADE AND ITS EFFECTS ON THE THIRD WORLD

1. Interreligious Taskforce on U.S. Food Policy, "The United States and the Changing International Economic Order," *Hunger,* no. 4 (1976):2.

2. Brennon Jones, "International Commodity Trade," Bread for the World, Background Paper, no. 35 (April 1979).

3. Samir Amin, *Accumulation on a World Scale* (1971, English ed., New York: Monthly Review Press, 1974); Arghiri Emmanuel, *Unequal Exchange: A Study of the Imperialism of Trade* (New York: Monthly Review Press, 1972).

4. Emmanuel, p. xxx.

5. Michael Harrington, *The Vast Majority: A Journey to the World's Poor* (New York: Simon & Schuster, 1977), p. 143.

6. Amin, p. 78.

7. Ibid., p. 61.

8. Cheryl Payer, *Commodity Trade of the Third World* (New York: John Wiley & Sons, 1975), p. viii.

9. Jones.

10. Ibid.

11. Payer, p. ix.

12. Ibid.

13. Ibid., p. viii.

14. Orlando Letelier and Michael Moffitt, "The International Economic Order," *TNI Pamphlet Series,* no. 2 (Washington, D.C.: Transnational Institute, 1977), p. 12.

15. Harald Malmgren, *Trade for Development* (Washington: Overseas Development Council, 1971), p. 15.

16. Harrington, p. 236.

17. Presidential Commission on World Hunger, *Overcoming World Hunger: The Challenge Ahead* (Washington, D.C.: U.S. Government Printing Office, 1980), p. 64.

18. Malmgren, p. 16.

19. Harrington, p. 237.

20. Presidential Commission on World Hunger, p. 61.

21. Hans W. Singer and Javed A. Ansari, *Rich and Poor Countries* (Baltimore: The Johns Hopkins University Press, 1977), pp. 80–81.

22. Ibid., p. 85.

23. Radha Sinha, *Food and Poverty* (New York: Holmes and Meier, 1976), p. 94.

24. Singer and Ansari, p. 130.

25. Sinha, p. 97.

26. Hal Sheets, "Big Money in Hunger," *Worldview Symposium on Food and Hunger* (New York: Council on Religion and International Affairs, 1976) and "ABC News Closeup," 27 June 1975, "Food: the Crisis of Price."

27. Seymour Melman, *The Permanent War Economy* (New York: Simon & Schuster, 1974), pp. 92–93.

28. Ibid., p. 89.

29. Ibid., p. 90.

30. For a more detailed study of the following see Sheets.

31. Dan Morgan, *Merchants of Grain* (New York: Viking Press, 1979), p. 153.

32. Ibid., p. 157.

33. Hal Sheets.

34. Ibid.

35. Emma Rothschild, "Food Politics," *Foreign Affairs* 54 (1976) :296.

36. Emma Rothschild, "For Some, a Feast of Crumbs," *New York Times*, 10 January 1977, p. 21.

CHAPTER 4
THE STRUCTURE OF AID AND ITS EFFECTS
ON THE THIRD WORLD

1. Leon Howell, "The Geopolitics of 'Aid': The Poorest Rank Lowest," *Christianity and Crisis*, 28 May 1979, p. 143.

2. Ibid., p. 143.

3. *Development: New Approaches*, Intercom 69 (New York: Center for War/Peace Studies of the New York Friends Group, 1972), p. 28.

4. Mahbub ul Haq, "Rich and Poor Nations—A New Formula for Closing the Gap," *Christian Science Monitor,* 29 August 1975, p. 15.

5. Cheryl Payer, *The Debt Trap* (New York: Monthly Review Press 1974), p. ix.

6. Ibid., p. 13.

7. Ibid., p. 33.

8. Ibid., pp. 41–42.

9. Bruce Nissen, "Building the World Bank," in *The Trojan Horse,* ed. Steve Weissman (San Francisco: Ramparts Press, 1974), p. 53.

10. John White, *The Politics of Foreign Aid* (New York: St. Martin's Press, 1974), p. 170.

11. Nissen, p. 54.

12. Susan George, *How the Other Half Dies: The Real Reasons for World Hunger* (Montclair, N.J.: Allanheld, Osmun, 1977), p. 209.

13. James Morrell, "Foreign Aid: Evading the Control of Congress," *International Policy Report*, Center for International Policy, III (January 1977):19–20.

14. Ibid., p. 1.

15. Denis Goulet and Michael Hudson, *The Myth of Aid: The Hidden Agenda of the Development Reports* (New York and Maryknoll: IDOC and Orbis Books, 1971), p. 80. This part of the book is by Hudson.

16. Overseas Development Council, *The United States and World Development: Agenda 1977* (New York and Washington: Praeger and ODC, 1977), p. 130.

17. Ann Crittenden, "A Tough Report Card for A.I.D. Program," *New York Times*, 26 February 1978, p. 9.

18. Howell, p. 143.

19. Susan DeMarco and Susan Sechler's study—*The Fields Have Turned Brown: Four Essays on World Hunger* (Washington, D.C.: The Agribusiness Accountability Project, 1975), pp. 36–52—has been especially helpful for this discussion of PL 480.

20. Marvin R. Duncan et al., *International Trade and American Agriculture* (Kansas City, Mo.: Federal Reserve Bank, 1975), p. 22.

21. U.S. General Accounting Office, *The Overseas Food Donation Program—Its Constraints and Problems*, Report of the Comptroller General of the United States to the Congress (Washington, D.C.: General Accounting Office, 1975), p. 1.

22. Hubert H. Humphrey (84th Congress, First Session, Senate Committee on

Agriculture and Forestry: *Hearings: Policies and Operations of Public Law 480*, 1957), p. 129.

23. U. S. General Accounting Office, *The Overseas Food Donation Program*, p. 1.

24. U. S. Congress, House, *Food for Peace Program 1974 Annual Report*, House Doc. 94-352, 94th Congress, 2d sess., 1976, p. 1.

25. Ibid., p. 5.

26. DeMarco and Sechler, p. 39.

27. *NARMIC* (National Action Research into the Military Industrial Complex) *Memo on PL 480*, Research Project of the American Friends Service Committee, 24 March 1975 (mimeographed).

28. U.S. Congress, House, *Food for Peace Program 1974 Annual Report*, p. 9.

29. Emma Rothschild, "Is It Time to End Food for Peace?" *New York Times Magazine*, 13 March 1977, p. 44.

30. U.S. Congress, Senate, Testimony of the Interreligious Taskforce, S 5351, and Rothschild, "Is It Time?" p. 15.

31. Daniel Balz, "Food for Peace—Or Politics," in *Food for People, Not for Profit*, ed. Catherine Lerza and Michael Jacobson (New York: Ballantine, 1975), p. 278.

32. Interreligious Taskforce on U.S. Food Policy, "Reforms Needed in Farm and Food Policy: The Price Support System, Food Aid, and the Food Stamp Program," *Hunger*, no. 9 (March 1977):5.

33. NARMIC Memo, p. 4.

34. Stephen S. Rosenfeld, "The Politics of Food," *Foreign Policy* 14 (Spring 1974), 17–29.

35. NARMIC Memo, p. 4, and Interreligious Taskforce, "Reforms," p. 5.

36. Emma Rothschild, "The Rats Don't Starve," *New York Times,* 11 January 1977, p. 33.

37. U.S. Congress, House, *Annual Report*, p. 9.

38. Kai Bird and Sue Goldmark, "Food Aid vs. Development," *Worldview* (January/February 1977): 40.

39. Interreligious Taskforce, "Reforms," p. 5.

40. Goulet and Hudson, p. 86.

41. DeMarco and Sechler, p. 44.

42. Goulet and Hudson, p. 86.

43. U.S. Congress, House, *Annual Report,* p. 9.

44. Goulet and Hudson, p. 86.

45. U.S. Congress, House, *Annual Report,* p. 2.

46. Ibid., p. 17.

47. Ibid.

48. Susan DeMarco and Susan Sechler's study *The Fields Have Turned Brown*, was especially helpful for this discussion of the Private Trade Entity Program.

49. DeMarco and Sechler, p. 47.

50. Dan Morgan, "Byzantine World of Cargo Contracts," *Washington Post*, 9 March 1975, p. 20.

51. Ibid.

52. U.S. Office of Political Research, *Potential Implications of Trends in World Population, Food Production, and Climate* (Washington: Library of Congress, 1974), pp. 39–40.

CHAPTER 5
MULTINATIONAL CORPORATIONS AND THE THIRD WORLD

1. Paul Sweezy, *Modern Capitalism and Other Essays* (New York and London: Monthly Review Press, 1972), pp. 6–12.

2. Ibid., p. 7.

3. Ibid., p. 8.

4. Ibid.

5. Richard J. Barnet and Ronald E. Müller, *Global Reach* (New York: Simon & Schuster, 1974), p. 153.

6. Ibid., p. 153.

7. Ibid., p. 139.

8. Robert J. Ledogar, *Hungry for Profits: U.S. Food and Drug Multinationals in Latin America* (New York: IDOC/ North America, 1975), p. 1.

9. Barnet and Müller, p. 157.

10. Ibid.

11. Ibid., pp. 157, 158.

12. Ibid., p. 159.

13. Ibid., p. 153.

14. Ibid., pp. 153–154.

15. Ibid., pp. 166–68.

16. Ronald Müller, "The Multinational Corporation and the Underdevelopment of the Third World, in *The Political Economy of Development and Underdevelopment,* ed. Charles K. Wilber (New York: Random House, 1973), p. 133.

17. Barnet and Müller, p. 169.

18. Ibid., p. 173 ff.

19. Ledogar, p. 96.

20. Ibid.

21. Ibid., p. 97.

22. Ibid., p. 98.

23. Corporate Information Center, "Gulf & Western in the Dominican Republic: II," *CIC Brief* (New York: Interfaith Center on Corporate Responsibility (November–December 1976): 3B.

24. Ibid., p. 3A.

25. Ledogar, p. 77.

26. Ibid., p. 83.

27. Ibid., pp. 85–86.

28. Ibid., p. 2.

29. Ibid., p. 122.

30. Ibid., p. 112.

31. Ibid., p. 127.

32. Henry J. Frundt with Douglas Clement, "Requirements for a Safe Bottle," *Agribusiness Manual* (New York: Interfaith Center on Corporate Responsibility, 1978), pp. iv, 25.

33. Ibid.

34. Leah Margulies, "A Critical Essay on the Role of Promotion in Bottle Feeding," *Agribusiness Manual* (New York: Interfaith Center on Corporate Responsibility, 1978), pp. iv, 16.

35. Leah Margulies, "Baby Formula Abroad: Exporting Infant Malnutrition," *Christianity and Crisis*, 10 November 1975, p. 3.

CHAPTER 6
PLANTING THE SEEDS OF CHANGE

1. Denis Goulet, *The Cruel Choice: A New Concept in the Theory of Development* (New York: Atheneum Publishers, 1971), pp. 294–98.

2. Ibid., p. 295.

3. Michael Harrington, *The Vast Majority: A Journey to the World's Poor* (New York: Simon & Schuster, 1977), p. 191.

4. Ibid., p. 218.

5. Goulet, p. x.

6. Paulo Freire, *Pedagogy of the Oppressed* (Brazilian edition, 1968; English translation: New York: Herder and Herder, 1972), p. 44.

7. Goulet, p. 292.

CHAPTER 7
RECOVERING OUR RELIGIOUS TRADITION

1. Robert N. Bellah, *The Broken Covenant* (New York: Seabury Press, 1975), p. 63. This discussion of the crisis in our society is based on Bellah's book.

2. Ibid., pp. 17–18.

3. Quoted in Ibid., p. 20.

4. Ibid., p. 152.

5. Denis Goulet, *The Cruel Choice: A New Concept in the Theory of Development* (New York: Atheneum Publishers, 1971). See especially Chapters 6 and 11 for a fuller discussion of this point.

6. Ibid., p. 143.

7. Ibid., p. 162.

8. Dorothee Sölle, *Death By Bread Alone* (Philadelphia: Fortress Press, 1978), p. 26.

CHAPTER 8
OUR RESPONSIBILITY TO THE POOR AND HUNGRY:
A NONRELIGIOUS PERSPECTIVE

1. Denis Goulet, *The Cruel Choice: A New Concept in the Theory of Development* (New York: Atheneum Publishers, 1971), p. 86.

2. Ibid., p. 129.

3. Ibid., p. 243.

4. Ibid., p. 91.

5. Ibid., p. 123–24.

6. Ibid., p. 237.

7. Ibid., p. 135.

8. I am indebted to Joseph Lombardi, S.J., for several conversations with him on Rawls and for a paper presented by him at a seminar, "Justice—A Philosophical Overview of the Term as Operative in Various Systems of Thought," St. Joseph's College, Philadelphia, Spring 1977.

9. John Rawls, *A Theory of Justice* (Cambridge: The Belknap Press of Harvard University Press, 1971), p. 75.

10. Lombardi, p. 5.

11. Ibid., app.

12. Ibid., p. 8.

13. Ibid., p. 9.

14. William K. Frankena, *Ethics*, 2nd ed. (Englewood Cliffs; N.J.: Prentice-Hall, 1973), p. 49.

15. Ibid., p. 51.

16. Ibid., pp. 42–52.

17. William K. Frankena, "Moral Philosophy and World Hunger," in *World Hunger and Moral Obligation*, ed. William Aiken and Hugh La Follette (Englewood Cliffs, N.J.: Prentice-Hall, 1977), pp. 66–84.

18. Ibid., p. 81.

19. Ibid.

20. Ibid., p. 83.

21. Brian Wren, *Education for Justice: Pedagogical Principles* (Maryknoll, N.Y.: Orbis Books, 1977), p. 53.

22. Ibid., p. 63.

23. Frankena, *Ethics*, p. 58.

24. Ibid.

25. Gene Outka, *Agape: An Ethical Analysis* (New Haven, Conn.: Yale University Press, 1972), p. 190.

26. Ibid., p. 263.

27. Ibid., pp. 263–66.

CHAPTER 9
POLITICAL THEOLOGY AND LIBERATION THEOLOGY

1. Juan Luis Segundo, S.J., *Our Idea of God* (Maryknoll N.Y.: Orbis Books, 1974), p. 182.

2. Ibid., p. 155.

3. Ibid., p. 180.

4. Robert McAfee Brown, *Theology in a New Key* (Philadelphia: Westminster Press, 1978), p. 81.

5. Ibid.

6. For this discussion, I am indebted to Francis Fiorenza for his clear analysis of the distinctions between liberation theology and political theology in his articles "Political Theology and Liberation Theology: An Inquiry into Their Fundamental Meaning," in *Liberation, Revolution, and Freedom*, ed. Thomas M. McFadden (New York: Seabury Press, 1975), pp. 3–29, and Francis P. Fiorenza, "Latin American Liberation Theology," *Interpretation* 28 (1974):441–57.

7. Francis P. Fiorenza, "Political Theology," p. 14.

8. Ibid., p. 9.

9. Claude Geffre and Gustavo Gutiérrez, *The Mystical and Political Dimension of the Christian Faith* (New York: Herder and Herder, 1974), p. 69.

10. Ibid., p. 10.

11. Ibid.

12. Fiorenza, "Political Theology," pp. 15–16.

13. Fiorenza, "Latin American Liberation Theology," p. 443. While this criticism may be true of some political theologians, it cannot be applied to all, particularly to Sölle.

14. Johannes B. Metz, "The Church's Social Function in the Light of a 'Political

Theology,' " in *Faith and the World of Politics*, ed. Johannes B. Metz (New York: Paulist Press, 1968), p. 8.

15. Ibid., p. 13.

16. Gustavo Gutiérrez, *A Theology of Liberation*, trans. Sister Caridad Inda and John Eagleson (Maryknoll, N.Y.: Orbis Books, 1973), p. 157.

17. Ibid., p. 231. Gutiérrez's first quote is from Wolfhart Pannenberg.

18. Hugo Assmann, *Theology for a Nomad Church* (1973, English ed.: Maryknoll, N.Y.: Orbis Books, 1976), pp. 34–35.

19. Ibid., p. 70.

20. Gutiérrez, *Theology of Liberation*, p. 267.

21. Quoted in ibid., p. 114.

22. Ibid., p. 113.

23. José María González-Ruiz, "The Public Character of the Christian Message and of Contemporary Society," in *Faith and the World of Politics*, ed. Metz, p. 58.

CHAPTER 10
THE METHODOLOGY OF LIBERATION THEOLOGY

1. Hugo Assmann, *Theology for a Nomad Church* (Maryknoll, N.Y.: Orbis Books, 1976), p. 54.

2. Juan Luis Segundo, S.J., *The Liberation of Theology*, trans. John Drury (Maryknoll, N.Y.: Orbis Books, 1976), p. 27.

3. Raul Vidales, "Methodological Issues in Liberation Theology," in *Frontiers of Theology in Latin America*, ed. Rosino Gibellini (Maryknoll, N.Y.: Orbis Books, 1979), p. 80.

4. Ibid., p. 85.

5. Assmann, p. 45.

6. Goulet's discussion of underdevelopment in *The Cruel Choice*, p. xv, is especially relevant here.

7. Gustavo Gutiérrez, *A Theology of Liberation* (Maryknoll, N.Y.: Orbis Books, 1973), p. 91.

8. Denis Goulet, *The Cruel Choice: A New Concept in the Theory of Development* (New York: Atheneum Publishers, 1971), p. 126.

9. Ibid., p. xix.

CHAPTER 11
WORLD HUNGER IN THE LIGHT OF FAITH

1. Gustavo Gutiérrez, *A Theology of Liberation* (Maryknoll, N.Y.: Orbis Books, 1973), p. 152.

2. Juan Luis Segundo, S.J., *Our Idea of God* (Maryknoll, N.Y.: Orbis Books, 1974), p. 66.

3. Ibid., p. 63.

4. Ibid., p. 66.

5. Antonio Pérez-Esclarín, *Atheism and Liberation* (Maryknoll, N.Y.: Orbis Books, 1978), p. 79.

6. Peréz-Esclarín, p. 80.

7. Ibid., p. 83.

8. Ibid., p. 93.

9. Gustavo Gutiérrez, "Liberation, Theology and Proclamation," in *Mystical and Political Dimension of the Christian faith*, ed. Geffre and Gutiérrez (New York: Herder and Herder, 1974), p. 59.

10. Ibid.

11. Dorothee Sölle, "Christ and Humanity: Their Role in the Search for Personal Identity," in *From Alienation to At-one-ness*, ed. Franics A. Eigo, O.S.A. (Villanova, Pa.: Villanova University Press, 1977), p. 175.

12. Gustavo Gutiérrez, "Liberation Praxis and Christian Faith," in *Frontiers of Theology in Latin America*, ed. Gibellini (Maryknoll: Orbis Books, 1979), p. 21.

13. Gutiérrez, *A Theology of Liberation*, p. 195.

14. Peréz-Esclarín, pp. 86–87.

15. Gutiérrcz, *A Theology of Liberation*, p. 177.

16. Ibid.

17. Dorothee Sölle, *Beyond Mere Dialogue: On Being Christian and Socialist*, (Detroit: American Christians Toward Socialism, 1978), p. 10.

18. Gutiérrez, *Frontiers*, p. 8.

19. Albert Camus, *The Plague,* trans. Stuart Gilbert (New York: The Modern Library, 1948), p. 228.

CHAPTER 12
THE SOCIAL TEACHINGS OF THE CHRISTIAN CHURCHES

1. David Hollenbach, *Claims in Conflict* (New York: Paulist Press, 1979).

2. Pius XI, *Quadragesimo Anno* in *Seven Great Encyclicals*, with an introduction by William J. Gibbons, S.J. (Glenrock, N.J.: Paulist Press, 1963), p. 149.

3. Ibid., p. 154.

4. Hollenbach, p. 52.

5. John XXIII, *Mater et Magistra* in *The Gospel of Peace and Justice*, ed. Joseph Gremillion (Maryknoll, N.Y.: Orbis Books, 1976), pp. 177–78.

6. Ibid., p. 180.

7. John XXIII, *Pacem in Terris* in Gremillion, p. 203.

8. Ibid., p. 204.

9. Ibid., p. 207.

10. Second Vatican Council, *Gaudium et Spes* in Gremillion, p. 264.

11. Ibid., pp. 299 and 301.

12. Ibid., p. 305.

13. Ibid., p. 321.

14. Ibid., p. 322.

15. Paul VI, *Populorum Progressio* in Gremillion, pp. 393–94.

16. Ibid., p. 394.

17. Ibid., pp. 392–93.

18. Ibid., p. 403.

19. Ibid., p. 395.

20. Ibid., pp. 400–01.

21. Ibid., p. 402.

22. Ibid., p. 405.

23. Ibid.

24. Ibid., pp. 405–06.

25. Ibid., pp. 401–02.

26. Synod of Bishops, Second General Assembly, *Justice in the World* in Gremillion, p. 515.

27. Ibid., p. 516.

28. Ibid., p. 517.

29. Ibid., pp. 520–21.

30. Ibid., p. 527.

31. Ibid., p. 528.

32. Ibid., p. 521.

33. Ibid., p. 529.

34. John Paul II, "Homily at Yankee Stadium," *Catholic Mind* 78 (January 1980): 23.

35. Ibid.

36. Ibid., p. 21.

37. Ibid., p. 22.

38. Ibid., p. 20.

39. Paul Bock, *In Search of a Responsible World Society* (Philadelphia: Westminster Press, 1974), p. 22. For a complete discussion of the social teaching of the Protestant churches, see Bock's study, which I found most helpful for this analysis.

40. Ibid., p. 23.

41. *Man's Disorder and God's Design*, The Amsterdam Assembly Series, 5 vols. (New York: Harper and Brothers, 1949). Vol. 5, *The First Assembly of the World Council of Churches, Official Report,* ed. W. A. Visser't Hooft, p. 128.

42. Bock, p. 23.

43. C. I. Itty, "Are We Yet Awake? The Development Debate Within the Ecumenical Movement," *The Ecumenical Review* (January 1974):15.

44. *Evanston Speaks: Reports from the Second Assembly of the World Council of Churches, 1954* (Geneva: WCC, 1955), pp. 42–43.

45. *The New Delhi Report: The Third Assembly of the World Council of Churches,* ed. W. A. Visser't Hooft (Association Press, 1962), pp. 94–95.

46. *The Uppsala Report 1968: Official Report of the Fourth Assembly of the World Council of Churches,* ed. Norman Goodall (Geneva: WCC, 1968), p. 45.

47. Ibid., pp. 47–48.

CHAPTER 13
THE ROLE OF RELIGION IN MAINTAINING THE STATUS QUO

1. Lawrence A. Cremin, *Traditions of American Education* (New York: Basic Books, 1977), p. 134.

2. John H. Westerhoff III and Gwen Kennedy Neville, *Generation to Generation* (New York: Pilgrim Press 1979), p. 119.

3. cf. Charles Y. Glock and Rodney Stark, *Religion and Society in Tension* (Chicago: Rand McNally, 1965); Andrew M. Greeley, *The Denominational Society: A Sociological Approach to Religion in America* (Glenview, Ill.: Scott, Foresman, 1972); Will Herberg, *Protestant, Catholic, Jew* (New York: Doubleday, 1960); Gerhard Lenski, *The Religious Factor: A Sociological Study of Religion's Impact on Politics, Economics and Family Life* (New York: Doubleday, Anchor, 1963); Talcott Parsons, *The System of Modern Societies* (Englewood Cliffs, N.J.: Prentice Hall,

1971); Max Weber, *The Protestant Ethic and the Spirit of Capitalism* (New York: Chas. Scribner's Sons, 1958).

4. Herberg, p. 265.

5. Ibid., p. 263.

6. Ibid., pp. 260–61.

7. Ibid., p. 260.

8. Juan Luis Segundo, S. J., *The Liberation of Theology* (Maryknoll, N.Y.: Orbis Books, 1976), pp. 42–43.

9. Hugo Assmann, *Theology for a Nomad Church* (Maryknoll, N.Y.: Orbis Books, 1975), p. 133.

10. Herberg, p. 260.

CHAPTER 14
THE ROLE OF EDUCATION IN MAINTAINING THE STATUS QUO

1. Colin Greer, *The Great School Legend: A Revisionist Interpretation of American Public Education* (New York: Basic Books, 1972), p. 108.

2. Ibid., p. vii.

3. Samuel Bowles and Herbert Gintis, *Schooling in Capitalist America* (New York: Basic Books, 1976), p. 265.

4. Raymond Callahan, *Education and the Cult of Efficiency* (Chicago: University of Chicago Press, 1962), pp. 28–34.

5. Ibid., p. 159.

6. Michael B. Katz, *Class, Bureaucracy, and Schools* (New York: Praeger Publishers, 1971), p. 122.

7. Ibid., pp. 108–09.

8. Samuel Bowles, "Unequal Education and the Reproduction of the Social Division of Labor," in *Schooling in a Corporate Society,* ed. Martin Carnoy (New York: David McKay, 1975), p. 45.

9. Bowles and Gintis, p. 192.

10. Joel Spring, *The Sorting Machine* (New York: David McKay, 1976), p. 57.

11. Joel Spring, *Education and the Rise of the Corporate State* (Boston: Beacon Press, 1972), p. 92.

12. Ibid., p. 95.

13. Clarence J. Karier, *Shaping the American Educational State* (New York: Free Press, 1975), p. 164.

14. Ibid., p. 161.

15. Alfred Binet and Th. Simon, *The Development of Intelligence in Children* (Baltimore: Williams and Wilkins Co., 1916), p. 266.

16. Ibid., p. 318.

17. Bowles and Gintis, p. 196.

18. Lewis Terman, *The Measurement of Intelligence* (Boston: Houghton Mifflin, 1916), pp. 27–28.

19. Bowles and Gintis, p. 102.

20. Ibid., p. 122.

21. Ibid., p. 120.

22. Ibid., p. 114.

23. Bowles and Gintis, p. 107.

24. Ibid., p. 132.

25. Ibid., p. 134.

26. For a more complete and detailed discussion of this point please refer to the fine study for the Carnegie Council on Children by Richard H. deLone, *Small Futures* (New York: Harcourt Brace Jovanovich, 1979).

27. Katz, p. 109.

28. deLone, p. 173.

29. Ibid., p. xiii.

30. Katz, p. 109.

CHAPTER 15
EDUCATING FOR CRITICAL CONSCIOUSNESS AND ACTION

1. Marie Augusta Neal, S.N.D. de N., *A Socio-Theology of Letting Go* (New York: Paulist Press, 1977), pp. 43–44.

2. Paulo Freire, *Pedagogy of the Oppressed* (New York: Herder and Herder, 1972), p. 58.

3. Ibid., p. 68.

4. Ronald Marstin, *Beyond Our Tribal Gods* (Maryknoll, N.Y.: Orbis Books, 1979), p. 52.

5. Ibid., p. 54.

6. Ibid., p. 68.

7. Harold Rugg, *Foundations for American Education* (Yonkers-on-Hudson, N.Y.: World Book Co., 1947), p. 580.

8. Harold Rugg, *Culture and Education in America* (New York: Harcourt, Brace, 1931), pp. 262–67.

9. George S. Counts, *The Social Foundations of Education* (New York: Charles Scribner's Sons, 1934), p. 137.

10. Ibid.

11. Ibid., pp. 514–15.

12. George S. Counts, *Dare the School Build a New Social Order?* (New York: John Day, 1932), p. 49.

13. Ibid., pp. 22–23.

14. Zalmen Slesinger, *Education and Class Struggle* (New York: Covici Friede Publishers, 1937), p. 18.

15. Ibid., p. 14.

16. Counts, *Dare the School,* p. 46.

17. George S. Counts, *Education and American Civilization* (New York: Teachers College Press, 1952), p. 308.

18. Counts, *Dare the School*, pp. 41–42.

19. George S. Counts and J. Crosby Chapman, *Principles of Education* (Boston: Houghton Mifflin, 1924), p. 243.

20. Counts, *Dare the School,* p. 55.

21. Synod of Bishops, Second General Assembly, *Justice in the World,* in *The Gospel of Peace and Justice,* ed. Joseph Gremillion (Maryknoll, N.Y.: Orbis Books: 1976), pp. 523–24.

22. Synod of Bishops, p. 524.

23. Ibid.

CHAPTER 16
THEORY AND PRACTICE OF EDUCATING FOR JUSTICE

1. Denis Goulet, *The Cruel Choice: A New Concept in the Theory of Development* (New York: Atheneum Publishers, 1971), especially Chapter 6.

2. Robert McAfee Brown, *Theology in a New Key* (Philadelphia: Westminster Press, 1978), p. 61.

3. Daniel Berrigan, *Love, Love at the End* (New York: Macmillan, 1971), pp. 7–9.

ANNOTATED BIBLIOGRAPHY

The following annotated bibliography has been prepared for Christian educators who want to study world hunger in more detail without having to research it themselves. All the books listed are readable, provide solid information, and are well documented. For those who wish to research the subject further, a more complete bibliography follows the Annotated Bibliography.

PART I:
THE PROBLEM OF WORLD HUNGER

Barnet, Richard J., and Müller, Ronald E. *Global Reach: The Power of the Multinational Corporations.* New York: Simon & Schuster, 1974. One of the most thorough studies of the character and activities of multinational corporations in the United States and the Third World.

DeMarco, Susan, and Sechler, Susan. *The Fields Have Turned Brown: Four Essays on World Hunger.* Washington: Agribusiness Accountability Project, 1975. Superb critical essays on the control of U.S. grain, PL 480, the Green Revolution, and agribusiness in the Third World. Includes an excellent annotated bibliography. Recommended for undergraduate classroom use.

Frundt, Henry J., ed. *Agribusiness Manual: Background Papers on Corporate Responsibility and Hunger Issues.* New York: Interfaith Center on Corporate Responsibility, 1978. A collection of some of the best articles published on agribusiness and its effect on the production and consumption of food in the United States and the Third World.

George, Susan. *How the Other Half Dies: The Real Reasons for World Hunger.* Montclair, N.J.: Allanheld, Osmun, 1977. One of the best critical studies of the economic and political causes of world hunger. Some of the areas covered include agribusiness, food aid, support for economic elites in the Third World, and the World Bank. If adopted for undergraduate classroom use, it will be necessary to provide background information on the history and nature of the problem of underdevelopment and the structures that keep the Third World poor.

Harrington, Michael. *The Vast Majority: A Journey to the World's Poor.* New York: Simon & Schuster, 1977. The best book on hunger and underdevelopment from a socialist perspective. Chapters containing personal reflections on the author's visit to India and Africa alternating with chapters on the political and economic analysis of the problem make the book especially attractive. Recommended for undergraduates with a solid foundation in the problem of underdevelopment.

Lappé, Frances Moore, and Collins, Joseph. *Food First: Beyond the Myth of Scarcity.* New York: Ballantine, 1979 (revised edition). The most comprehensive study of the political and economic causes of world hunger today. Question/answer format. Like Susan George's book, it may require some background information if adopted for undergraduate classroom use but can be easily understood by senior high school students and undergraduates.

Lappé, Frances Moore, Collins, Joseph, and Kinley, David. *Aid as Obstacle: Twenty Questions about Our Foreign Aid and the Hungry.* San Francisco: Institute for Food and Development Policy, 1980. An excellent exposé on the failure of United States foreign aid. Answers some of the most important questions about United States foreign aid and provides a fact sheet on the various aid agencies.

Ledogar, Robert J. *Hungry for Profits: U.S. Food and Drug Multinationals in Latin America.* New York: IDOC/North America, 1975. One of the best brief studies of the activities and effects of U.S. food and pharmaceutical corporations in the Third World.

Lernoux, Penny. "When Moneylenders Go Broke: World Banking at the Brink." *National Catholic Reporter,* 25 January–9 May 1980 Reprint. One of the finest critical studies to date on the operation and effects of world banking on the Third World. Recommended for undergraduate classroom use.

Nelson, Jack A. *Hunger for Justice: The Politics of Food and Faith.* Maryknoll, N.Y.: Orbis Books, 1980. A thorough study of the lengths to which the United States has gone to insure the integration of the Third World into the international free market system and the effect it has had on the Third World's poverty and hunger. Provides an important biblical perspective on the problem. Also relates the problem of military spending to world hunger.

Payer, Cheryl. *The Debt Trap.* New York: Monthly Review Press, 1974. One of the most thorough studies of the International Monetary Fund, its structure, policies, and effect on the Third World.

Sivard, Ruth Leger. *World Military and Social Expenditures.* Leesburg, Va.: WMSE Publications. An annual publication detailing the amount proportionately spent on military vs. social needs worldwide. Examines the effect of escalating military expenditure on areas such as education, health care and other social services.

PART II:
THE PUBLIC AND POLITICAL RESPONSIBILITY OF CHRISTIANS

Bock, Paul. *In Search of a Responsible World Society.* Philadelphia: Westminster Press, 1974. One of the most comprehensive studies of the social teachings of the World Council of Churches.

Brown, Robert McAfee. *Theology in a New Key: Responding to Liberation Themes.* Philadelphia: Westminster Press, 1978. A fine introduction to liberation theology. Provides a brief overview of the social teaching of the Christian churches, the distinguishing features of liberation theology and criticisms of liberation theology. Persuasively argues the need for North Americans to take the challenge of liberation theologians seriously. If adopted for classroom use, combine with several essays by the liberation theologians themselves.

Goulet, Denis. *The Cruel Choice: A New Concept in the Theory of Development.* New York: Atheneum Publishers, 1971. One of the best studies of development ethics. Questions the meaning of development, proposes ends toward which development in the First as well as the Third World ought to be directed. If adopted for classroom use, assign chapters selectively. Preface, Chapters 1, 2, 5, 6, 11, 12, and conclusion are especially good.

Gremillion, Joseph, ed. *The Gospel of Peace and Justice: Catholic Social Teaching Since Pope John.* Maryknoll, N.Y.: Orbis Books, 1976. Collection of the social teaching of the Roman Catholic Church from John XXIII to Paul VI. Gremillion's overview provides a good introduction to and perspective for understanding the documents. If adopted for classroom use, select most pertinent sections of documents.

Gutiérrez, Gustavo. *A Theology of Liberation: History, Politics and Salvation.* 1971; English ed., Maryknoll, N.Y.: Orbis Books, 1973. The classic in liberation theology. Probes the relationship between salvation and the historical process of liberation. Must reading for teachers, but difficult for undergraduates with no theological background.

Metz, Johannes B., ed. *Faith and the World of Politics.* Concilium: Theology in the Age of Renewal, Fundamental Theology, vol. 36. New York: Paulist Press, 1968. A good collection of essays on the political dimension of faith and the church. Could be adopted for classroom use for undergraduates.

Sider, Ronald J. *Rich Christians in an Age of Hunger: A Biblical Study.* New York: Paulist Press, 1977. A fine biblical study of the problem of hunger written from an evangelical perspective.

PART III:
EDUCATING FOR JUSTICE

Beckmann, David M., and Donnelly, Elizabeth Anne. *The Overseas List.* Minneapolis: Augsburg Publishing House, 1979. A comprehensive guide to volunteer service and employment overseas.

Bobo, Kimberley, A., ed. *World Food/Hunger Studies.* New York: Transnational University Program, Institute for World Order, 1977. A collection of course outlines and syllabi for courses on world hunger taught from generalist, ethical, international agriculture development, nutritional, policy, and political economic perspectives. Contains an excellent listing of books, periodicals, resource packets, multimedia materials, and organizations. Especially suited to the college teacher.

Bowles, Samuel, and Gintis, Herbert. *Schooling in Capitalist America.* New York: Basic Books, 1976. A critical study of the role of the school in reproducing inequality in a capitalist society. Argues against the popular belief that IQ and the development of technical or cognitive skills in school are significant contributing factors to economic success.

deLone, Richard H. *Small Futures: Children, Inequality, and the Limits of Liberal Reform.* New York: Harcourt Brace Jovanovich, 1979. The most recent of the fine studies done for the Carnegie Council on Children. Argues persuasively that poverty cannot be reduced to individual failure but is rooted in our economic system. Efforts to overcome poverty by improving the lot of poor children through education are doomed to fail without concomitant efforts to change the structure of our economic system.

Fenton, Thomas P., ed. *Education for Justice: A Resource Manual.* Maryknoll, N.Y.: Orbis Books, 1975. A practical sourcebook for educators involved in planning and implementing courses and programs in justice. Provides an especially good annotated listing of audiovisual materials, learning activities, action resources, and groups involved in justice.

Freire, Paulo. *Education for Critical Consciousness.* 1969; English ed., New York: Seabury Press, 1973; Continuum Books, 1974.

———. *Pedagogy of the Oppressed.* 1968; New York: Herder and Herder, 1972. The exiled Brazilian educator's educational philosophy and methodology.

Marstin, Ronald. *Beyond Our Tribal Gods: The Maturing of Faith.* Maryknoll, N.Y.: Orbis Books, 1979. One of the finest books on the issue of faith development and social justice. Builds on the work of James Fowler. Presents a convincing argument for outer change as a necessary component of inner growth. Excellent for undergraduate and adult students.

McGinnis, James B. *Bread and Justice: Toward a New International Economic Order.* New York: Paulist Press, 1979. Also *Bread and Justice: Toward a New International Economic Order, Teacher's Book.* Provides a readable summary of the root causes of world hunger for the high-school and college student. Especially helpful are the suggestions for action and list of resources following each chapter. The teacher's book is a good source for student activities, films, speakers, and additional readings for each chapter of the text.

Millar, Jayne C. *Focusing on Global Poverty and Development: A Resource Book for Educators.* Washington: Overseas Deveopment Council, 1974. Good articles, charts, bibliography, and film resources on the problem of underdevelopment. Especially helpful for high-school teachers.

Wren, Brian. *Education for Justice: Pedagogical Principles.* Maryknoll, N.Y.: Orbis Books, 1977. One of the best books available on the relationship of education to social justice. Builds on and draws out the implications of Freire's problem-posing education. Discusses the obstacles to justice and changes needed to build a more just social order. Excellent for undergraduate and adult students.

SELECTED BIBLIOGRAPHY

ABC—"ABC News Closeup," 27 June 1975. "Food: The Crisis of Price."

Abelson, Philip H., ed. *Food: Politics, Economics, Nutrition and Research.* Washington: American Association for the Advancement of Science, 1975.

Aiken, William, and LaFollette, Hugh, eds. *World Hunger and Moral Obligation.* Englewood Cliffs, N.J.: Prentice-Hall, 1977.

Alavi, Hamza. *Imperialism, Old and New.* Originally appeared in the *Socialist Register,* 1964. Boston: New England Free Press, n.d.

Alves, Rubem, A. *A Theology of Human Hope.* New York: World Publishing, 1969; St. Meinrad, Ind. Abbey Press, 1972.

Amin, Samir. *Accumulation on a World Scale.* 1971; English ed., New York: Monthly Review Press, 1974.

Anderson, Gerald H., and Stransky, Thomas F., eds. *Third World Theologies.* Mission Trends, no. 3. New York: Paulist Press, 1976.

Arnstine, Barbara. "Reconstructing George S. Counts: An Essay Review." *Educational Theory* 24 (1974): 110–19.

Aronowitz, Stanley. *Food, Shelter and the American Dream.* New York: Seabury Press, 1974.

Arrupe, Pedro, S.J. *Men for Others: Education for Justice and Social Action Today.* 1973; English ed., Washington: Jesuit Secondary Education Association, 1974.

Assmann, Hugo. *Theology for a Nomad Church.* 1973; English ed., Maryknoll, N.Y.: Orbis Books, 1976.

Aziz, Sartaj, ed. *Hunger, Politics and Markets: The Real Issues in the Food Crisis.* New York: New York University Press, 1975.

Baier, Kurt, *The Moral Point of View: A Rational Basis of Ethics,* abridged ed. New York: Random House, 1965.

Baran, Paul A. *The Political Economy of Growth.* New York: Monthly Review Press, 1957; Modern Reader Paperbacks, 1968.

Baran, Paul A., and Sweezy, Paul M. *Monopoly Capital: An Essay on American Economic and Social Order.* New York: Monthly Review Press, 1966; Modern Reader Paperback, 1968.

Barnet, Richard J. *The Economy of Death.* New York: Atheneum Publishers, 1969.

Barnet, Richard J., and Müller, Ronald E. *Global Reach: The Power of the Multinational Corporations.* New York: Simon & Schuster, 1974.

Barraclough, Geoffrey. "The Great World Crisis I." *New York Review of Books,* 23 January 1975, pp. 20–29.

———. "The Haves and the Have Nots." *New York Review of Books,* 13 May 1976, pp. 31–41.

———. "Wealth and Power: The Politics of Food and Oil." *New York Review of Books*, 7 August 1975, pp. 23–30.

Barratt Brown, Michael. *The Economics of Imperialism.* Baltimore: Penguin Books, 1974.

Barry, Brian. *The Liberal Theory of Justice: A Critical Examination of the Principal Doctrines in "A Theory of Justice" by John Rawls.* Oxford: Clarendon Press, 1973.

Becker, James M., and Mehlinger, Howard D., eds. *International Dimensions in the Social Studies,* 38th Yearbook. Washington: National Council for the Social Studies, 1968.

Beckford, George L. *Persistent Poverty: Underdevelopment in Plantation Economies of the Third World.* New York: Oxford University Press, 1972.

Berg, Alan, *The Nutrition Factor.* Washington: The Brookings Institution, 1973.

Berger, Peter, *The Sacred Canopy.* Garden City N.Y.: Doubleday, 1969.

Bhagwati, Jagdish N., ed. *Economics and World Order: From the 1970s to the 1990s.* New York: Free Press, 1972; Macmillan, 1974.

———. *Trade, Tariffs and Growth.* Cambridge, Mass.: MIT Press, 1969.

Bhagwati, Jagdish N., and Eckhaus, Richard S., eds. *Development and Planning: Essays in Honour of Paul Rosenstein-Rodan.* Cambridge, Mass.: MIT Press, 1973.

Bhagwati, Jagdish N.; Jones, Ronald W.; Mundell, Robert A.; and Vanek, Jaroslav, eds. *Trade, Balance of Payments and Growth.* Amsterdam and London: North Holland Publishing Co., 1971.

Bird, Kai, and Goldmark, Sue. "Food Aid vs. Development." *Worldview,* January/February 1977, pp. 38–41.

Blakeslee, Leroy; Heady, Earl O.; Framingham, Charles F. *World Food Production, Demand, and Trade.* Ames, Iowa: Iowa State University Press, 1973.

Bobo, Kimberley A., ed. *World Food/Hunger Studies.* New York: Transnational University Program, Institute for World Order, 1977.

Bock, Paul. *In Search of a Responsible World Society.* Philadelphia: Westminster Press, 1974.

Böckle, Franz, ed. *War, Poverty, Freedom: The Christian Response.* Concilium: Theology in the Age of Renewal, Moral Theology, vol. 15. New York: Paulist Press, 1966.

Borgstrom, Georg. *Focal Points: A Global Food Strategy.* New York: Macmillan, 1973.

———. *The Food and People Dilemma.* The Man-Environment System Series. North Scituate, Mass.: Duxbury Press, a Division of Wadsworth Publishing Co., 1973.

———. *The Hungry Planet: The Modern World on the Edge of Famine,* 2nd ed. Rev. New York: Collier, 1972.

Bowen, Howard R., et al. *Investment in Learning: The Individual and Social Value of American Higher Education.* San Francisco: Jossey-Bass, 1977.

Bowles, Samuel, and Gintis, Herbert. *Schooling in Capitalist America.* New York: Basic Books, 1976.

Brown, Lester R. *By Bread Alone.* New York: Praeger Publishers, 1974.

———. *The Changing Face of Food Scarcity.* Communiqué on Development Issues, no. 21. Washington: Overseas Development Council, 1973.

———. *The Politics and Responsibility of the North American Breadbasket.* Worldwatch Paper 2. Washington: Worldwatch Institute, 1975.

———. *Population and Affluence: Growing Pressures on World Food Resources.* Population Bulletin, vol. 29, no. 2. Washington: Population Reference Bureau, 1973.

———. *Seeds of Change: The Green Revolution and Development in the 1970's.* New York: Praeger Publishers, 1970.

———. *The Twenty-Ninth Day: Accommodating Human Needs and Numbers to the Earth's Resources.* New York: W.W. Norton, 1978.

———. *Why Hunger?* Communiqué on Development Issues, no. 9. Washington: Overseas Development Council, 1971.

———. *World Population Trends: Signs of Hope, Signs of Stress.* Worldwatch Paper 8. Washington: Worldwatch Institute, 1976.

———. *World Without Borders.* New York: Random House, 1972; Vintage Books, 1973.

Business as Usual: Corporate Influence in Food Policy. Washington: Agribusiness Accountability Project, 1973.

Callahan, Daniel. "Doing Well by Doing Good: Garrett Hardin's *Lifeboat Ethic.*" *The Hastings Center Report* 4 (1974): 1-4.

Callahan, Daniel, ed. *The American Population Debate.* Garden City, N.Y.: Doubleday Anchor Books, 1971.

Callahan, Raymond E. *Education and the Cult of Efficiency.* Chicago: University of Chicago Press, 1962.

Campaign for Human Development, United States Catholic Conference. *Poverty in American Democracy: A Study of Social Power.* Washington: United States Catholic Conference, 1974.

Carbone, Peter F., Jr. *The Social and Educational Thought of Harold Rugg.* Durham, N.C.: Duke University Press, 1977.

Carnoy, Martin. *Education as Cultural Imperialism.* New York: David McKay, 1974.

Carnoy, Martin, ed. *Schooling in a Corporate Society.* New York: David McKay, 1975.

"The Catholic University in the Modern World." Final Document of the Second International Congress of Delegates of Catholic Universities, Rome, 20-29 November 1972. *College Newsletter,* March 1973, pp. 1-10.

Center for International Policy. "Foreign Aid: Evading the Control of Congress." *International Policy Report,* January 1977.

Christianity and Crisis. Special Issue on the Human and Social Costs of the U.S. Economic System. 29 November and 13 December 1976, pp. 271-300.

Cochrane, Willard W. *Feast or Famine: The Uncertain World of Food and Agriculture and its Policy Implications for the United States.* Ninth District Exponent. Minneapolis: Federal Reserve Bank, 1974.

Collins, Denis E., S.J. *Paulo Freire: His Life, Works and Thought.* New York: Paulist Press, 1977.

Collins, Randall. Review of *Schooling in Capitalist America,* by Samuel Bowles and Herbert Gintis. *Harvard Educational Review* 46 (1976): 246-51.

Commoner, Barry. *The Closing Circle: Nature, Man and Technology.* New York: Alfred A. Knopf, 1971; Bantam Books, 1972.

Cooper, Richard N., ed. *A Reordered World: Emerging International Economic Problems.* Washington: Potomac Associates, 1973.

Coover, Virginia, et al. *Resource Manual for a Living Revolution.* Philadelphia: New Society Press, 1977.

Cottingham, Jane, ed. *Bottle Babies: a Guide to the Baby Foods Issue.* Carouge and

Geneva: ISIS—Women's International Information and Communication Service, and the World Council of Churches, 1976.

Counts, George S. *Dare the School Build a New Social Order?* New York: John Day, 1932.

———. *Education and American Civilization.* New York: Teachers College Press, 1952.

———. *The Social Foundations of Education.* New York: Charles Scribner's Sons, 1934.

Counts, George S., and Chapman, J. Crosby. *Principles of Education.* Boston: Houghton Mifflin, 1924.

"Creating Undergraduate Peace Studies Programs." A Special Issue of *Peace and Change* 1 (Winter 1973).

Cremin, Lawrence A. *The Genius of American Education.* New York: Random House, Vintage Books, 1965.

———. *Public Education.* New York: Basic Books, 1976.

———. *Traditions of American Education.* New York: Basic Books, 1977.

———. *The Transformation of the School.* New York: Alfred A. Knopf, 1961.

Crittenden, Brian. *Education and Social Ideals: A Study in Philosophy of Education.* Don Mills, Ontario: Longman Canada, 1973.

Daniels, Norman, ed. *Reading Rawls: Critical Studies on Rawls' "A Theory of Justice."* New York: Basic Books, n.d.

Davies, J. G. *Christians, Politics and Violent Revolution.* Maryknoll, N.Y.: Orbis Books, 1976.

deLone, Richard H. *Small Futures: Children, Inequality, and the Limits of Liberal Reform.* New York: Harcourt Brace Jovanovich, 1979.

DeMarco, Susan, and Sechler, Susan. *The Fields Have Turned Brown: Four Essays on World Hunger.* Washington: Agribusiness Accountability Project, 1975.

Development: New Approaches: A Guide for Educators with Issues and Resources. Intercom 69. New York: Center for War/Peace Studies of the New York Friends Group, 1972.

Dewey, John. *Democracy and Education: An Introduction to the Philosophy of Education.* New York: Macmillan, 1916; The Free Press, 1966.

Du Boff, Richard B. "Converting Military Spending to Social Welfare: The Real Obstacles." *The Quarterly Review of Economics and Business* 12 (1972): 7–22.

Duncan, Marvin R.; Bickel, Blaine W.; and Miller, Glenn H., Jr. *International Trade and American Agriculture.* Kansas City, Mo.: Federal Reserve Bank of Kansas City, 1975.

Dussel, Enrique. *History and the Theology of Liberation: A Latin American Perspective.* English ed., Maryknoll, N.Y.: Orbis Books, 1976.

Eagleson, John, ed. *Christians and Socialism: Documentation of the Christians for Socialism Movement in Latin America.* Maryknoll, N.Y.: Orbis Books, 1975.

Eberstadt, Nick. "Myths of the Food Crisis." *New York Review of Books,* 19 February 1976, pp. 32–37.

Eckholm, Eric P. *Losing Ground: Environmental Stress and World Food Prospects.* New York: W. W. Norton, 1976.

Eckholm, Eric P., and Record, Frank. *The Two Faces of Malnutrition.* Worldwatch Paper 9. Washington: Worldwatch Institute, 1976.

Ehrlich, Paul R., *The Population Bomb,* rev. ed. New York: Ballantine Books, 1971.

Ehrlich, Paul R., and Ehrlich, Anne H. *The End of Affluence: A Blueprint for Your Future.* New York: Ballantine Books, 1974.

Elliott, Charles. *Patterns of Poverty in the Third World.* New York: Praeger Publishers, 1975.

Emmanuel, Arghiri. *Unequal Exchange: A Study of the Imperialism of Trade.* New York: Monthly Review Press, 1972.

Encyclopedia of Philosophy, 1967 ed. S.v. "Problems of Ethics," by Kai Nielsen.

Erb, Guy F., and Kallab, Valeriana, ed. *Beyond Dependency: The Developing World Speaks Out.* Washington: Overseas Development Council, 1975.

Fann, K. T., and Hodges, Donald C., eds. *Readings in U.S. Imperialism.* Boston: Porter Sargent, 1971.

Feinberg, Walter. *Reason and Rhetoric: The Intellectual Foundations of 20th Century Liberal Education Policies.* New York: John Wiley, 1975.

————. "Revisionist Scholarship and the Problem of Historical Context." *Teachers College Record* 78 (1977): 311–36.

Feinberg, Walter, and Rosemont, Henry, Jr., eds. *Work, Technology, and Education: Dissenting Essays in the Intellectual Foundations of American Education.* Urbana, Ill.: University of Illinois Press, 1975.

Fenton, Thomas P. *Coffee: The Rules of the Game and You.* New York: The Christophers, n.d.

Fenton, Thomas P., ed. *Education for Justice: A Resource Manual.* Maryknoll, N.Y.: Orbis Books, 1975.

Fierro, Alfredo. *The Militant Gospel: A Critical Introduction to Political Theologies.* 1975; English ed., Maryknoll, N.Y.: Orbis Books, 1977.

Finnerty, Adam Daniel. *No More Plastic Jesus: Global Justice and Christian Lifestyle.* Maryknoll, N.Y.: Orbis Books, 1977.

Fiorenza, Francis P. "Latin American Liberation Theology." *Interpretation* 28 (1974): 441–457.

————. "Political Theology and Liberation Theology: An Inquiry into Their Fundamental Meaning." In *Liberation, Revolution, and Freedom,* pp. 3–29. Edited by Thomas M. McFadden. New York: Seabury Press, 1975.

Frank, André Gunder. *Latin America: Underdevelopment or Revolution: Essays on the Development of Underdevelopment and the Immediate Enemy.* New York: Monthly Review Press, 1969.

Frank, Charles R. *Debt and Terms of Aid.* Overseas Development Council Monograph, no. 1. Washington: Overseas Development Council, 1970.

Frankena, William K. "Conversations with Carney and Hauerwas." *Journal of Religious Ethics* 3 (1975): 45–62.

————. *Ethics,* 2nd ed. Englewood Cliffs, N.J.: Prentice-Hall, 1973.

————. "The Ethics of Love Conceived as an Ethics of Virtue." *Journal of Religious Ethics* 1 (1973): 21–36.

————. "Love and Principle in Christian Ethics." In *Faith and Philosophy,* pp. 203–25. Edited by Alvin Plantinga. Grand Rapids: William B. Eerdmans, 1964.

————. *Perspectives on Morality: Essays by William K. Frankena.* Edited by K. E. Goodpastor. Notre Dame, Ind.: University of Notre Dame Press, 1976.

Freire, Paulo. *Education for Critical Consciousness.* 1969; English ed., New York: Seabury Press, 1973; Continuum Books, 1974.

————. *Pedagogy of the Oppressed.* 1968; New York: Herder and Herder, 1972.

French, David S. "Does the U.S. Exploit the Developing Nations?" *Commonweal,* 19 May 1967, pp. 257–59.

Freudenberger, C. Dean, and Minus, Paul M., Jr. *Christian Responsibility in a Hungry World.* Nashville, Tenn.: Abingdon Press, 1976.

From the Ground Up: Building a Grass Roots Food Policy. Washington: Center for Science in the Public Interest, 1976.

Frundt, Henry J., ed. *Agribusiness Manual: Background Papers on Corporate Responsibility and Hunger Issues.* New York: Interfaith Center on Corporate Responsibility, 1978.

Gallis, Marion. *Trade for Justice: Myth or Mandate.* Geneva: Commission on the Churches' Participation in Development, World Council of Churches, 1972.

Gardner, Richard N., ed. *The World Food and Energy Crisis: The Role of International Organizations.* Rensselaerville, N.Y.: Institute on Man and Science, 1974.

Geffre, Claude, and Gutiérrez, Gustavo. *The Mystical and Political Dimension of the Christian Faith.* New York: Herder and Herder, 1974.

Gelb, Leslie H., and Lake, Anthony. "Washington Dateline: Less Food, More Politics." *Foreign Policy* 17 (Winter 1974–75): 176–189.

George, Susan. *How the Other Half Dies: The Real Reasons for World Hunger.* Montclair, N.J.: Allanheld, Osmun, 1977.

Global Justice and Development. Report of the Aspen Interreligious Consultation, Aspen, Colorado, June 1974. Washington: Overseas Development Council, 1975.

Gollwitzer, Helmut. *The Rich Christians and Poor Lazarus.* New York: Macmillan, 1970.

González-Ruiz, José María. *The New Creation: Marxist and Christian?* Maryknoll, N.Y.: Orbis Books, 1976.

Goulet, Denis. *The Cruel Choice: A New Concept in the Theory of Development.* New York: Atheneum, 1971.

———. "An Ethical Model for the Study of Values." *Harvard Educational Review* 41 (1971): 205–27.

———. *Is Gradualism Dead? Reflections on Order, Change and Force.* New York: The Council on Religion and International Affairs, 1970.

———. *A New Moral Order: Studies in Development Ethics and Liberation Theology.* Maryknoll, N.Y.: Orbis Books, 1974.

———. *The Uncertain Promise: Value Conflicts in Technology Transfer.* New York: IDOC; Washington: Overseas Development Council, 1977.

———. "Voluntary Austerity: The Necessary Art." *Christian Century,* 8 June 1966, pp. 748–752.

———"World Hunger: Putting Development Ethics to the Test." *Christianity and Crisis,* 26 May 1975, pp. 125–32.

———. *World Interdependence: Verbal Smokescreen or New Ethic?* Development Paper 21. Washington: Overseas Development Council, 1976.

Goulet, Denis, and Hudson, Michael. *The Myth of Aid: The Hidden Agenda of the Development Reports.* New York: IDOC; Maryknoll, N.Y.: Orbis Books, 1971.

Gowan, Susanne et al. *Moving Toward a New Society.* Philadelphia: New Society Press, 1976.

Gran, Guy. "Is Poverty Really Inevitable?" *Sojourners,* April 1977, pp. 29–32.

Gray, David Dodson. *Triage: Its Variants and Alternatives.* 1975.

Greene, Wade. "Triage: Who Shall Be Fed? Who Shall Starve?" *New York Times Magazine,* 5 January 1975, pp. 9–11.

Greer, Colin. *The Great School Legend: A Revisionist Interpretation of American Public Education.* New York: Basic Books, 1972.

Gremillion, Joseph, ed. *Food/Energy and the Major Faiths.* Maryknoll, N.Y.: Orbis Books, 1978.

Gremillion, Joseph, ed. *The Gospel of Peace and Justice: Catholic Social Teaching Since Pope John.* Maryknoll, N.Y.: Orbis Books, 1976.

Griffin, Keithe. *The Political Economy of Agrarian Change.* Cambridge: Harvard University Press, 1974.

Gussow, Joan Dye. "Barriers to Action." Paper delivered at the National University Conference on Hunger, University of Texas at Austin, 22 November 1975.

———. *The Feeding Web: Issues in Nutritional Ecology.* Palo Alto, Calif.: Bull Publishing, 1978.

Gustafson, James M. *Can Ethics Be Christian?* Chicago: University of Chicago Press, 1975.

———. *The Church as Moral Decision-Maker.* Philadelphia: The Pilgrim Press, 1970.

Gustafson, James M.; Peters, Richard S.; Kohlberg, Lawrence; Bettelheim, Bruno: and Keniston, Kenneth. *Moral Education: Five Lectures.* Cambridge: Harvard University Press, 1970.

Gutek, Gerald L. *The Educational Theory of George S. Counts.* Studies in Educational Theory of the John Dewey Society, no. 8. Ohio State University Press, 1970.

Gutiérrez, Gustavo. *A Theology of Liberation: History, Politics and Salvation.* 1971; English ed., Maryknoll, N.Y.: Orbis Books, 1973.

———. "Where Hunger Is, God Suffers." Reprinted from *Witness,* April 1977. In *Why Are People Hungry?* New York: United Presbyterian Church, n.d.

Gutiérrez, Gustavo, and Shaull, Richard. *Liberation and Change.* Atlanta: John Knox Press, 1977.

Haavelsrud, Magnus. "The Hidden Connection." In *Mutual Understanding of Peoples and Minority Group Education,* pp. 81–95. Edited by Rikio Kimura. Proceedings of the 2nd Asian Convention of the International Association of Educators for World Peace, Sendai, Japan. August 1976.

———. "The Negation of Peace Education." In *Expanding Dimensions of World Education,* pp. 144–49. Edited by Nasrine Adibe and Frank A. Stone. Proceedings of an International Conference, Hacettepe University, Ankara, Turkey, 21–24 June 1976.

———. "Raising Consciousness Through a Global Community Curriculum." *Bulletin of Peace Proposals* 5 (1974): 274–79.

———. "Towards a Vision of the Role of Formal Education in Quest of Peace." *Peace Progress—IAEWP Journal of Education* 1 (1975): 57–63.

Haavelsrud, Magnus, ed. *Education for Peace.* Surrey, Eng.: IPC Science and Technology Press, 1974.

Habermas, Jürgen. *Knowledge and Human Interests.* 1968; English ed., Boston: Beacon Press, 1971.

———. *Toward a Rational Society: Student Protest, Science, and Politics.* 1968 & 1969; English ed., Boston: Beacon Press, 1970.

Hall, Ross Hume. *Food for Thought: The Decline in Nutrition.* Hagerstown, Md.: Harper & Row Publishers, 1974.

Hamilton, Martha M. *The Great American Grain Robbery and Other Stories.* Washington: Agribusiness Accountability Project, 1972.

Harle, Vilho. *Political Economy of Food: Proceedings of an International Seminar.*

Research Reports, no. 12, 1976. Tampere, Finland: Tampere Peace Research Institute, 1976.

Harrington, Michael. *The Vast Majority: A Journey to the World's Poor.* New York: Simon & Schuster, 1977.

Haughey, John C., S.J., ed. *The Faith That Does Justice: Examining the Christian Sources for Social Change.* New York: Paulist Press, 1977.

Hayter, Teresa. *Aid as Imperialism.* Baltimore: Penguin Books, 1971.

Heilbroner, Robert L. *Business Civilization in Decline.* New York: W. W. Norton, 1976.

————. *The Great Ascent: The Struggle for Economic Development in Our Time.* New York: Harper & Row Publishers, Harper Torchbook, 1963.

————. *An Inquiry into the Human Prospect.* New York: W. W. Norton, 1974.

————. *The Limits of American Capitalism.* New York: Harper & Row Publishers, Harper Torchbooks, 1967.

————. "None of Your Business." *New York Review of Books,* 20 March 1975, pp. 6–10.

Henderson, George, ed. *Education for Peace: Focus on Mankind.* Washington: Association for Supervision and Curriculum Development Yearbook Committee, 1973.

Henriot, Peter J. *Development Alternatives: Problems, Strategies, Values.* Institute of Society, Ethics, and the Life Sciences, 1976.

Hertzberg, Hazel W. "The New Curriculum Movement in the Social Studies: Uses of the Past and Implications for the Future." *Social Science Education Consortium Newsletter,* April 1973, pp. 1–5.

Hessel, Dieter T., ed. *Beyond Survival: Bread and Justice in Christian Perspective.* New York: Friendship Press, 1977.

Hightower, Jim. *Eat Your Heart Out: Food Profiteering in America.* New York: Random House, 1975; Vintage Books, 1976.

————. *Food, Farmers, Corporations, Earl Butz . . . And You.* Washington: Agribusiness Accountability Project, 1973.

————. *Hard Tomatoes, Hard Times: A Report of the Agribusiness Accountability Project on the Failure of the Land Grant College Complex.* Cambridge, Mass.: Schenkman Publishing, 1973.

Hill, Judah. *Class Analysis: United States in the 1970's.* San Francisco: Synthesis Publications, 1975.

Holland, Joe. *The American Journey: A Theology in the Americas Working Paper.* New York: IDOC; Washington: Center of Concern, 1976.

Hudson, Michael. *Super-Imperialism.* New York: Holt, Rinehart and Winston, 1972.

Hudson, W. D. *Modern Moral Philosophy.* Garden City, N.Y.: Doubleday & Company, Anchor Books, 1970.

Huebner, Dwayne. "Curriculum '. . . With Liberty and Justice for All.' " Paper presented at the Conference on Craft, Conflict, and Symbol: Their Import for Curriculum and Schooling, Tennessee Technological University, 25–26 April 1974.

————. "Moral Values and the Curriculum." Paper delivered at the Conference on Moral Dilemma of Public Schooling, Madison, Wisconsin, 12 May 1965.

Hurn, Christopher. *The Limits and Possibilities of Schooling: An Introduction to the Sociology of Education.* Boston: Allyn & Bacon, 1978.

Illich, Ivan. *Deschooling Society.* New York: Harper & Row, Publishers, 1970; Harrow Books, 1972.

"The Incredible Empire of Michel Fribourg." *Business Week,* 11 March 1972, pp. 84–90.

International Peace Research Association, Communication and Consciousness Raising Working Group. "A Global Strategy for Communication and Conscious-Raising in Various Local Settings." *International Peace Research Newsletter* 14 (1976): 7–10.

Interreligious Taskforce on U.S. Food Policy. "Reforms Needed in Farm and Food Policy: The Price Support System, Food Aid, and the Food Stamp Program." *Hunger,* no. 9. March 1977.

———. "The United States and the Changing International Economic Order." *Hunger,* no. 4, 1976.

Iowa State University, Center for Agricultural and Rural Development. *U.S. Trade Policy and Agricultural Exports.* Ames, Iowa: Iowa State University Press, 1973.

Isenman, Paul J., and Singer, H. W. *Food Aid: Disincentive Effects and their Policy Implications.* AID Discussion Paper, no. 31. Washington: Agency for International Development, Bureau for Program and Policy Coordination, 1975.

Jalee, Pierre. *Imperialism in the Seventies.* New York: Joseph Okpaku Publishing, 1972.

———. *The Pillage of the Third World.* New York: Monthly Review Press, 1968.

———. *The Third World in World Economy.* New York: Monthly Review Press, 1969.

Jegen, Mary Evelyn, and Manno, Bruce V., eds. *The Earth Is the Lord's: Essays on Stewardship.* New York: Paulist Press, 1978.

Johnson, D. Gale. *World Agriculture in Disarray.* New York: Franklin Watts, 1973.

———. *World Food Problems and Prospects.* Washington: American Enterprise Institute for Public Policy Research, 1975.

Jones, Brendan. "Bankers Cautioned on Third World's Debt Burden." *New York Times,* 5 October 1977.

Jones, Brennon. *Export Cropping and Development: We Need to Know More.* Background Paper, no. 25. Washington: Bread for the World, 1975.

———. "Of Fat Years and Lean Years—and Food Reserves." *New York Times,* 27 August 1977.

———. "Rx for Carter: Heed the Poor Nations." *Commonweal,* 7 January 1977, pp. 9–12.

Karier, Clarence J. *Shaping the American Educational State.* New York: Free Press, 1975.

Karier, Clarence J.; Violas, Paul C.; and Spring, Joel. *Roots of Crisis: American Education in the Twentieth Century.* Chicago: Rand McNally, 1973.

Katz, Deborah, and Goodwin, Mary T. *Food: Where Nutrition, Politics, and Culture Meet.* Washington: Center for Science in the Public Interest, 1976.

Katz, Michael B. *Class, Bureaucracy, and Schools.* New York: Praeger Publishers, 1971.

———. *The Irony of Early School Reform.* Cambridge: Harvard University Press, 1968.

Katz, Michael B., ed. *School Reform: Past and Present.* Boston: Little, Brown and Company, 1971.

King, Seth S. "2 Nations Accept Human-Rights Clause Linked to U.S. Aid Program." *New York Times,* 18 December 1977.

Knox, Francis. *The Common Market and World Agriculture.* New York: Praeger Publishers, 1972.

Kolko, Gabriel. *Wealth and Power in America: An Analysis of Social Class and Income Distribution.* New York: Praeger Publishers, 1962.

Kotz, Nick. *Let Them Eat Promises: The Politics of Hunger in America.* Garden City, N.Y.: Doubleday & Company, 1969; Anchor Books, 1971.

Lappé, Frances Moore, and Collins, Joseph. *Food First: Beyond the Myth of Scarcity.* Boston: Houghton Mifflin, 1977.

Laslett, Peter, and Runciman, W. G., eds. *Philosophy, Politics and Society,* second series. New York: Barnes & Noble Books, 1962.

Laudicina, Paul A. *World Poverty and Development: a Survey of American Opinion.* Washington: Overseas Development Council, 1973.

Ledogar, Robert J. *Hungry for Profits: U.S. Food and Drug Multinationals in Latin America.* New York: IDOC/North America, 1975.

Lernoux, Penny. "When Moneylanders Go Broke: World Banking at the Brink." *National Catholic Reporter,* 25 January–9 May, 1980, Reprint.

Lerza, Catherine. "The Private Government of Grain." *Elements: A Journal of World Resources,* November 1976, pp. 4–5.

Lerza, Catherine, and Jacobson, Michael, eds. *Food for People, Not for Profit: A Source Book on the Food Crisis.* New York: Ballantine, 1975.

Lewis, Sir W. Arthur. *Dynamic Factors in Economic Growth.* Bombay: Priya Adakar, Orient Longman, 1974.

———. *Reflections of Nigeria's Economic Growth.* Paris, 1967.

———. *Some Aspects of Economic Development.* Ghana: Ghana Publishing, 1971.

Lichtheim, George. *Imperialism.* New York: Praeger Publishers, 1971.

Lombardi, Joseph, S.J. Paper presented at the seminar entitled "Justice—a Philosophical Overview of the Term as Operative in Various Systems of Thought," St. Joseph's College, Philadelphia, Spring 1977.

Long, Edward LeRoy, Jr. *A Survey of Christian Ethics.* New York: Oxford University Press, 1967.

Lucas, George R., Jr., and Ogletree, Thomas W. *Lifeboat Ethics: The Moral Dilemmas of World Hunger.* New York: Harper & Row Publishers, 1976.

Lundberg, Ferdinand. *The Rich and the Super-Rich: A Study in the Power of Money Today.* Secaucus, N.J.: Lyle Stuart, 1968; New York: Bantam Books, 1969.

MacDonald, James B., and Zaret, Esther. *Schools in Search of Meaning.* Washington: Association for Supervision and Curriculum Development, 1975.

McFadden, Thomas M., ed. *Theology Confronts a Changing World.* The Annual Publication of the College Theology Society. West Mystic, Conn.: Twenty-Third Publications, 1977.

McGinnis, James B. *Bread and Justice: Toward a New International Economic Order* and *Teacher's Book.* New York, Paulist Press, 1979.

McLaughlin, Martin M. *World Food Insecurity:Has Anything Happened Since Rome?* Communiqué on Development Issues, no. 27. Washington: Overseas Development Council, 1975.

McNamara, Robert S. *One Hundred Countries, Two Billion People: The Dimensions of Development.* New York: Praeger Publishers, 1973.

"The MacNeil/Lehrer Report." WNET/WETA telecast, 18 October 1977. "Agency for International Development." Library #537, Show #3077.

Magdoff, Harry. *The Age of Imperialism.* New York: Monthly Review Press, 1969.

Malmgren, Harald. *Trade for Development*. Overseas Development Council Monograph, no. 4. Washington: Overseas Development Council, 1971.

Marcuse, Herbert. *One-Dimensional Man: Studies in the Ideology of Advanced Industrial Society*. Boston: Beacon Press, 1964.

Margulies, Leah. "Baby Formula Abroad: Exporting Infant Malnutrition." *Christianity and Crisis*, 10 November 1975, pp. 1-4.

Marstin, Ronald. *Beyond Our Tribal Gods: the Maturing of Faith*. Maryknoll, N.Y.: Orbis Books, 1979.

Marx, Karl. *The Grundrisse*. Edited by David McLellan. New York: Harper & Row Publishers, 1971; Harper Torchbooks, 1972.

Mayer, Jean, ed. *U.S. Nutrition Policies in the Seventies*. San Francisco: W. H. Freeman, 1973.

Mermelstein, David, ed. *Economics: Mainstream Readings and Radical Critiques*. New York: Random House, 1970.

Merrill, Richard, ed. *Radical Agriculture*. New York: Harper Colophon Books, 1976.

Mesarovic, Mihajlo, and Pestel, Eduard. *Mankind at the Turning Point: The Second Report to the Club of Rome*. New York: E. P. Dutton, 1974.

Metz, Johannes B., ed. *Faith and the World of Politics*. Concilium: Theology in the Age of Renewal, Fundamental Theology, vol. 36. New York: Paulist Press, 1968.

Míguez, Bonino, José. *Doing Theology in a Revolutionary Situation*. Philadelphia: Fortress Press, 1975.

Millar, Jayne C. *Focusing on Global Poverty and Development: A Resource Book for Educators*. Washington: Overseas Development Council, 1974.

Mills, C. Wright. *Power, Politics and People: The Collected Essays of C. Wright Mills*. New York: Oxford University Press, 1963.

Minear, Larry. *New Hope for the Hungry? The Challenge of the World Food Crisis*. New York: Friendship Press, 1975.

———. *Whatever Happened to the World Food Crisis? Hunger*, No. 5. Washington: Impact, the Interrreligious Taskforce on U.S. Food Policy, 1976.

Miranda, José Porfirio. *Marx and the Bible: A Critique of the Philosophy of Oppression*. 1971; English ed., Maryknoll, N.Y.: Orbis Books, 1974.

Mische, Gerald, and Mische, Patricia. *Toward a Human World Order: Beyond the National Security Straitjacket*. New York: Paulist Press, 1977.

Morgan, Dan. "American Agripower and the Future of a Hungry World." *Saturday Review*, 13 November 1976, pp. 7-12.

———. Series on Food Aid Business. *Washington Post*, 9-14 March 1975.

———. Series on the Merchants of Grain. *Washington Post*, 2-5 January 1976.

Morton, Kathryn, and Tulloch, Peter. *Trade and Developing Countries*. New York: A Halsted Press Book of John Wiley, 1977.

Moyer, William, and Thorne, Erika. *Food/Hunger Macro-Analysis Seminar: A Do-It-Yourself Manual for College Courses and Action Groups*. New York: Transnational Academic Program, Institute for World Order, 1977.

Müller, Ronald E. "The Multinational Corporation: Asset or Impediment to World Justice?" *IDOC: International/North American Edition*. A Special Issue on Poverty, Environment and Power. Papers on Issues of Justice in the Americas from the Tenth Annual Conference of Catholic Inter-American Co-operation Program, 1-4 February 1973, Dallas, Texas, New York: IDOC, May 1973.

NARMIC Memo on PL 480. 24 March 1975.

National Conference of Catholic Bishops. *The Ministerial Priesthood and Justice in the World*. Synod of Bishops. Washington: United States Catholic Conference, 1972.

Neal, Marie Augusta. *A Socio-Theology of Letting Go: The Role of a First World Church Facing Third World Peoples*. New York: Paulist Press, 1977.

Nell, Onora. "Lifeboat Earth." *Philosophy and Public Affairs* 4 (1975): 273–92.

Nelson, C. Ellis. *Where Faith Begins*. Richmond: John Knox, 1952.

Nelson, Jack A. *Hunger for Justice: The Politics of Food and Faith*. Maryknoll, N.Y.: Orbis Books, 1980.

Nelson, Jack. "The U.S. and World Hunger: Food as Weapon." *Christianity and Crisis*, 24 January 1977, pp. 319–26.

A New International Economic Order: Education/Action Kit. Cambridge, Mass.: American Friends Service Committee, New England Regional Office, 1976.

New York Times. Food and Population: The World in Crisis. New York: Arno Press, 1975.

Niebuhr, H. Richard. *Christ and Culture*. New York: Harper & Row Publishers, 1951.

Nielsen, Kai. *Ethics Without God*. London: Pemberton Books, 1973.

North American Congress on Latin America. "Del Monte: Bitter Fruits." *NACLA's Latin America and Empire Report* 10 (September 1976).

———. "U.S. Grain Arsenal." *NACLA's Latin America and Empire Report* 9 (October 1975).

Nowell-Smith, P. H. *Ethics*. Oxford: Basil Blackwell, 1957.

Oglesby, Carl, and Shaull, Richard. *Containment and Change: Two Dissenting Views of American Foreign Policy*. New York: Macmillan, 1967.

Oliver, Donald W. *Education and Community: A Radical Critique of Innovative Schooling*. Berkeley, Calif.: McCutchan, 1976.

Option for Struggle: Three Documents of Christians for Socialism. New York: Church Research and Information Projects, 1974.

Ossowska, Maria. *Social Determinants of Moral Ideas*. Philadelphia: University of Pennsylvania Press, 1970.

Outka, Gene. *Agape: An Ethical Analysis*. New Haven, Conn.: Yale University Press, 1972.

Overseas Development Council. *The U.S. and the Developing World: Agenda for Action 1974*. Washington & New York: Overseas Development Council and Praeger Publishers, 1974.

———. *The U.S. and World Development: Agenda for Action 1975*. Edited by James W. Howe. Washington & New York: Overseas Development Council and Praeger Publishers, 1975.

———. *The U.S. and World Development: Agenda for Action 1976*. Edited by Roger D. Hansen. Washington & New York: Overseas Development Council and Praeger Publishers, 1976.

———. *The United States and World Development: Agenda 1977*. Edited by John W. Sewell. Washington & New York: Overseas Development Council and Praeger Publishers, 1977.

Packenham, Robert A. *Liberal America and the Third World: Political Development Ideas in Foreign Aid and Social Science*. Princeton, N.J.: Princeton University Press, 1973.

Paddock, William and Paul. *Famine 1975! America's Decision: Who Will Survive?* Boston: Little, Brown and Company, 1967.

——. *Time of Famines: America and the World Food Crisis* (a new edition of *Famine 1975!*) Boston: Little, Brown and Company, 1976.

Palo Alto Packet Committee and the Simple Living Program. *Taking Charge: A Process Packet for Simple Living: Personal and Social Change.* San Francisco: American Friends Service Committee, 1975.

Paul VI, Pope. *Encyclical Letter on the Development of Peoples*, commentary by Barbara Ward. New York: Paulist Press, 1967.

Payer, Cheryl. *Commodity Trade of the Third World.* New York: John Wiley, 1975.

——. *The Debt Trap.* New York: Monthly Review Press, 1974.

"Peace Education." *Transnational Perspectives* 3 (1976): 34–38.

Peterson, Peter G. "A New International Economic Order—I. Sharing the Bounty" and "II. Helping Others—and Ourselves." *New York Times*, 12 & 13 May 1977.

Phenix, Philip H. *Education and the Common Good: A Moral Philosophy of the Curriculum.* New York: Harper and Brothers, 1961.

——. "Orientation to Value Education." Paper presented to the Program Committee for Education in the Society, Division of Education and Ministry, National Council of Churches, Greenwich, Conn., 11 June 1976.

The Philadelphia Macro-analysis Collective. *Organizing Macro-analysis Seminars: A Manual*, 3rd ed., 2nd printing. Philadelphia: Philadelphia Macro-analysis Collective, 1975.

Phillips, Michael J. "The Status of Cooperatives in the Imperfectly Competitive Grain Export Market." *Congressional Record—Senate*, 17 December 1975, pp. S 22613-14.

Pinar, William, ed. *Curriculum Theorizing.* Berkeley, Calif.: McCutchan Publishing, 1975.

Pinar, William, ed. *Heightened Consciousness, Cultural Revolution and Curriculm Theory.* Berkeley, Calif.: McCutchan Publishing, 1974.

Plantinga, Alvin, ed. *Faith and Philosophy: Philosophical Studies in Religion and Ethics.* Grand Rapids, Mich.: Eerdmans, 1964.

Poleman, Thomas T., and Freebairn, Donald K. *Food, Population, and Employment.* New York: Praeger Publishers, 1973.

Procopio, Mariellen, and Perella, Frederick J., Jr. *Poverty Profile USA.* New York: Paulist Press, 1976.

The Public Interest, no. 13, Fall 1968. Special Issue: The Universities.

Punzo, Vincent J. *Reflective Naturalism: An Introduction to Moral Philosophy.* New York: Macmillan, 1969.

Quigley, Thomas E. *Freedom and Unfreedom in the Americas: Towards a Theology of Liberation.* New York: IDOC, 1971.

Raines, John Curtis. *Attack on Privacy.* Valley Forge, Pa.: Judson Press, 1974.

——. *Illusions of Success.* Valley Forge, Pa.: Judson Press, 1975.

Ravitch, Diane. *The Revisionists Revised: Studies in the Historiography of American Education.* National Academy of Education, 1977.

——. "60's Education, 70's Benefits." *New York Times*, 29 June 1978, p. 35.

Rawls, John. *A Theory of Justice.* Cambridge, Mass.: Belknap Press of Harvard University Press, 1971.

Reardon, Betty. "Education for Peace and Social Justice." *Geographical Perspectives* 34 (Fall 1974).

Reutlinger, Shlomo, and Selowsky, Marcelo. *Malnutrition and Poverty: Magnitude and Policy Options.* World Bank Staff Occasional Papers, no. 23. Washington: The World Bank, 1976.

Rhodes, Robert I., ed. *Imperialism and Underdevelopment: A Reader.* New York: Monthly Review Press, Modern Reader Paperback, 1970.

Rich, William. *Smaller Families Through Social and Economic Progress.* Washington: Overseas Development Council, 1973.

Richardson, Robin. "A Small Project for a Small Planet—A Personal Account." *World Studies Bulletin* 39 (July 1976).

———. "Tensions in World and School: An Outline of Certain Current Controversies." *Bulletin of Peace Proposals* 5 (1974): 263–73.

Ridgeway, James. *The Closed Corporation: The American University in Crisis.* New York: Random House, 1968.

Robbins, William. *The American Food Scandal: Why You Can't Eat Well on What You Earn.* New York: William Morrow & Co., 1974.

———. "U.S. Grain Inquiry Hints at Rigging of Ship Subsidies." *New York Times,* 7 December 1975.

Rodney, Walter. *How Europe Underdeveloped Africa.* Washington: Howard University Press, 1974.

Rothschild, Emma. "America's Offal Policy." *New York Times,* 16 April 1978, p. 19.

———. "Food Politics." *Foreign Affairs* 54 (1976): 285–307.

———. "For Some, a Feast of Crumbs" and "The Rats Don't Starve." *New York Times,* 10 & 11 January 1977.

———. "Is It Time to End Food for Peace?" *New York Times Magazine,* 13 March 1977, pp. 15–48.

———. "The Politics of Food." *New York Review of Books,* 16 May 1974, pp. 16–17.

Rugg, Harold. *Culture and Education in America.* New York: Harcourt, Brace, 1931.

———. *Democracy and the Curriculum: The Life and Program of the American School.* Third Yearbook of the John Dewey Society. New York: D. Appleton-Century, 1939.

———. *Foundations for American Education.* Yonkers-on-Hudson, N.Y.: World Book, 1947.

Rugg, Harold, and Withers, William. *Social Foundations of Education.* Englewood Cliffs, N.J.: Prentice-Hall, 1955.

Ryan, William. *Blaming the Victim,* rev. ed. New York: Vintage, Random House, 1976.

Sanderson, Fred H. *The Great Food Fumble.* Washington: The Brookings Institution, 1975.

Schertz, Lyle P. "World Food Prices and the Poor." *Foreign Affairs* 52 (1974): 511–37.

Schroyer, Trent. *The Critique of Domination: The Origins and Development of Critical Theory.* New York: George Braziller, 1973.

Schumacher, E. F. *Small Is Beautiful: Economics as if People Mattered.* New York: Harper & Row, 1973; Harper Colophon Books, 1975.

Schwab, Joseph J. *College Curriculum and Student Protest.* Chicago: University of Chicago Press, 1969.

Scientific American. Special Issue on Food and Agriculture (September 1976).

Segal, Judith A. *Food for the Hungry: The Reluctant Society.* Baltimore: The Johns Hopkins Press, 1970.

Segundo, Juan Luis. *Liberation of Theology.* 1975; English ed., Maryknoll, N.Y.: Orbis Books, 1976.

———. *A Theology for Artisans of a New Humanity.* vol. 3: *Our Idea of God.* 1970; English ed., Maryknoll, N.Y.: Orbis Books, 1974.

Sennett, Richard, and Cobb, Jonathan. *The Hidden Injuries of Class.* New York: Random House, Vintage, 1972.

Sheerin, William E. "Educational Scholarship and the Legacy of George S. Counts." *Educational Theory* 26 (1976): 107–12.

Sheets, Hal. "Big Money in Hunger." *Worldview Symposium on Food and Hunger.* New York: Council on Religion and International Affairs, 1976.

———. *Disaster in the Desert.* New York: Carnegie Endowment for International Peace, 1974.

Shepherd, Jack. *The Politics of Starvation.* New York: Carnegie Endowment for International Peace, 1975.

Shonfield, Andrew, ed. *International Economic Relations of the Western World 1959–1971,* vol. 1: *Politics and Trade,* vol. 2: *International Monetary Relations.* London: Oxford University Press and The Royal Institute of International Affairs, 1976.

Sider, Ronald J. *Rich Christians in an Age of Hunger: A Biblical Study.* New York: Paulist Press, 1977.

Sideri, S. "Prospectives for the Third World." *Internationale Spectator* 25 (1971): 469–98.

Silk, Leonard. "Industrial vs. Poor Nations: A Battle on Untrod Ground." *New York Times,* 9 May 1977.

Silk, Leonard, and Vogel, David. *Ethics and Profits: The Crisis of Confidence in American Business.* New York: Simon & Schuster, 1976.

Simon, Arthur. *Bread for the World.* New York: Paulist Press, 1975.

Simon, Paul and Arthur. *The Politics of World Hunger: Grass Roots Politics and World Poverty.* New York: Harper's Magazine Press, 1973.

Singer, Lester. Review of *Pedagogy of the Oppressed,* by Paulo Freire. *Educational Theory* 24 (1974): 426–32.

Sinha, Radha. *Food and Poverty.* New York: Holmes and Meier, 1976.

Sivard, Ruth Leger. *World Military and Social Expenditures 1976* and *1977.* Leesburg, Va.: WMSE Publications, 1976 and 1977.

Slesinger, Zalmen. *Education and the Class Struggle.* New York: Covici Friede, 1937.

Smith, Brian H. "Chile: A Memo for Multinational Corporations." *America,* 20 January 1973, pp. 34–36.

Sölle, Dorothee. *Beyond Mere Dialogue: On Being Christian and Socialist.* The 1977 Earl Lectures at the Pacific School of Religion. Detroit: American Christians Toward Socialism, 1978.

———. *Beyond Mere Obedience: Reflections on a Christian Ethic for the Future.* 1968; English ed., Minneapolis: Augsburg Publishing House, 1970.

———. *Christ the Representative: An Essay in Theology after the "Death of God."* 1965; English ed., Philadelphia: Fortress Press, 1967.

———. *Death by Bread Alone: Texts and Reflections on Religious Experience.* 1975; English ed., Philadelphia: Fortress Press, 1978.

———. *Political Theology.* 1971; English ed., Philadelphia: Fortress Press, 1974.

Solkoff, Joel. "The Grain Drain: Cargill's Private Empire." *The New Republic,* 18 December 1976, pp. 9–11.

Spivey, J. Carlisle. *World Food Supply: A Global Development Case Study.* New York: Management Institute for National Development, 1974.

Spring, Joel H. *Education and the Rise of the Corporate State*. Boston: Beacon Press, 1972.

———. *A Primer of Libertarian Education*. New York: Free Life Editions, 1975.

———. *The Sorting Machine*. New York: David McKay, 1976.

Sweezy, Paul M. *Modern Capitalism and Other Essays*. New York: Monthly Review Press, 1972.

Sweezy, Paul M., and Magdoff, Harry. *The Dynamics of U.S. Capitalism*. New York: Monthly Review Press, 1972.

Talbot, Ross B., ed. *The World Food Problem and U.S. Food Politics and Policies: 1972-1976*. Ames, Iowa: Iowa State University Press, 1977.

Theobald, Robert. *An Alternative Future for America II,* 2nd ed. Chicago: Swallow Press, 1970.

Toma, Peter A. *The Politics of Food for Peace: Executive-Legislative Interaction*. The Institute of Government Research, American Government Studies, no. 2. Tuscon Ariz.: University of Arizona Press, 1967.

Torres, Sergio, and Eagleson, John, eds. *Theology in the Americas*. Maryknoll, N.Y.: Orbis Books, 1976.

Toulmin, Stephen Edelston. *An Examination of the Place of Reason in Ethics*. Cambridge: Cambridge University Press, 1950.

Trager, James. *Amber Waves of Grain*. New York: Arthur Fields Books, 1973.

Transnational Institute. *World Hunger: Causes and Remedies*. Amsterdam: Transnational Institute & Institute for Policy Studies, Washington, 1974.

Trezise, Philip H. *Rebuilding Grain Reserves: Toward an International System*. Washington: The Brookings Institution, 1976.

Turner, James S. *The Chemical Feast: The Ralph Nader Study Group Report on Food Protection and the Food and Drug Administration*. 1970; Harmondsworth, Eng.: Penguin Books, 1976.

Tyack, David B. *The One Best System: A History of American Urban Education*. Cambridge, Mass.: Harvard University Press, 1974.

ul Haq, Mahbub. *The Poverty Curtain: Choices for the Third World*. New York: Columbia University Press, 1976.

———. "Rich and Poor Nations—A New Formula for Closing the Gap." *Christian Science Monitor*, 29 August 1975, pp. 14-15.

United Nations. Action for Development/Food and Agriculture Organization. *Higher Education and Third World Development Issues—An International Comparative Study*. Report of a Survey and Evaluation of Post-Secondary Level Development Education in Some Industrialized Countries, by Robin J. Burns. Rome: Action for Development/FAO, 1975.

United Nations, Educational, Scientific and Cultural Organization. *Recommendation Concerning Education for International Understanding, Co-operation and Peace and Education Relating to Human Rights and Fundamenta Freedoms*, adopted by the General Conference at its 18th Session. Paris, 19 November 1974.

United Nations, General Assembly, 6th Special Session, 1 May 1974. *Declaration on the Establishment of a New International Economic Order.*

U.S. Congress, House. *Food for Peace Program 1974 Annual Report,* H. Doc. 94-352, 94th Congress, 2nd sess. 1976.

U.S. Congress, Senate. Select Committee on Nutrition and Human Needs. *Report on Nutrition and the International Situation*. 93rd Congress, 2nd sess., 1974.

U.S. Congress, Senate. *Testimony* [to the Foreign Assistance Subcommittee] *of the*

Interreligious Taskforce on U.S. Food Policy—A Comprehensive Look at Development. *Congressional Record*, 1 April 1977, S 5351.

U.S. Department of Agriculture. *The Annual Report on Activities Carried out under Public Law 480, 83rd Congress, as Amended, during the Period July 1, 1974 through June 30, 1975.*

U.S. Department of Agriculture, Economic Research Service. *The World Food Situation and Prospects to 1985*. Foreign Agricultural Economic Report, no. 98. Washington: Government Printing Office, 1974.

U.S. Department of State, Agency for International Development. *AID's Challenge in an Interdependent World*. Washington: AID, 1977.

U.S. Department of State, Agency for International Development, Office of Public Affairs. "For a Better World." *War on Hunger: A Report from the Agency for International Development,* by Betty Snead (July 1976).

U.S. General Accounting Office. *Grain Reserves: a Potential U.S. Food Policy Tool*. Report of the Comptroller General of the United States to the Select Committee on Nutrition and Human Needs. Washington: General Accounting Office, 1976.

U.S. General Accounting Office. *The Overseas Food Donation Program—Its Constraints and Problems*. Report of the Comptroller General of the United States to the Congress. Washington: General Accounting Office, 1975.

U.S. General Accounting Office. *The World Food Program—How the U.S. Can Help Improve It*. Report of the Comptroller General of the United States to the Senate Committee on Government Affairs. Washington: General Accounting Office, 1977.

U.S. Catholic Conference, International Justice and Peace Office. *Our Daily Bread*, 3 vols. Washington: U.S. Catholic Conference, 1975–76.

"U.S. Food Power: Ultimate Weapon in World Politics?" *Business Week*, 15 December 1975, pp. 54–60.

Veatch, Henry B. *For an Ontology of Morals: A Critique of Contemporary Ethical Theory*. Evanston, Ill.: Northwestern University Press, 1971.

Vernon, Raymond. *Sovereignty at Bay*. New York: Basic Books, 1971.

Wall, David. *The Charity of Nations: The Political Economy of Foreign Aid*. New York: Basic Books, 1973.

Warnock, G. J. *Contemporary Moral Philosophy*. London: Macmillan, 1967.

Warwick, Donald P. "Compulsory Sterilization in India." *Commonweal*, 10 September 1976, pp. 582–85.

Weissman, Steve, ed. *The Trojan Horse*. San Francisco: Ramparts Press, 1974.

White, John. *The Politics of Foreign Aid*. New York: St. Martin's Press, 1974.

Wellmer, Albrecht. *Critical Theory of Society*. 1969; English ed., New York: Seabury Press, Continuum Books, 1974.

Wilber, Charles K., ed. *The Political Economy of Development and Underdevelopment*. New York: Random House, 1973.

Williams, William Appleman. *The Roots of the Modern American Empire*. New York: Random House, 1969.

Wogaman, J. Philip. *The Great Economic Debate: An Ethical Analysis*. Philadelphia: Westminster Press, 1977.

Wolff, Robert Paul. *The Poverty of Liberalism*. Boston: Beacon Press, 1968.

Wren, Brian. *Education for Justice: Pedagogical Principles*. Maryknoll, N.Y.: Orbis Books, 1977.

Young, Michael F. D., ed. *Knowledge and Control: New Directions for the Sociology of Education*. London: Collier-Macmillan, 1971.

RELIGIOUSLY AFFILIATED
ORGANIZATIONS INVOLVED WITH
WORLD POVERTY AND HUNGER

The most comprehensive listing and description of organizations involved with hunger can be found in *Who's Involved with Hunger: An Organization Guide*, published by the World Hunger Education Service, 2000 P Street, N.W., Room 205, Washington, DC 20036, price $2.00 plus postage. For general information and updating on underdevelopment and hunger, the best organization to keep in touch with is *The Institute for Food and Development Policy*, founded by Frances Moore Lappé and Joseph Collins, 2588 Mission Street, San Francisco, Calif. 94110, (415) 648-6090.

Educators might want to write to the *Institute for World Order*, 777 United Nations Plaza, New York, NY 10017. The Institute is an educational and research organization devoted to building a world order of peace and social justice, economic well-being and ecological balance. They develop educational material on peace and justice for the high school and college curriculum. The Institute has also published a *Directory of Organizations and Publications for Peace and World Order Education*, which provides information on how to find services and material useful for developing programs, courses, and study units on peace and world order for educators at all levels.

Another source of educational material is the *Institute for Education in Peace and Justice*, 2913 Locust St., St. Louis, MO 63103. The Institute publishes material for teachers on peace and justice issues and is involved in teacher-education on hunger, global awareness, racism, multicultural education, and mutuality in education.

The *Consortium on Peace Research, Education and Development* (COPRED), Kent State University, Kent, OH 44242, is an excellent source for current national and international developments in peace and justice education. It is a membership organization devoted to networking, catalyzing, and serving persons and institutions interested in scientific study, action, research, and education on problems of peace and social justice. Its newsletter provides up-to-date information on national and international conferences, curriculum, and audiovisual material.

Finally, *Global Education Associates*, 552 Park Avenue, East Orange, NJ 07017, conducts educational and research programs, publishes educational materials, and seeks to catalyze a transcultural, multi-issue movement for world order based on the values of social and economic justice, peace, ecological balance, and participation in decision-making. The associates have conducted over 800 workshops, institutes, and leadership seminars throughout the world.

Here follows a list of religiously affiliated organizations working for structural and systematic change in the areas of poverty and hunger in the Third World and the United States. All publish valuable material on the subject.

American Friends Service Committee, National Office, 1501 Cherry Street, Philadelphia, PA 19102 (215-241-7000). A Quaker organization based on a belief in the dignity and worth of all people and the ability of love and nonviolence to bring about change. Involved in domestic and international works of service, development, justice, and peace. Publishes excellent material in all these areas.

Bread for the World, Bread for the World Educational Fund, 32 Union Square East, New York, NY 10003 (212-260-7000). A Christian citizens' movement that seeks to influence government policies that address the basic causes of hunger. Publishes a monthly newsletter to inform members on issues and action. The Educational Fund researches and publishes material and holds seminars on college campuses and seminaries for the purpose of educating the public on issues of development and hunger.

Campaign for Human Development, 1312 Massachusetts Ave., N.W., Washington, DC 20005 (202-659-6600). A Catholic education and action program. Assists poor people in the United States to help themselves find long-range solutions to the problems of poverty. The Campaign for Human Development serves as a research center and clearing house for information on poverty. It provides poverty-related justice educational material, coordinates justice education programs, consults with poor people's groups, and provides training and workshops on a national and diocesan level.

Clergy and Laity Concerned, 198 Broadway, Room 302, New York, NY 10038 (212-964-6730). Founded to mobilize opposition to American intervention in Southeast Asia, Clergy and Laity Concerned is today involved in challenging and changing government and corporate policies that oppress people personally, politically, or economically. Publishes a monthly journal and has printed material, speakers, and audiovisual materials available on issues such as the arms race, the environment, hunger, and development.

Interfaith Center on Corporate Responsibility, 475 Riverside Drive, Room 566, New York, NY 10115 (212-870-2295). A coalition of church investors concerned about corporate responsibility. Member agencies include representatives of fourteen Protestant denominations and more than 150 Catholic religious communities that seek to have their program concerns reflected in the practices of corporations in which they hold stock. Some of the issues of concern to ICCR members include: agribusiness, bank voting of stocks, energy, infant formula, militarism, transnational corporations, and human development. Publishes *The Corporate Examiner,* a monthly newsletter, and the *CIC Brief,* which offers an in-depth study of a particular social area.

Interreligious Taskforce on U.S. Food Policy, 110 Maryland Ave., N.E., Washington, DC 20002 (800-424-7292). A grassroots network of committed persons who, on the basis of religious and moral conviction, seek to influence public policy. Sponsored by twenty national Protestant, Roman Catholic, and Jewish agencies, the Taskforce prepares publications and makes recommendations on public policy issues such as U.S. food policy, U.S. farming policy, military spending, health care, and issues affecting women. Regularly publishes *Impact,* containing information and recommendations on U.S. food policy and other federal policy issues.

Maryknoll Justice and Peace Office, Maryknoll, NY 10545. Regularly publishes *NEWSNOTES,* a newsletter containing the most current information on international peace and justice issues and recent publications in the area of peace and justice.

NETWORK, 806 Rhode Island Avenue, N.E., Washington, DC 20018 (202-526-4070). A Catholic social justice lobby that seeks to influence Congress on issues that affect the poor and powerless. Besides lobbying, NETWORK publishes a bi-monthly journal and periodic action alerts, conducts workshops, seminars, and intern programs, and testifies at congressional hearings.

INDEX